accidental agreements(TM) with the enemy

natalie wolfe

accidental agreements with the enemy(TM)
natalie wolfe

Published by Your Family Blessings, LLC YourFamilyBlessings.com

Design & Layout by LifeWise Books – LifeWiseBooks.com
Book Cover & Interior Design by Yvonne Parks | PearCreative.ca

All Bible copyright statements are found in the back of this book.

Printed in the U.S.A.

ISBN (Print): 978-0-9976062-2-5
ISBN (Kindle): 978-0-9976062-3-2
Library of Congress Control Number (LCCN): applied for

dedication

This book is dedicated to the family saints who went before me. It is also dedicated to my children, Wendy, Brad and Alexis: and the saints to follow. May God bless you, and may your God-ordained destinies come forth—on Earth as it is in Heaven—in Jesus' name.

table of contents

Dear Reader,

My hope is the book's title caught your attention! The truth is, we unintentionally make unhealthy, unscriptural *Accidental Agreements with the Enemy*. We deny it is possible to be aligned with the enemy and change our outcome. The Bible says, "You will know the truth (Jesus), and the truth will set you free."

Facing many challenges, I became frustrated with my circumstances. Watching my friend's journeys, there appeared to be little advancement or God-sized answers to their prayers. They were not experiencing substantial breakthroughs. It was difficult to understand why they were not receiving more blessings.

For many years, I had been actively seeking the Lord's guidance and wondered why abundant blessings were not happening for me and my friends who pray. God allows trials in life. When trials and circumstances become prolonged, unexplainable, and abnormal, there is a Biblical misalignment.

Having experienced God's movement in the past, I knew He was present even in hard circumstances. I kept saying to myself, "Where is the good God in the Bible I trust and believe in?" "Where are the breakthroughs?" It did not make sense. This is when my "pursuit of the Lord" began, persistently knocking on heaven's door asking for answers. This led to divine revelation, which is what I am sharing with you in this book.

I am convinced God is trustworthy, faithful, and eager to bless us at every turn. We have been indoctrinated into believing blessings are primarily dispensed upon our arrival in heaven. So we settle for less, assuming God is not big enough to handle our problems. I am here to tell you He blesses us on earth!

However, we have been missing important pieces in our spiritual blessing puzzle. These critical pieces lead to an alignment with blessings for you on earth.

Without this alignment, we give in, give up, and keep saying prayers with halfhearted belief in answers. We eventually wallow in mud, self-pity, hopelessness, and lack of knowledge. We are settling for bread crumbs of blessings. We perceive what we receive as big blessings, but in our hearts, we know there is more. The Bible says we perish for lack of knowledge, but we need more than mere human knowledge.

The key to receiving Holy Spirit revelation about the lies in your belief system is becoming divinely educated. The Lord identified seven areas commonly hijacked by the enemy. These Accidental Agreements are interwoven within our body, soul and spirit, not to be addressed independently. When we ask Holy Spirit to reveal our Agreements, He will be faithful to help us quickly eliminate them. Our Heavenly Father is excited to give us good gifts!

This book contains people's stories who have followed the Accidental Agreement program and received dramatic blessings. These individuals learned to understand God's blessing economy. There are no exceptions, as God loves us all the same. Blockages may cause delays, but after removing the blockages, blessings abound. My prayer is for your heightened pursuit of the Lord to receive the God-ordained blessings waiting for ***YOU***. It is an exhilarating journey!

Blessings!

Natalie

Please share your blessing stories on our website:
AccidentalAgreements.com

CHAPTER 1
introduction

Princess for a Day. That's me, I'm told. I feel good. I feel special. I have just heard a Christian speaker explain that every believer is royalty. I'm a princess, a daughter (or son) of the King of Kings! The speaker even hands out a little tiara with a notepad that says, "I am Royalty." I can't express how great I feel. It continues the rest of the day, and I fall asleep feeling content.

I wake up the next morning and get slammed by the world...slammed with an insult, a situation that does not go as planned, a betrayal by a friend, or a disappointment with my kids. My emotions change from feeling like a beautiful princess with a tiara who is on top of the world, to Cinderella, sitting in ashes with limited hope.

My earthly view of a princess envisions someone with special privileges, honor, favor, and influence. It also includes a matching dress, coat, hat, and gloves like Princess Diana or Princess Kate. That's my earthly perception of royalty. But that's not what my life looks like.

Why not? What happened?

I can tell you exactly what happened. I've had IDENTITY THEFT! But, instead of my credit cards and social security number, I've had my God-given, true identity stolen. Suddenly, I don't know who I am and who I belong to. The vision of the princess and royalty is just a long-lost fantasy I once had. Where did it all go wrong?

> The problem was, I did not understand the true identity God gave me. I heard the words but did not embrace them in my heart.

The problem was, I did not understand the true identity God gave me. I heard the words but did not embrace them in my heart. I had head knowledge of the scriptures and God's Biblical promises, but did not understand the nature and extent of God's love for me in my heart and soul. I had misconceptions about who my Father in Heaven really was based upon my experiences with my earthly father and mother. My mother and father were a blessing to me. Don't we all base our assessment of our Heavenly Father on a human being? Yes, that's what we do until we see and experience the difference between the two kinds of love. My Father in Heaven is perfect and offers unconditional love. My Father in Heaven loves me so much and has an incredible plan for me. These plans are full of real promises He wants to bless me with daily. When I lose sight of God's perspective, I lose sight of my own identity.

Everything that has happened to you from birth until now creates a memory, affecting how you feel. Hence, it can hinder you from being free to embrace the love God has for you. To embrace and reclaim our true identity as royalty, the way God sees us, we must ask the Holy Spirit to reveal our broken areas. These areas cause misconceptions about how much our Father in Heaven loves and adores us.

We have all had identity theft. Our Godly identity has been stolen, hijacked, and altered. Our Heavenly Father is the King of the Universe, full of love, mercy, and grace. He gives us royal attributes through His Holy Spirit, who lives inside of each one of us if we have accepted Jesus Christ as Savior. He gives us royal attributes, but not as the world identifies them. They are His values and His characteristics, which are far better than we could ever imagine: "Now to him who is able to do immeasurably more than we ask or imagine, according to His power at work within us."[1] Yet, we get stuck in life due to our imagination and our soul wounds, which tell us, and God, what our life is supposed to look like. Therefore, it is vitally important to bind our body, spirit, and soul (mind, will, emotions, and imagination) to Jesus daily, maybe hourly. "For as he thinks in his heart, so is he."[2] Our view of God, ourselves, and others (God's perspective of them) influences our heart and every thought, action, and motive. These beliefs, thoughts, or lies are called "strongholds" in the Bible. These lead, or mislead, our thoughts about what we believe about God, others, or ourselves, from childhood to adulthood.

We become mixed up about our identity in Christ. Just when we think we've moved into a wonderful place with the Lord, we find ourselves right back where we started. Why are we on a larger-than-life-sized roller coaster? It's because of this identity theft I've referred to earlier. Deeper than this, identity theft is a result of a term I will refer to as an "Accidental Agreement" (AA). An Accidental Agreement occurs when we come into agreement with a lie the enemy has perpetrated about who we are, who God is, or who someone else is. Now, you are probably scouring your mind thinking, "I say my daily prayer, try to love everyone, and go to church… I couldn't possibly have an Accidental Agreement! I love the Lord. I would never do that!"

May I share something? It usually doesn't happen consciously, but rather by accident. Hence, the term! For many of us, we don't even know we have made an Accidental Agreement, and ultimately don't even understand what's truly holding us back from receiving more of God's blessings! Accidental Agreements typically come from a hurtful experience, which has caused a deep soul wound. Because of these soul wounds we often lose sight of truth, not on purpose, but by accident. We all have Accidental Agreements at one time or another. Common examples are believing God is punitive or believing God is limited in His time, ability, or resources. These beliefs can lead to behavior such as spending money the wrong way; spending too much time at the office; food issues; engaging in church activities that replace God; exercising too much or not exercising at all; fantasizing; "zoning out" by playing computer games; or watching too much or inappropriate television or movies to name a few.

Let me give you a real-life example of how Accidental Agreements played a big role in the life of a friend, Kimberly. When Kimberly and I began discussing the challenges facing her, she was in the middle of a stalled, three-year divorce. Kimberly had been released from her marriage by the Lord because of unfortunate circumstances and had sought counseling to make sure she was hearing correctly. She was left alone, in an empty house, finances in shambles as well as mentally, physically, emotionally, and spiritually drained.

Kimberly was a strong Christian for most of her life, despite a tough childhood. She diligently sought the Lord for many years, regularly participating in church, conferences, and small groups. She devoured a multitude of Christian books. On the surface, she had it all together, but this divorce was one of the biggest hurdles she had ever faced in life.

As we began to talk, it quickly became evident she had believed many of the lies the enemy had been whispering in her ear, such as, "I'll never be able to finish this divorce. People will think poorly of me because of this failure, and I'll be disgraced. I'll never be able to support myself. I'm not smart enough," and so on. She had been frozen in fear, afraid of losing her home, believing she was not smart enough to understand financial issues or the legalities of the divorce process. She was afraid of never finding a man she could trust, fearful her Christian friends would ostracize her and she would end up forever alone in a low-paying, unfulfilling job.

With this mindset, she was mentally exhausted and in a constant state of stress, anxiety, and fear. She was not eating or sleeping well and couldn't keep her mind off the divorce. She was left wondering why the Lord wasn't helping her more. She felt alone, as though she had to go through this on her own. Overall, she felt abandoned, stuck, and unworthy.

All the lies she had been hearing from the enemy were lies she had started believing. She was under a full-blown attack of Accidental Agreements and didn't know it. They had taken over her mind, will, emotions, and imagination, hijacking her identity and leaving her in a state of chaos—managed chaos. She was still functioning, carrying on with life but not happy nor fulfilled.

The only way she was going to find relief and successfully move forward was by coming out of agreement with the lies of the enemy. She had to *retrieve* her God given identity! We did this by identifying her specific Accidental Agreements, combined with prayer. We started with the first lie which came to her mind! Once the lies were identified, they arose out of her subconscious mind. Now, she would be able to deal with them in her conscious thoughts on an hour-by-hour basis for the next few days. Everything she believed which did not line up with scripture were Accidental Agreements.

Next, through a series of "Truth Statements"—the opposite of the lies—she reversed the hurtful emotions and mental damage. She began to speak these Truth Statements out loud over her life every time she heard the whisper of condemnation, negativity, or a lie. This constant divine revelation let the truth penetrate her heart and soul. I will disclose more detail on how this works later in the book. Essentially, it's a combination of acknowledgement of the specific lie, while declaring and aligning with the truth that God is good and He will work everything out for good in every circumstance. This reconfigures the brain's wiring to correctly believe the truth about your noble and trustworthy Heavenly Father. The result is you ACT and REACT correctly. This will move you closer to being in alignment with your God-ordained destiny.

Within two weeks, Kimberly's circumstances started changing. Once she came out of agreement with the enemy, something shifted within and outside of her. It was as if someone flipped a switch. Her divorce began moving forward, her finances took an incredible turn as totally unexpected financial resources appeared, and most importantly, her stress levels dropped significantly. All the lies she had believed were exposed! She felt God's love and experienced His provision. The peace that passes all understanding swept over her. She was no longer paralyzed. Motivation was restored, and relationships changed and flourished. God loves to bless His children!

This is only one example of God's abundant blessings as one gets out from underneath Accidental Agreements! It literally transforms your life. When identity is shifted back to its proper place, meaning God is a good Father, we come out of agreement with the enemy. Our whole lives can and will shift! I have seen it happen hundreds of times, both in my own life and the lives of many I've met. The spiritual key is recognizing where our specific beliefs and the enemy's lies overlap. Replacing those misguided beliefs with trust in the Truth of God's Word provides true clarity. This is exactly what I'm going to show you in the next chapters. It sounds easy, and it is, but you must be willing to allow the Holy Spirit to download the lie and be vigilant in breaking the lie pattern.

In this book, my goal is to help you understand what Accidental Agreements are and how they seriously disrupt your well-being in seven important areas of your life. It is far too easy for you to pass from day to day, shrouded in a haze of accepting that life "is what it is," and there is nothing you can do to change it. When you understand how Accidental Agreements are often the root cause of many problems in your life, you will immediately want to know how to rid yourself of them. After all, who doesn't want a better life? Who doesn't want a more fulfilling life? Who doesn't want to receive more blessings? God has so much more for you! Don't settle for less than you are entitled to receive! God loves to bless his kids extravagantly.

YOUR EXPECTATIONS

Removing Accidental Agreements is a simple and uncomplicated process. God says to have childlike faith.[3] You can expect to see changes and blessings in a matter of a few weeks only when you truly get out of agreement with the enemy. The hurts and wounds of your past intensify your resistance to forgiveness and healing. Anger, resentment, stubbornness and thoughts of retribution have immense power, and the enemy uses those emotions to validate the Accidental Agreements. The path to wholeness and healing is one which will create genuine mental and emotional changes, resulting in freedom you never knew was possible. Instead of believing the lies Satan has whispered in your ear, you will soon learn to replace those lies with the truth God has spoken to you. In turn, this will bring you into a closer and more intimate relationship with Him. And the bonus? You become extravagantly blessed.

> Accidental Agreements primarily occur within your mind and emotions and have ripple effects into all facets of your life.

Accidental Agreements primarily occur within your mind and emotions and have ripple effects into all facets of your life. They can be agreements about any aspect of your life—how you feel, how you look, how you think and react, how you perceive God, the possessions you own, who you associate with throughout the day, how you perceive others, or even how you perceive and react with those closest to you. They can be broad or specific in scope, often manifesting in very subtle ways. We are going to focus on specific lies you believe because this allows you to pinpoint the exact source of your problem. Because of their hidden nature, it's imperative to see and understand where and how they invade your life. As you go through this book and begin to recognize some of your Accidental Agreements, I will show you how to identify and conquer the major obstacles which obstruct your healing. I believe you should have complete freedom and wholeness to love God with all of your heart, all of your soul, all of your mind, and all of your strength.[4]

CONVICTION VS CONDEMNATION

Before we begin dealing with your Accidental Agreements, it is important to clearly understand something. Condemning thoughts and words you hear, all negativity, and even words you hear yourself repeating, are from the enemy, not from God. There is no condemnation in Christ Jesus[5], meaning anytime you feel condemned for something in the past, present, or future, it's coming directly from the enemy. However, it's important to recognize the difference between conviction from the Holy Spirit vs. condemnation. Conviction comes when you go against your conscience, falling into sin when you know better. But conviction brings you into repentance with the Lord, ultimately leading you back to Him.

Condemnation, on the other hand, comes in the form of negative and detrimental lies spoken to your mind, saying you now have little value in the eyes of God or others because of what you've done. Condemnation tells you not to approach God because of your sin. Condemnation tells you God is too busy to care about the details in your life or your family's lives. Condemnation tears you down, while conviction has the ability to lift you up and bring you back into alignment with God.

Many people live with guilt and shame their entire lives. Instead of embracing the concept that Christ died for our sins and when we confess our sins we are forgiven, people choose to carry these false burdens around. They get heavier by the year! Romans 8:1 says, "So now there is no condemnation for those who belong to Christ Jesus."[6] James 5:16 says, "Confess your sins to each other and pray for each other so that you may be healed. The earnest prayer of a righteous person has great power and produces wonderful results."[7] You have a choice to make right now. Do you believe the words of the Bible that say you are not to live with guilt, shame and condemnation? It is your choice to believe truth or carry extra baggage, tied to the enemy.

Condemnation tears you down, while conviction has the ability to lift you up and bring you back into alignment with God.

When breaking your Accidental Agreements, if you hear condemnation, it's okay to say out loud, "Get behind me Satan. My Father in Heaven doesn't talk to me that way. He loves me and speaks gently!"

To give you an example of this in action, let's take my friend John. Originating from childhood, John has dealt with deep emotional wounds inflicted by his father. His dad wasn't around as he grew up, and when he was, he was more of an angry dictator than a loving father. John was often ridiculed for not living up to his dad's standards. He felt the physical discipline he endured from his dad was often a manifestation of the disappointment his dad felt toward him. He felt like a failure.

Fast forward to present day where John has four grown children. He finds himself looking back on the parenting of his children as an exact replica of the way his dad treated him. John wasn't actively involved with his kids, and when he was, he was not a good father. The condemnation he feels toward how he treated his children is even deeper than the hurt he felt from his own father's rejection. "Why did I ever let myself get so angry at them? Knowing the pain I'd felt when I grew up, how could I inflict this on my own children?" He now suffers from lies such as: "You don't deserve their love because of the way you treated them. You are a horrible father. You knew better and still treated them that way… You shouldn't even try to ask for their forgiveness because simply put—you don't deserve it. There is no way this damage can be reversed to create the loving relationship you really want with your kids."

This same scenario happened to June, whose mother was critical of her life, which could never measure up to her mother's expectations. It played out in her parenting skills, and the pattern of judgmental criticism was repeated. The lie John and June believed was, "I have screwed up too much in my life for God to fix me or my relationship with my children."

Do you think this is conviction speaking, or condemnation? Do these thoughts edify John and June, bringing them closer to the Lord, or do they send them into a tailspin? Again, conviction leads to repentance and forgiveness, while condemnation leads to our value being entirely diminished. John and June are dealing with a harsh case of the enemy's condemnation. Jesus came to set them free from condemnation. This type of scenario happens much too often in life. I will show you how to find freedom from it.

Later in the book, I will share examples from people who had problems with Accidental Agreements and have found healing and blessings by overcoming them. They found their freedom by identifying the lies they were believing and replacing those lies with Truth Statements. Truth Statements are simple declarations of what God says in Scripture about your identity, God's perception of you, and your perception of others. Repeating OUT LOUD the truth in Scripture, from your gut, each time you are influenced by lies or negative thoughts produces great power. The lies become so obvious that after only a few hours—yes, only a few hours—you will easily come into agreement with the Lord.

Bill Johnson, pastor of Bethel church in Redding, California, is an author of many books including *God is Good: He's Better Than You Think*. He often says in his messages, "When you believe a lie, you empower the lie. We know who the father of lies is." Therefore, we are empowering Satan's position when we believe lies.

It's your choice. Do you want to empower God, who loves to bless you, or the enemy? Don't believe the lies!

---

[1] Ephesians 3:20 (NLT)
[2] Proverbs 23:7 (NKJV)
[3] Matt. 18:2–4; Luke 18:17 (NKJV)
[4] Mark 12:30–31 (NKJV)
[5] Romans 8:1 (NKJV)
[6] Romans 8:1 (ESV)
[7] James 5:16 (NLT)

CHAPTER 2

what is an accidental agreement?

An Accidental Agreement (AA) occurs when your perspective about a life situation or circumstance does not align with God's perspective. An Accidental Agreement happens when you unconsciously accept the enemy's lies about anything that deprives you of your God-ordained destiny and identity, and the blessings you are entitled to receive as a child of God. An Accidental Agreement can stem from almost anything: words, circumstances, past experiences, activities, or even objects.

Simple, everyday incidents can become hurtful events when experienced through the lens of a soul wound. There may be nothing inherently evil or wrong about a particular instance or circumstance, yet the wound can project something untrue, resulting in deep emotional scars and unhappy feelings. Because these are negative emotional strongholds, or Accidental Agreements, they are established and rooted in our body and soul (mind, will, emotions and imagination). They cause further emotional and physical pain, gaining enormous strength with each passing month and year. One interesting characteristic of a soul wound is it does not remain stagnant. It expands with time and circumstances. Synonyms for "agreement" include arrangement, covenant, treaty, promise, pact, bargain, understanding, deal, and bond. Therefore, an Accidental Agreement becomes a treaty or covenant with the enemy. Yikes!

We all have heart/soul wounds from life, from childhood, adulthood and everything in between. Rita Bennett says in her book, *You Can Be Emotionally Free*:

> It is not the memory of the event itself that hurts us as much as the memory of our feelings about and our interpretation of the event. Hurts of the past that have sunk into the subconscious may continue to cause pain without our knowing where it comes from, and may cause us to react in ways we don't mean to, or may even cause physical illness.[1]

The soul, or psychological nature, needs healing from hurts of the past. Many of these hurts are not of our doing at all. Others are from our own wrong decisions to go our way and not God's. The healing of the soul helps to bring wholeness to the total person.

Rita goes on to say:

> When I you received Jesus, the Holy Spirit came in and brought my spirit alive to God. His image or likeness was restored in my spirit, and greatest of all miracles, His spirit came to take up permanent residence in me. But, my "soul" part is another matter. The Greek for "soul" is "*psyche*." My soul is my *psych*ological nature: mind, will and emotions—my feelings, my thoughts, my desires and drives.[2]

This soul part of me is in the process of BEING made whole or healed, day by day. The soul still struggles against the Spirit of God. Paul tells the Philippians to "work out your own salvation with fear and trembling,"[3] but he goes on to say, "it is God who works in you both to will and to do for his good pleasure."[4]

Each one of us faces this problem on a daily basis, and it is easy to fall prey to an Accidental Agreement. Interestingly, the first people the Lord led me to teach this concept to were intercessors, teachers, and pastors. No one is exempt from the schemes of the enemy. The important thing to understand is we are not meant to live under these constraints, creating strings to the enemy and resulting in delayed blessings and freedom. We should and can be freed from them very easily! The more you dive in and find the lies you're believing in your conscious and subconscious mind, the greater your ability to renounce them and move into alignment with the way God sees you. When you move into the place of agreement with the Lord, you get blessed in the very area that held you hostage! It is fun to watch God bless people in miraculous and unusual ways!

Accidental Agreements with the enemy occur because people believe inaccurate concepts or outright lies about who God is, who they are, or who others are. The misconceptions we have about God's nature, character, and love will often be reflected in the way we see ourselves and the way we treat others. Whether we realize it or not, we are reflecting our view of God. This is why it's imperative to understand the truth about who He is. He is a good Father who loves you more than you can ever fathom. He is NOT the one who causes the bad things in your life to teach you lessons. Rather, He is the one who is always faithful to redeem everything the enemy hijacks. God is love, and in Him there is no darkness.[5] The enemy comes to steal, kill, and destroy.[6] His main strategy is to trick you into believing God is causing all your harm. He comes like a snake in the grass, bites, and slithers away while God takes the blame. In fact, God promises to refine and teach us through these experiences, but it's important to understand who is the source of your grief. It is NOT your wonderful Creator. Let me repeat this. The source of your grief and problems is NOT God. Understand God is good and His Will is to show you the love He has for you through blessings, not curses.

Whether we realize it or not, we are reflecting our view of God.

God detests curses. One of the biggest lies perpetrated today by the enemy is there are no curses operating right now in civilized countries. Satan deceitfully convinces many people in North America and First World countries there are no curses or spiritual battles afflicting them. The belief is this only happens in Third World countries aimed at harming "uneducated" people. The enemy has pulled a lie over on us! Through soul wounds caused by sin, whether hereditary or self-inflicted, we have come into agreement with the enemy. Any area of our life tied to darkness cannot be blessed.

STRINGS

Try to grasp this simple concept. If, in any area of your life, you have one string tied to the Lord and another string tied to the enemy, you must know the Lord is not going to bless this area. However, when you break your agreement with the enemy, you cut the string and come into agreement with God. Now, the Lord can bless you in this exact area. You do this by aligning with what He says in scripture. Whether accidentally or intentionally, you cannot expect the Lord to condone or bless an alignment you have with Satan. Light and darkness simply do not coexist. In 1 John 1:5, it says "This is the message we have heard from him and declare to you; God is light; in him there is no darkness at all."[7]

Yet, more than you might imagine, Christians do expect God to bless those areas. Most believers have Accidental Agreements, far more than they imagine or are willing to admit. Once these lies are identified, it becomes easy to see the deception and renounce all alignments with the enemy.

For example, imagine you are having lunch with a co-worker who is passionate about health and fitness and is certified to offer personal training advice. She begins to share some of the information she has learned, but you immediately view it as a personal accusation, as if she thinks you're overweight and need to exercise. You become quiet, shut down, and leave lunch internally upset at her as well as insecure about yourself. What happened? Upon reflection, you realize it stirred up feelings from childhood when school kids made fun of you. Perhaps it was due to your weight or because you were not the "best" at sports. Even though you maintain a healthy weight now, the soul wound you incurred as a child, buried in your subconscious mind, began to manifest. The result was you felt hurt and offended over a conversation which was never meant to be a personal accusation. Accusations are a common ploy of the enemy.

It is important to recognize when you agree with the enemy as it will reflect negatively in your health. In fact, the level of agreement you have with the enemy will reflect the health of your spirit, soul, and body including your mind, will, emotions, and imagination.

> The level of agreement you have with the enemy will reflect the health of your spirit, soul, and body.

The Bible says you have been created in the image of God.[8] When you pick yourself apart, it unintentionally causes you to change the perception of the image God made you to be. Instead of believing you are a child created in His image, you begin to distort this identity and hurt your ability to receive His blessing in the VERY SAME AREA in which you believed the lie. Satan always presents a counterfeit.

Often, we only see ourselves as physical and emotional beings, forgetting we are also spirit beings as well. Each one of us was created with a unique design and purpose. Fulfilling this purpose and God's will for our lives involves effort on our part. In other words, we must surrender our agenda to the Lord. When we allow the Holy Spirit inside of us to completely control our lives and govern our minds, will, emotions, bodies, and imaginations, we come into perfect alignment with Him.

Romans 12:1–2 says, "Offer your bodies as a living sacrifice, holy and pleasing before God. Do not conform to the pattern of this world, but be transformed by the renewing of your mind. Then, you will be able to test and approve what God's will is."[9]

It requires us to give up, throw in the towel, and let the Holy Spirit dominate every facet of our life. By recognizing our identities in Christ, agreeing with God about who He thinks we really are and what He's capable of doing in our lives, we open ourselves up to receive blessings. These were once hindered by our Accidental Agreements.

> An Accidental Agreement will hijack your God-ordained destiny.

Bill Johnson states in *The Supernatural Ways of Royalty:* "what I do with God's promises determines the direction of my thought-life, and eventually affects my reality. It is essential to understand what God thinks of me (and others) in order to step into my destiny."[10]

Being out of alignment with God's word is like having your spine out of alignment in your body. It creates a condition which causes aggressive, often nagging pain, which can disrupt your thinking, comfort, and ability to complete everyday tasks. It limits you from enjoying many of life's blessings.

An Accidental Agreement with the enemy seriously handicaps your life and will severely hurt your ability to accomplish all God intends for you to do. It will delay or sabotage all of the fun blessings He is excited to give you! An Accidental Agreement will hijack your God-ordained destiny.

MARY'S STORY:

Mary has struggled with a poor, physical self-image since childhood. She is a lovely woman who thought she had outgrown this problem. Years later, the same feelings were present at age 34 as they were at 13. Even though physically fit, Mary expressed unhappiness with her appearance because of a previous weight issue. She always compared herself to other women, whether at the grocery store, work, the gym, or church.

Mary's self-image problems began as a child in elementary school. She was often picked on by girls making fun of her physical appearance. High school and college were difficult for Mary. She began working out excessively to keep her body in shape. She thought this would protect her from hurtful words. When friends complimented her physical beauty for being in excellent physical condition, she never believed them. She thought they had ulterior motives, or they felt sorry for her.

This created what would become a deep-seated SOUL WOUND. A soul wound is something in your past that wounded you to the point of causing current emotional pain. Many are not even aware of their soul wounds. Most people do not realize childhood experiences have such a profound impact on adulthood.

Critical words can often be the most damaging emotions we face in this world. Words ring through our ears and hearts, inflicting deep emotional pain. This is precisely what happened to Mary. She listened to the lies of the enemy whispered in her ear and began to believe them with her whole heart. A real soul wound had formed, and it would be years later before she recognized she needed help. She had accidentally come into agreement with the enemy's lies, and they were stealing her joy and peace.

What was Mary's Accidental Agreement? Mary never believed she was pretty or thin enough to be lovable. This is describing conditional love. Unconditional love is what our soul yearns for. Everyone craves, and we were designed, for unconditional love. Our Heavenly Father is the only one who can truly provide absolute, no strings attached, deep in our soul, unconditional love. He created our individual DNA, and He knows what is essential for our complete happiness.

This is precisely how Accidental Agreements work in all of us. They creep in unnoticed, causing us to believe a lie perpetrated by the enemy to interrupt our God-ordained destiny in life. These subtle AA's prevent us from experiencing God's ultimate love and power. The Accidental Agreements act as literal walls between our Heavenly Father and ourselves. The walls destroy the potential intimacy the Lord desires to have with us. In turn, it drives us into a place where we're unable to help others because of our own hurt.

You may be emotionally injured, mentally wounded, offended, struggling, barely getting by, or drifting through life, believing an AA you don't even know exists. My hope is to help you identify your Accidental Agreements and show you how to be freed from them. God deeply desires to have an intimate relationship with you. He wants these barrier walls to come down. Let's trust the Holy Spirit to bring your AA's to light, ultimately leading you into an amazing walk with God and new blessings!

SEVEN TYPES OF ACCIDENTAL AGREEMENTS

Accidental Agreements (AA) appear in assorted shapes and sizes. Some AA's are less obvious because you have been living with them for a long time. You don't realize the impact until they are revealed by the Holy Spirit, sending a resonating wave through your spirit. I will help you explore the different areas AA's tend to pop up in and how they potentially manifest. Some will be so hidden and subtle, you might be tempted to justify them away! The good news is the enemy is not very creative. His lies look and sound similar once presented to your conscious mind. I pray you will give thoughtful and prayerful consideration to what you're about to learn.

It is possible to overlook some of your Accidental Agreements, simply because you think they are too small and don't make a difference. Keep in mind, as the Bible puts it: "a little leaven leavens the whole lump."[11] In other words, a little contamination can poison the entire loaf of bread. An AA can contaminate your entire life: your body, soul, mind, will, emotions, imagination, passions, and desires. While all Accidental Agreements are activated within the soul, they are not all the same type or category. They are divided into seven main categories:

Spiritual – Inaccurate beliefs about God; how He sees you and how you see Him.

Mental and Imagination– False conclusions caused by wrong thinking and beliefs, leading to wrong actions and insecurities.

Emotional – Unhealthy or misguided feelings resulting from soul wounds.

Physical – Physical illness, generational infirmity, and false agreements about your physical body.

Financial – Incorrect beliefs about God's promises concerning wealth and blessing His children; generational problems or tendencies operating through the bloodline regarding money.

Relational – Unhealthy relationships or parts of relationships influenced by negative soul wounds that skew your perception; subtle acceptance of negativity, moral compromise, or sinful behavior.

Willful – An unconscious choice to deliberately hurt or cause harm to oneself or another person based upon incorrect beliefs or wounds.

CYNTHIA'S TESTIMONY

Here is a testimony of a mental agreement and the result when it was broken.

Cynthia was a lifelong Christian who loved the Lord, attended church, was involved with a small group and prayed daily. She knew God loved her, but she also recognized He had a big job running the world. One day, Cynthia decided to "test" God to see if He was really aware of the details concerning her life. She wanted to decide if she could trust God in every situation. She began asking Him for a parking space when she attended a weekly lunch appointment at a restaurant with limited parking. What do you know! A parking space appeared in front. Cynthia, being a businesswoman, thought this was an accident. The following week, she asked the Lord for a parking space in front of the restaurant and again, one appeared. She thought it was a lucky break. Then, Cynthia realized it was God answering her prayers. This scenario repeated itself so many times, the people at her meeting noticed and began to comment. She was ministering to them by simply asking God to help her with a parking request! God is interested in the details of your life!

Cynthia's Accidental Agreements included:

1. God is too busy to help her with a parking spot.
2. God is not interested in the small details.
3. God isn't omnipresent to watch over her life.

We all have hidden Accidental Agreements. Everyone. We will work on ridding ourselves of AA's until we go to heaven because we are not Jesus. Jesus was the only perfect person.

If you do not remember one point in this book, please remember this: praise God, spend time studying and memorizing the truth in God's Word, and thank Him for every detail. Allowing the Word to penetrate into your innermost being (heart, soul and gut) daily is the key to creating changes. Learn to hear the voice of God when He speaks to you. We only know a small piece of God's plan. Instead of jumping to false, "logical," or human conclusions when circumstances look terrible, make a choice to align with scripture and worship the Lord. Singing songs to the Lord, memorizing scriptures (truth), and being grateful even for things which appear bad changes the atmosphere! If you're not convinced, try it!

In the next few sections, let's dive into each category and explore the hidden Accidental Agreements. Remember, everyone has them. We are human. This will be an incredible time with the Holy Spirit revealing issues which have undermined your blessings for years. So strap on your seatbelt and let's go!

---

[1] Rita Bennett. *You Can Be Emotionally Free* (Alachua, FL: Bridge-Logos) 1982. 45.
[2] Rita Bennett. *You Can Be Emotionally Free*, 41.
[3] Philippians 2:12 (NKJV)
[4] Philippians 2:13 (NKJV)
[5] 1 John 1:5 (NKJV)
[6] John 10:10 (NKJV)
[7] 1 John 1:5 (NLT)
[8] Genesis 1:27 (NKJV)
[9] Romans 12:1–2 (NIV)
[10] Bill Johnson, *The Supernatural Ways of Royalty* (Shippensburg, PA: Destiny Image) 2006. 57.
[11] Galatians 5:9 (NKJV)

CHAPTER 3
spiritual accidental agreements

Spiritual Accidental Agreements (AA) are inaccurate beliefs about God, His love for you, and how He views you. Many of these develop because of incomplete or inaccurate teaching. We are tainted by our view of earthly fathers instead of correctly representing the truth of what a perfect Heavenly Father looks like. Unfortunately, many of these teachings come from well-meaning pastors but are taken severely out of context. The pastor may teach from his or her own place of hurt, relying more on their experiences in life rather than what the Word teaches. When you accept inaccurate concepts of God, you will find yourself acting on those false beliefs. Regardless of how it entered your life, this misconception dilutes or nullifies your understanding of how much God loves you.

Heavenly Father misconceptions are a slippery slope, which can lead to a religious life of harsh legalism or false grace. Legalism is when a person follows a strict set of rules in order to *earn* God's love and favor. It results in harsh judgment of others, a critical spirit rooted in bitterness, and extreme spiritual bondage. Jesus came to set us free from the law, giving us grace to freely live. John 8:32 says, "And you shall know the Truth and the Truth shall set you free."[1] We are no longer under an Old Testament law-based system. Rather, the New Testament commandment of love empowers us to walk more righteously out of choice than we could have through obligation!

No one purposely determines to be legalistic, but instead must be taught through a life experience or instructional teaching. The Word of God does not preach this message. It typically comes from a misguided or false teacher or from a strict religious upbringing. In fact, Paul uses some of the harshest and most colorful language in the Bible to lash out against legalism in Galatians. Legalism comes from the enemy. If you can be convinced you must earn God's favor or you will never be good enough, the enemy will blind you to God's infinite and unconditional love.

We are all saved by grace, through Jesus Christ alone. On the other hand, false grace can creep in on the opposite side of the religion spectrum. This is when a person believes they are simply "saved by grace," and can do anything and everything sinful in this world without consequences. They believe God has no real standards and they can do whatever they please because God won't care. Yes, God will still love all, regardless of their sin. Sin has earthly consequences and has the power to open the door wide to the enemy. Satan will use our choices to entangle us in lies and deceptions, keeping us from reaching our true destiny. Twisted and false grace utterly misses the point of why Jesus came, but instead of bringing freedom, it keeps people in bondage! They will be unable to live and walk in the genuine love and peace the Holy Spirit brings because they have Accidental Agreements with the enemy in many areas.

Spiritually developed Accidental Agreements are some of the most subtle agreements. They are shrouded in our religious beliefs, which we tend to hold very sacred. Religion is extremely powerful because people inherently believe in God in one form or another and often having their own beliefs formed from their life's experiences. Because of this, it feels like a personal attack when a religious teaching or belief opposes their own views. This is why we must center our belief systems on what the Word of God states, not on what we see with our eyes. This is why we rely on the Holy Spirit to reveal our Accidental Agreements.

Spiritual Accidental Agreements are uniquely important because they have the power to influence all other AA's. A misguided understanding about God's character or who you are in Christ when you accepted Him as Lord and Savior can have disastrous and far-reaching effects. Now, the real question is: Do you have any Spiritual Accidental Agreements? How can you possibly know if your beliefs are misguided or false? What a scary question to ask! After all, you have confidence in what you believe because you think it's right.

The first place to confirm is always the Word of God. Do you have a belief which comes more from your own past experiences rather than what the Bible teaches? Really dig into scripture and let the Holy Spirit guide you. Have you ever read the Bible and thought to yourself, "Oh, I don't know that I agree with that scripture?" Your reaction would be a prime indication you have a past experience determining what you think about a specific topic. The Holy Spirit guides you into ALL truth so ask Him where your beliefs are incorrect. Be sure to stay quiet long enough to hear the answer! No guessing allowed!

Perhaps you have been wounded by Christians in your church or Bible study. The very people who are supposed to know God and act in accordance with the Bible are the people who betrayed you the most! Satan wants to steal your faith. He is hoping you will walk away from God, or you will believe only parts of the Bible as truth. Remember, part of identity theft is altering your identity by mixing—mixing up people, situations, or events. This mixing twists communication, creates chaos, and divides. One of Satan's best strategies is to divide and conquer. He strives to divide the church, believers, and friends. When you begin to observe ungodly division approaching, be aware this is an enemy trick. Something good and effective to advance the kingdom of God is at hand. Press on!

Remember, part of identity theft is altering your identity by mixing—mixing up people, situations, or events.

MARGARET'S STORY

Margaret was raised in a legalistic church. The church characterized their denomination as the only church allowed in heaven. It viewed all other Christians as sinners. Her legalistic upbringing taught her God was angry and wrathful, one who would penalize and hate people if they sinned. Even as a believer, she thought by sinning, God would show His wrath by punishing to teach her a painful lesson. She even thought He would bring sickness or harm on people. She believed He would take all she had, forcing her into poverty if she messed up. The phrase "the Lord giveth, and the Lord taketh away" was used entirely out of context and formulated the belief system she stood upon. Essentially, she lived in spiritual bondage, believing she had to be perfect for God to be pleased with her. She felt unworthy for God to speak to her heart and counsel her. It was a fear-based religion, not one of understanding the true love of God towards His kids!

When Margaret approached me for counseling, she was in a state of turmoil and lived a fear-filled life. She thought, "God is giving me what I deserve." As we discussed the true nature of God, Jesus, and the Holy Spirit, she understood God loves us unconditionally in our current condition. She began to realize she had a Spiritual Accidental Agreement. She had fallen into the legalistic trap of the enemy. God knew she was going to make this mistake before it happened. God is all-knowing. Understanding this, she renounced the agreement with the enemy and believed God loved her regardless of her faults or sin. Going forward, she had to evaluate every part of her life to eliminate her critical perception of not only her Heavenly Father, but herself and how she perceived and judged others. She grew up judging with a critical spirit, which had crept into all sections of her life. There is a fine line between judging and discerning. God is the only one allowed to judge. She eventually broke the Spiritual Accidental Agreements. Margaret lives with less fear, loves others more freely, and sees her Heavenly Father as a loving Father who gently corrects. Grace has empowered her to live closer to Jesus than she ever could have through the law.

Here's another real-life example of a Spiritual Accidental Agreement with the enemy and the blessings which followed breaking the agreement.

MINISTRY BETRAYAL ONE

A couple built a large ministry over a number of years. It required many years of hard work, creating programs, obtaining volunteers, hiring employees, and establishing a loyal following of Christians. They built up the size and identity of this integrity-filled ministry. They produced marketing and media programs, conducted speaking engagements, and even arranged trips abroad to expand this mission for Christ.

A trusted person with ulterior motives was mentored and slowly promoted within their organization. Gossip, slander, and innuendos began swirling behind their backs, resulting in a corporate takeover similar to Wall Street. The ministry, company, programs, and money were hijacked. This is exactly the type of behavior we read about in national corporate financial news. The last place they expected this to happen would have been in their Christian ministry, especially by a friend.

This betrayal creates a soul wound or Accidental Agreement with the enemy. If you view this as unjust and you desire to get even, become bitter, or have self-pity, you have made a judgment about the situation which created an Accidental Agreement. Judgments are tied to unforgiveness which blocks prayers and causes delayed blessings. The Lord won't bless an area which is tied to the enemy.

This is when the Holy Spirit must be consulted to determine your perspective about the situation and heal your heart. The next steps should be taken carefully, directed by the Lord. The Lord is the only one allowed to judge.

This ministry couple had a choice to respond in one of two ways. Their first choice was not to retaliate but negotiate in good faith with the offending party. When the person did not respond appropriately, they asked the Lord what to do. When the Lord said to leave it alone, they backed off, prayed a lot, and gave the offense to the Lord to resolve. This choice was very difficult, given the emotional pain associated with such a betrayal on a business and personal level. However, the Lord is the judge and jury of every situation. They had hoped the Lord would have intervened differently in the negotiation, which would have resolved the problem. God is the only one who can change and heal your heart and soul wounds.

The potential Accidental Agreements were enormous. They could have been bitter; mad at God for allowing this to happen; felt abandoned and betrayed; become distrustful of all Christians; waged a legal war; slandered the thieves; allowed self-pity to form; become withdrawn, given up on life and God; believed God was not paying attention or He was against them; believed God was punitive; and the list goes on. Maybe you have been in their shoes with a slightly different scenario. Perhaps someone betrayed you at church or in ministry, gossiped about you, deceived you, stole from you, etc. Do not let Satan whisper lies in your ears or put thoughts in your head. An alignment with the enemy empowers the father of lies.

In Ministry Betrayal One, the ministry founders chose to forgive, not become bitter or feel like victims. They made a choice to continue believing God was good and in charge of all circumstances. They chose to not gossip or respond to slanderous comments.

They made a choice to continue believing God was good and in charge of all circumstances.

The result of this true situation is an example of God's miraculous redemption. The ministry was restored and is better than before; the people who surround them are loyal, faith filled friends; the employees are of higher quality; the programs are excellent; their reputation of integrity has been restored; they did not allow Satan to steal their faith or alter their belief that God is good-no matter what the circumstances look like; and God continues to bless them more than before! It was a difficult journey, but this miraculous redemption story required them to not believe the lies of the enemy, which would have created Accidental Agreements. I am reminded of Job, chapter forty-two, in which Job prays for his friends and his fortunes are restored.

MINISTRY BETRAYAL TWO

In the second scenario, a ministry was built from the ground up, beginning with only a few employees. A minister worked hard, built the ministry, and after many years, enjoyed great success. The same situation occurred as in the above scenario; a trusted coworker hijacked the ministry and took over the operation.

When negotiating with the ministry partner who stole the company failed, the man who was wronged defaulted to the second, and most common, scenario. He became mad, angry, gossiped, tried to retaliate, and harbored unforgiveness for years. He was furious, disappointed, betrayed, felt like he was punished by God and had a difficult time in life. As a result, it brought hardship on the family. This situation created a soul wound or stronghold. Bitterness and unforgiveness blocked his prayers and blessings were delayed. The bitterness soul wound created a legal right for the enemy to have access to him. The enemy invited "buddies" to attach to him and whispered lies in his ears about this situation and many situations. The facts were twisted, creating additional issues. (See the *Forgiveness* section in Appendix I on blocked prayers).

The result of Betrayal Two? The founder maintained bitter feelings over this split for many years. A religious betrayal cut deeply into his soul. Eventually, he tried to forgive but did not really forgive ALL of the offenses. The result: a perpetual string to the enemy was created. The founder kept seeking the Lord about this issue. The Holy Spirit told him, "This ministry belonged to the Lord, not him. Let it go." He had been judging the situation incorrectly. This revelation changed everything, including his outlook. When the founder of the ministry finally decided to fully forgive and surrender the results to the Lord, he was blessed immediately! He was given a new ministry even more exciting and fulfilling; his other business began to flourish; his personal relationships multiplied; his joy and happiness returned; he is stress free and healthier than ever. His love and trust for the Lord were restored and grew stronger. Remember, God is the "better than" God who loves to bless His kids. What fun to watch!

To summarize these real life spiritual Accidental Agreements:

The first scenario, in which the offended person released the situation to the Lord, refusing to align with the enemy, eliminated an Accidental Agreement. They experienced a huge blessing, one not imaginable at the time. It was difficult to understand how this seemingly catastrophic situation could have occurred; ministry, friendships, and years of work and money were lost. They retained their faith, believing God was good and still in control. The blessings they later received were far better than they could have asked or imagined.

The second scenario, the one in which the wronged man held the offense and bitterness, remained stuck for several years until his life became so painful that he was desperate to hear God and truly repented. It took some time for this to happen, but when God restored, He blessed him in unique ways which delighted his heart and made him laugh out loud. Yes, that's the good Father we have! Blessings abound when you align with the Lord!

Kerry Kirkwood, author of *The Power of Right Thinking*, writes:

> Ephesians 4:6–27 says to not give the devil a place…the Greek word for place here (in this scripture) is "topos" meaning geographical ground or territory. The strategy of the devil is to set up a base or staging area for greater infiltration on a later day. If he can start by suggesting that someone doesn't like us and letting us think it is our discernment at work, then we have given ground. The devil is a squatter; he will take anything that we are willing to concede through agreement. Agreement to our enemy is simply not disagreeing or pushing back in that suggestive thought.[2]

Coming out of agreement with a Spiritual AA will be life changing. As I stated earlier, since they can affect all areas of our lives, the simple truth will come out of believing who God is and what He says about you. This will set you free. Base it on the Word. If you are wondering what freedom is or what it would truly look like in your life, then you haven't fully experienced it yet. When you experience the true freedom of what Jesus did for you on the cross, you'll know it! Freedom is an exhilarating, peaceful, and joy filled life experienced all at the same time. It's truly life changing, filled with blessings every day!

LIES AND TRUTH STATEMENTS

Read through the following lies which are relevant to you and circle the top three. These are your Accidental Agreements, which we will use later in the book when implementing our AA Freedom Program.

Rather than waiting to begin the program at the end of the book, you can begin now if you prefer. However, when you read the rest of the book, you will find a common theme in the lies you are believing, which may help you break the Accidental Agreement faster. In the Appendix, you will find the corresponding Truth Statements." Circle the Truth Statements and scriptures that resonate with you. Write the Lie and Truth Statements on a note card and put a mark by the lie each time you hear it, whether it's every minute or hour. Each time you hear the lie, repeat the Truth Statement and appropriate scripture out loud (dunamis power-Holy Spirit). Continue this for one week, and each day the number of lie whispers should diminish. You will be able to recognize the lies quickly because they are being moved out of your subconscious mind, creating new brain patterns. The more consistently you practice this exercise, the faster the Accidental Agreements will be broken. Once broken, you will see movement in the heavenlies very quickly. Watch for the Lord's blessings! If you are not seeing blessings, read the rest of the book and check the Appendix for *Common Hindrances to Healing*. Ask the Holy Spirit which one applies to your situation. The Holy Spirit will highlight an issue quickly because He wants to see you blessed!

The Holy Spirit will highlight an issue quickly because He wants to see you blessed!

1. LIE: God can't possibly hear everyone's prayers, much less answer them! God is too busy to care about the details in my life. God would never talk to little old me. He is busy with more important things than me and my problems. This problem is unsolvable. I will have to deal with this problem the rest of my life.

2. LIE: God can't heal me and my children from our spiritual issues when we try but fail or are rebellious.

3. LIE: The way I speak and the words I use don't really matter. They are just figures of speech, and everyone says them. It's just the way I am. It's the way I was raised.

4. LIE: God is a God of grace, so it doesn't matter if I sin a little or a lot.

5. LIE: If I work harder and smarter, God will love me more.

6. LIE: It doesn't really matter if I fast and pray. Fasting and prayer won't really move God's hand or make a difference in my problems or my family's lives. Fasting is just too hard. I have to fast completely from all food to be pleasing to You. Fasting is not for today, and it doesn't make a difference.

7. LIE: I don't have time for daily prayer. If I pray once per day, that's enough. Too many of my little prayers bother Him. I don't have time to read the Bible daily. God won't speak to me through the Bible—that's just for preachers.

8. LIE: Surely God doesn't expect me to follow His guidelines in the Bible in everyday life. God doesn't really mean what He says in the Bible.

Listed below are additional lies. You may use different truth statements for these from the Appendix.

9. LIE: God doesn't really care about me or love me. He doesn't want to talk to me. He doesn't even have time to talk to me; He's too busy running the world.

10. LIE: God prefers to communicate with certain people in authority in church. He won't talk to me much.

11. LIE: I have lost hope about ________________________.

12. LIE: God is mad at me. God doesn't want to talk to me.

13. LIE: The Bible doesn't have wisdom for my life, my marriage, raising children, for business, relationships, etc. It is old-fashioned and outdated. The Bible has guidelines intended to hurt me or hold me back. It isn't relevant for today.

14. LIE: I don't have time to learn scripture. I can't memorize scripture very well. I don't think memorizing scripture will help me very much.

15. LIE: I don't need to know what the New and Old Testament scriptures really mean. I don't need to know or understand the Old Testament and how it relates to the New Testament.

16. LIE: Bible studies are for women who don't work outside the home. They are full of gossips. I don't have time to join a Bible study, and if I did, I wouldn't learn anything important. Bible studies aren't for men.

17. LIE: God doesn't really understand my life, and I can't figure it out.

18. 18. LIE: It's okay if I don't bless the food I eat.

19. LIE: It's okay if I don't regularly take communion.

---

[1] John 8:32 (NKJV)

[2] Kerry Kirkwood. *The Power of Right Thinking*, (Shippensburg, PA: Destiny Image) 2016. 32.

CHAPTER 4

mental accidental agreements (and imagination)

Accidental Agreements (AA) occur in many areas of your life, but all of them start in the mind. After all, the mind is the center of reason, conclusion, activation, and response. Everything you do, say, think, or feel is experienced and expressed through the mind. The mind is where consciousness, perception, thinking, judgment, and memory originates. It's the center of imagination, passions, desires, ego, recognition, gratitude, reasoning, and attitudes. Thus, the mind is either a powerful ally or a demoralizing enemy.

The mind is separated between the conscious and subconscious. The conscious mind is responsible for logic and reasoning, enabling you to make right and wrong decisions at any given moment. The subconscious is the underlying part of the mind, which controls involuntary actions while also intensely affecting your voluntary actions and emotions. It is also where beliefs and memories are locked away, largely without your knowledge.

Your mind, will, and emotions are based upon life events which have happened to you and how you have interpreted and assessed them. These memories are then stored in your subconscious, waiting to be called upon to tell the mind how to: answer a question; assess whether a situation is dangerous; decide whether to attend an event; determine where you spend your money; know whether to stay in your job; understand how to raise your kids; learn how to deal, or not deal with stress; consider whether you will exercise or not; commit to spend time daily reading the Bible; or select what you eat. Every life decision you make is affected. Everything is a choice.

Your mind, will, and emotions are based upon life events which have happened to you and how you have interpreted and assessed them.

Emotions are attached to these events and help determine how you feel based on your current situation. When something happens to you, the subconscious appears on the scene whispering to your mind. The whisper tells you how to feel about a person, a situation, or how you should react. These thoughts, emotions, and evaluations are stored in your cells. Wow! That's a lot of preconceived ideas. It's a lot of imagination which may or may not line up with the Word of God, not to mention God's perspective about a situation. Can you even begin to fathom the kind of deceit and trickery the enemy uses in this area of your life? He wants to deceive you into believing lies about God and others, and especially about yourself.

In scripture, Satan is referred to as a deceiver, presenting counterfeits to every blessing God has for you. He delights in playing "mind games," tricking you into believing bad things will happen. He tries to make you believe God is incapable of accomplishing good in the face of evil. He tries to convince you God cannot and will not work in your life because of your own corruption, past wounds, and abuses. The lies of the enemy can be very strong and seemingly unbearable at times. Thankfully, God has given us a sound mind[1] and always promises a way out.[2] He wants to help you gain freedom from these lies. Remember this concept, as it is very important: The Lord always promises a way out. Call on Him for help, and He will direct you. I have several personal testimonies about this and have witnessed people escaping from seemingly impossible circumstances.

The Lord always promises a way out.

Dr. Carolyn Leaf, a famous scientist and Christian author, has written several books about the power of the mind over the body. She is well known for her scientific explanation of how negative or skewed thinking creates literal grooves or pathways in the brain. The good news is this skewed thinking can be redeemed. There is a way to get your God-given groove back. In her book, *Switch On Your Brain*, she explains,

> Now scientists know that the brain has the amazing ability to reorganize throughout life, changing its structure and function through mental experience alone. If the brain can get worse by constantly focusing on the problem, then the brain can get better by understanding how to eliminate and replace the problem.[3]

She is referring to a term called Neuroplasticity, which is the brain's ability to change itself through the formation of new neural pathways. At its root, Neuroplasticity is using conscious thought to change the subconscious. Remember how the subconscious controls the emotions you feel in any given situation? Imagine if you were able to rewire how you felt toward someone or something. You would, in turn, have power to control your emotions, thoughts, actions, and words. Those stored lies, or Accidental Agreements, are what lead you to say or act in inappropriate or ungodly ways.

Dr. Leaf goes on to say,

> Neuroplasticity can operate for us as well as against us, because whatever we think about most will grow (in the brain). This theory applies to both the positive and negative ends of the spectrum. The overriding concept is to apply Neuroplasticity in the correct direction by rewiring the event with the positive thinking of Philippians 4:8: "Finally, brothers, whatever is true, whatever is honorable, whatever is just, whatever is pure, whatever is lovely, whatever is commendable, if there is any excellence, if there is anything worthy of praise, think about these things." (ESV)[4]

God knew what He was doing when He told us to focus on things that are honorable and true. By focusing on them, the brain literally creates new pathways of thought. Many people let their minds run free, letting circumstances around them determine their thought processes. In turn, this is a recipe for letting life run them over.

Dr. Leaf states:

> Those who believe you are just your brain believe you have no free will. The active mind changes the brain; the brain is the passive part of existence. As we think, we are making the brain fire in different patterns and combinations, and whenever we make the brain fire differently, we change the brain. Epigenetics research demonstrates that our lifestyles and environment can transform the way our genes are expressed, and evidence

from this field shows we are not being controlled by the structure of our brains.[5]

It takes conscious effort to cause the brain to fire differently; conscious effort to change the way the past is thought about; conscious effort to ultimately change the way a memory affects the mind, will, and emotions. How amazing! Instead of letting the past define who you are, you have the power to rewire your brain and change the way you feel about certain things. You might be thinking, "Well, my brain isn't as strong as you think it is."

To that, Dr. Leaf says: "One brain generates more energy (electrical impulses) in one day than all the cell phones on the planet. So we have the power to make changes; we do not have a spirit of fear, but of love, power and a sound mind."[6, 7]

Your brain is immensely powerful, more so than you can even fathom. Negative thinking may feel as though it has a death grip on you, and it will never let go. It may seem like no amount of conscious thought could reverse the damage already done on your mind. However, as a believer, the spiritual power you have is more powerful than anything on the face of the planet. You have the same spirit inside of you that raised Jesus Christ from the dead and healed deaf ears, blind eyes, and leprosy. Don't you think the same spirit has the power to heal your mind?

IMAGINATION

Merriam Webster defines imagination as "the ability to imagine things that are not real; the ability to form a picture in your mind of something that you have not seen or experienced; the ability to think of new things; something that only exists or happens in your mind."[8]

Our imagination can play an enormous part in halting us from fulfilling our God-ordained destiny. We create ideas in our imagination of what our life should look like; what our marriage should be like; what our kids should do in life; how they should act or react; what our careers should be; how our family dynamics should play out; how our health should be; and the list goes on. Fill in the blank right now of what you are dissatisfied with in life. I am dissatisfied or disappointed with ______________________________. I wish ________________ was different. There is an Accidental Agreement tied to this area. Keep this in mind later.

These ideas are our ideas, not God's! We cannot imagine extravagantly enough to figure out His plans for us, our lives, and our family's lives. It is staggering. It will astonish you! Your jaw will drop when His plan is unfolded to reveal your God-ordained destiny. You will laugh out loud! It is impossible to think or dream up what our lives will look like because, "My thoughts *are* not your thoughts, nor *are* your ways My ways," says the Lord. "For *as* the heavens are higher than the earth, so are My ways higher than your ways, and My thoughts than your thoughts." Isaiah 55:8–9 (NKJV).

But we do exactly that. We create a vision for our lives, and when unfulfilled, it causes disappointment. Everyone does this, from retired grandparents to top executives. We make choices and decisions based upon these preconceived ideas, originating from our imagination. It is extremely important to submit our imagination daily, perhaps hourly, to the Lord by binding it to Jesus each morning. By consecrating, or cleansing our imagination to align with God's intentions, we are positioning ourselves to receive blessings. In my counseling, I find most Accidental Agreements are tied to unforgiveness and unfulfilled expectations in the imagination. This is the primary reason for grumbling. Grumbling is when something is not going the direction we hoped it would go. We become discontent, complain, and are unhappy about something when we truly don't have a clue what God's big picture is for our life. It's our imagination at work!

By consecrating, or cleansing our imagination to align with God's intentions, we are positioning ourselves to receive blessings.

Here is a good example of how this works. A recent incident occurred as Christian volunteers were driving to an important meeting. They were taking my friend, Pastor Paul Varghese from India, to pray over a family with an upcoming marriage. They became lost when all four phones received incorrect directions from their GPS maps. It caused hours of delays, and eventually they were lost. Upon arriving late at the destination, they prayed about the upcoming wedding. Within minutes, the bride-to-be received a call from her doctor announcing the kidney she had waited 14 years to receive had been found and was ready to be transplanted into her body. She had surgery the next day and was married seven days later. That's God! The volunteers could have started grumbling and complaining about the phones, bad directions, how far away they had to drive, how inconvenient this was, or simply turned around and driven home. They chose to believe God was in charge of this delay and made a choice to trust God. Instead, they witnessed a miracle!

Remember Kimberly's testimony at the beginning of the book: she was dealing with many Accidental Agreements. Her mental agreement with the enemy was strong. She had been frozen in fear, unsure how to take forward steps. Nearly every lie was rooted in fear, manifesting in whispers like: "I will never be able to support myself," "My life will be miserable" and "I am not smart enough to get through this."

Do you see how her mind played such a significant role? The lies were repeated subtly in her ear, so she believed them, and they infiltrated and dominated her thinking. Her mind was plagued with negativity, stress, and fear. Her identity had been hijacked. Thankfully, in God's amazing design of the human brain, she was able to overcome the negative thinking by renouncing the Accidental Agreements and replacing them with Truth Statements.

Kimberly decided to record each time she heard the lie and counter it with a Truth Statement, speaking it out loud. She had a job that required typing during the day, allowing her to record the lies as she heard them. After studying her notes at the end of each day, she realized Lie #1 was similar to Lie #5, which was in turn similar to Lie #9. This helped her become aware of the lies, quickly moving them from her subconscious to her conscious mind. She was able to identify the enemy's whispers and the variations of the original lie. When she started receiving blessings, her hope returned and she became excited about life again. She received an "Innocent Spouse" letter from the IRS saving her $50,000; a high-risk loan payable over a ridiculous number of years was suddenly paid in full. There were many other unbelievable God blessings. She began to see how Accidental Agreements work and how her caring Heavenly Father loved to pour out His blessings upon her. They were such outrageous and unexpected blessings it could only be attributed as unmistakably God at work! She was blessed in the very areas in which she had once held Accidental Agreements. Kimberly was finally able to release the mental and emotional stress which had plagued her for years. Relationships were also restored! She was in awe of how great God was towards her and how quickly He extravagantly blessed her.

As with Kimberly, the Holy Spirit will enable you to overcome even the darkest, most deeply hidden thoughts and situations. The Holy Spirit will reveal the areas where you have come into wrongful agreement. One by one, the Holy Spirit will expose the root of each negative thought so it can be dealt with and removed. God will turn the situation or circumstances into something positive for you, not against you, enabling you to receive greater blessings! Utilize the power of Neuroplasticity (changing the physical structure of your brain) along with the power of the Holy Spirit. Ask the Holy Spirit what lie you may be believing right now! Let His Spirit reveal your Accidental Agreement. It's time for blessings!

LIES AND TRUTH STATEMENTS

Read through the following lies which are relevant to you and circle the top three. These are your Accidental Agreements, which we will use later in the book when implementing our AA Freedom Program.

Rather than waiting to begin the program at the end of the book, you can begin now if you prefer. However, when you read the rest of the book, you will find a common theme in the lies you are believing which may help you break the Accidental Agreement more quickly. In the Appendix, you will find the corresponding Truth Statements. Circle the Truth Statements and scriptures that resonate with you. Write the Lie and Truth Statements on a note card and put a mark by the lie each time you hear it, whether it's every minute or every hour. Each time you hear the lie, repeat the Truth Statement and appropriate scripture out loud (dunamis power-Holy Spirit). Continue this for one week, and each day the number of lie whispers should diminish. You will be able to recognize the lies quickly because they are being moved out of your subconscious mind, creating new brain patterns. The more consistently you practice this exercise, the faster the Accidental Agreements will be broken. Once broken, you will see movement in the heavenlies very quickly. Watch for the Lord's blessings! If you are not seeing blessings, read the rest of the book and check the Appendix for *Common Hindrances to Healing*. Ask the Holy Spirit which one applies to your situation. The Holy Spirit will highlight an issue very quickly because He wants to see you blessed!

1. LIE: There's no way for God to correct the mistakes and bad choices I've made. There's no way for God to work everything out for my good.

2. LIE: I'm too tired to continue this battle. This battle is too hard. My whole life is too hard.

3. LIE: I can't accomplish or do ____________________. I'm not smart enough; capable enough; and I lack the resources, etc.

4. LIE: I'm never going to get ahead. I'm going to be stuck in this situation/place/position/ forever.

5. LIE: God doesn't have time for me. God is too busy to bother with the details of my life. God can't be everywhere all of the time. God has bigger things to worry about than me.

6. LIE: God does the best He can (like your perception of an earthly father). God loves me conditionally, like my dad and mother did.

7. LIE: I'm not worthy for someone like God to love me.

8. LIE: God can't really take care of all of my needs or desires.

9. LIE: I won't amount to anything because my (parents, teacher, boss, friends) said I won't.

10. LIE: God is mad at me. God doesn't want to talk to me.

Listed below are additional lies. You may use different Truth Statements for these from the Appendix.

11. LIE: I have lost hope about doing ____________________.

12. LIE: I've messed up too much for God to really use me.

13. LIE: I'm too young or too old for God to use me.

14. LIE: I don't have enough experience for God to use me.

15. LIE: God is mad at me.

16. LIE: God doesn't really love me.

17. LIE: God messed up when he made me.

18. LIE: I will always have a limited life. I am slow. I am not smart enough. I will never be successful.

19. LIE: I don't have enough time to ________________________.

20. LIE: I will never be able to change. I will never be able to ____________________.

21. LIE: I'm going to be (fat, unhappy, unsuccessful, ____________________ like my (mom, dad, brother, sister, family).

22. LIE: God can't heal me and my children from mental issues.

---

[1] 2 Timothy 1:7 (NKJV)
[2] 1 Corinthians 10:13 (NKJV)
[3] Dr. Carolyn Leaf, *Switch On Your Brain* (Grand Rapids, MI: Baker Books) 2015. 61.
[4] Leaf, 63.
[5] Leaf, 65.
[6] Leaf, 65.
[7] 2 Timothy 1:7 (NKJV)
[8] "Imagination." Merriam-Webster.com.

CHAPTER 5
emotional accidental agreements

I decided to divide the categories of mind and emotions due to the impact buried emotions can have in life. Many times, people are confused or react in ways that are less than godly, because of a strong emotion operating in the soul realm, buried deeply in the subconscious. These buried wounds lead to bad conclusions. Bad conclusions lead to hurt feelings and eventually get acted upon in the physical realm. Emotional Accidental Agreements (AA's) are fostered by soul wounds or strongholds which are unhealed, unresolved and twisted. Let's face the facts: hateful and hate filled words yield some of the most penetrating wounds you will endure. Harsh criticism causes deep emotional tearing in the soul, especially when there is a measure of truth in the criticism. Proverbs 18:8 says, "The words of a talebearer are as wounds and they go down into the innermost parts of the belly."[1]

This false truth forces an agreement with the critic, and the enemy rushes in to pour salt on the wound. His taunting words are like poisonous darts. "They are right. You really are no-good." "Nobody loves you."

"Why don't you just go into the darkness and pull the covers over your life." The wound gets stored in the subconscious and off we go with the rest of our week. These wounds don't mysteriously go away. In fact, they are responsible for determining how we deal with stress, anxiety, fear, love, guilt, shame, rejection, and relationships. They influence how we think and how we feel in virtually every aspect of our lives! Please don't downplay the importance of this, because it is very powerful.

SWISS CHEESE–THE HOLE IN YOUR HEART

Soul wounds are as though a hole penetrated your heart and soul. I refer to this as the "Swiss cheese" heart example. It provides a good visual example of what your heart and soul look like when penetrated with soul wounds. Picture a heart looking like a piece of Swiss cheese. It has an outer edge which is complete but the inside is full of little holes. Some of the holes have merged together, causing a bigger hole. This is exactly what your heart and soul look like in the spiritual realm when you have soul wounds from strongholds, or as I call them, Accidental Agreements. The greater the number of soul wounds (holes), the less effective the heart is going to be. Conversely, the fewer the holes (Accidental Agreements or wounds) the better your heart and soul will operate.

> Soul wounds are as though a hole penetrated your heart and soul.

SHALOM WHOLENESS

This is exactly why in Jewish culture the word shalom means, "How are you doing in body, soul, and spirit?" The Jewish people understand we are a whole person. Jesus repeated this in the Old and New Testament when He said, "Love the Lord your God with all your heart and with all your soul and with all your strength and with all your mind."[2] This phrase was repeated in Deut.6:5; Matt. 22:36–40; and Mark 12:30–31. To be repeated four times, it is obviously very important to the Lord. In fact, Jewish people today use this scripture in their mezuzah, which is placed on the doorframe on the outside of their home and the inside doors to invite the presence of the Lord into all parts of their lives.

Our goal is to be able to love God with all of our heart, soul, mind, and strength by being 100% FULL of the Holy Spirit. This is similar to the Jewish concept of shalom. In Paul's day, many Jews greeted each other saying, "shalom." The Hebraic meaning of shalom is both a noun and an action word. Most know the Hebrew word shalom is understood around the world to mean "peace." However, "peace" is only one small part of the meaning. Shalom is used to both greet people and to bid them farewell, and it means much more than "peace, hello, or goodbye."

Hebrew words go beyond their spoken pronunciation. Each Hebrew word conveys feeling, intent, and emotion. Shalom is more than just peace; it is *complete peace.* According to Strong's Concordance, Shalom means "completeness, wholeness, (good) health, peace, welfare, safe, soundness, tranquility, prosperity, perfectness, fullness, rest, harmony, the absence of agitation or discord." Shalom means to be complete, perfect, and full, which is the goal of ridding oneself of Accidental Agreements.

MEDICAL CONFIRMATION

A skewed emotional soul wound will cause chaos in all other areas of your life if left untreated. It will affect all seven Accidental Agreement areas: spiritual, mental (and imagination), emotional, physical, financial, relationships, as well as in your will. It steals the peace promised by Jesus in your life. It will literally make you physically sick. Proverbs 17:22 says, "A merry heart does good like medicine: but a broken spirit dries the bones."[3] A merry heart has healing power! When we are aligned with the

Lord, we are able to reap the benefits of joy the Spirit promises, including tangible blessings! Proverbs 13:12 says, "Hope deferred makes the heart sick."[4] This is a description of how our skewed imagination causes hopelessness, self-pity, depression, jealousy, gossip, lying, and physical illnesses to flourish. There is an underlying Accidental Agreement.

I don't think most people understand the power our hearts, emotions, and minds have over our physical bodies. I will talk about this more in the physical section. Joy and happiness in your heart has been biochemically proven to release positive chemicals in the brain. Likewise, negativity and unhealthy emotional wounds have the power to release toxic chemicals into your body derailing you.

In her book, *Switch On Your Brain*, Dr. Leaf says, "When you think, you also feel. This is because thoughts have an emotional component in addition to the information, or what the actual memory is about."[5]

She goes on to say, "You can choose to reject the presently activated thoughts and the incoming information, or you can let the information make its way into your mind, soul, and spirit, eventually subsiding in your nonconscious and becoming automatized, dominating who you are."[6]

Many medical studies have been conducted which conclusively prove healthy emotions lead to a healthy body, a whole body. In his book, *Raising the Dead*, Dr. Chauncey Crandall, IV, a famous cardiologist, says, "The truth remains that sin can create illness, psychiatric disorders, heart disease, and many other afflictions. Morality is essentially God's description of the way He intended things to work. When we neglect His "operating instructions," our physical health often starts to suffer."[7]

In his book, *Touching Heaven*, Dr. Crandall says:

> Third World believers, who live in cultures where spiritual things are not covered over by the sophistications of

> education or religion, understand that we are always wrestling against the powers of darkness, and that evil spirits have to leave when we bind them up through the name of Jesus. Not so much those of us in First World countries. We are too caught up in the spirit of materialism and entitlement to realize who our true opponent is or how to combat him."[8]

Eph. 6:12 says, "Our struggle is not against flesh and blood, but against the rulers, against the authorities, against the powers of this dark world and against the spiritual forces of evil in the heavenly realms."[9]

Jesus said, "Unless you change and become like little children, you will never enter the kingdom of heaven."[10] Dr. Crandall said:

> He (Jesus) wasn't promoting the immaturity of childlike behavior, but rather the unhindered trust of a child's belief. Such trust is a gift, not a reason for condemnation. It should be no surprise, then, that He (Jesus) urged little children to come to Him, "for the kingdom of heaven belongs to such as these."

Dr. Henry Wright, of Be in Health Ministry, studies the emotional effects on the body and how they are linked to disease. He says in his national bestselling book, *A More Excellent Way to Be in Health*, "More holiness in your life will result in more wholeness. Less holiness in your life will result in less holiness."[13] He says, "I believe there is a connection between sin and disease because Deuteronomy 28 says so. Disobedience to God and His Word and not staying in covenant with Him will open the door to the curse. In Deuteronomy 28, in the section on curses, we found all manner of disease... I do not think God is going to bless us and let us keep our sin."[14]

Many Christians do not believe this because we all know wonderful Christians who have passed to heaven from diseases like cancer. The truth is, there is a spiritual root to almost every disease, which is a barrier to healing and wholeness.

Psalm 103:2–3 says, "Praise the Lord, my soul, and forget not all his benefits who forgives all your sins and heals all your diseases."[15]

The body is an interconnected combination of cells, blood, tissues, organs and intricately designed systems. The brain contains an important combination of glands, secreting chemicals throughout the body. The hypothalamus is important because it links the nervous system to the endocrine system via the pituitary gland. The hypothalamus tells the brain to release chemicals like serotonin and glutamate, which responds to your thoughts and emotions. It interacts with the amygdala, which interacts with the thalamus and hippocampus. Hippocampus helps us process short and long-term memories and helps us stay calm.

Dr. Henry Wright says:

> In fact, all your enemy has to do to produce over 100 major syndromes and diseases is control the activity of your hypothalamus through the mind-body connection...the hypothalamus gland is the facilitator and the originator of the following life circumstances: all expressions of fear, anxiety, stress, tension, panic, panic attacks, phobia, rage, anger and aggression. These are all released and facilitated by this one gland. It only responds to you emotionally and spiritually.[16]

Therefore, when unhealthy memories and emotions are triggered, your internal body, cells, glands, and organs react negatively, releasing the wrong chemicals into your body because of wounded emotions and wrong thinking. Thus, you actually get worse the longer you embrace these Accidental Agreements.

The truth is, there is a spiritual root to almost every disease, which is a barrier to healing and wholeness.

It is as though our heart and soul have little holes in them, little tears, from the soul wounds. Therefore, important pieces of healthy emotional information are missing. This causes misinformation, wrong interpretation of events, skewed feelings and emotions. Wrong beliefs about ourselves invade our body. We have literally created an alliance, or contract, with the enemy in these emotional and mental areas. As we are dominant in our reasoning, tainted by our incorrect assumptions and emotions, we react to situations incorrectly.

Dr. Wright says,

> The only way your soul knows anything is through theta or beta brainwave activity. Satan's invisible spirit world knows this. The only way it can access or influence your thinking is through temptation. It either has to materialize in the physical world, where you can see it, and perceive it through your five senses through beta (brainwaves), or it speaks to your spirit. You hear it and apprehend it through thoughts, impressions and feelings through theta brainwave activity. Your soul is your bridge. There is no entrance to it except through these two brainwaves.[17]

Besides the symptoms mentioned above, emotional agreements can lead to depression, high blood pressure, illness, and even suicide. While a person may never physically take their own life, their health slowly deteriorates as they give up emotional and soul territory to the enemy. In doing so, they give up on a victorious future and live their lives in compromise or defeat. But God is the God of Resurrection. Even when we dig our own graves, He is faithful to dig us out. In fact, the Lord promises a way out. When Accidental Agreements are removed and the truth of God's perspective becomes the emotional standard, people begin to live lives of victory, value, and virtue. God wants us to be whole in body, spirit, and soul. First Thessalonians 5:23 says, "May God himself, the God of peace, sanctify you through and through. May your WHOLE spirit, soul and body be kept blameless at the coming of our Lord Jesus Christ (my emphasis)."[18] God knew what He was saying in this verse. We read these scriptures and fly right past the true meaning.

FEAR

The Bible tells us the only fear we are to have is the fear of the Lord. The world tells us otherwise. Fear sneaks into our world as we deal with life experiences. Fear opens the door to the enemy to harass us with dark thoughts, causing doubt, dread, and distrust. The Lord is clear about asking Him for wisdom. He expects us to exercise wisdom and caution. However, there is a difference between fear and caution. When caution becomes obsessive and fearful, Holy Spirit needs to be consulted about the root of this emotion. It could have entered at birth, from a shocking experience, the possibility of a loss (job, health, loved one, etc.), or dread.

The Bible tells us the only fear we are to have is the fear of the Lord.

There is also a difference between fear and fright. Fright occurs at the moment of danger. Fear is an evil spirit which must be dealt with as sin. Fear opens the door to other types of fear, causing a gaping hole in your soul. Remember the Swiss cheese example? It will dictate your behavior until booted out by asking for forgiveness and repenting. Fear is the opposite of faith. Fear produces worry, leading to many illnesses as described in the section above. Fear robs you of your peace, trust, and even faith. It anticipates trouble through your imagination and is a type of mental cruelty.

Fear can manifest in the following ways: fear of man, abandonment, rejection, failure, being wrong, being abused, dying, being a victim, being controlled, not having an identity, being vulnerable, losing control, the future, poverty, being attacked, being alone, the dark, being unprotected, enclosed places, flying, public speaking, heights, being injured, something bad happening, emotional pain, losing a loved one, or physical pain. It can also manifest as codependency from rejection, talkativeness, attention getting tactics, worry, dread, anxiety, panic attacks, phobias and terror. This is a long list of fears, but finding the original entry point tied to a memory is critical to finding freedom from the controlling fear. Holy Spirit is faithful to reveal exactly where the issue began. It is safe to assume past generations may have had an issue with fear.

Our Heavenly Father desires for us to live a life free from harassment, fear, and anxiety. He lists peace as a Fruit of the Spirit in Galatians 5:22–23. Don't let the enemy entangle you in an Accidental Agreement with fear. We have been given all authority over the enemy through the shed blood of Jesus Christ. Seek the Lord for His perspective about your fear. He wants to bless you in the very area in which you have fear!

Second Timothy 1:7 says, "God has not given us a spirit of fear but of power and of love and of a sound mind."[19]

Philippians 4:6: "Don't worry about anything; instead, pray about everything. Tell God what you need, and thank him for all he has done."[20]

1 Thessalonians 5:23: "Now may the God of peace make you holy in every way, and may your whole spirit and soul and body be kept blameless until our Lord Jesus Christ comes again."[21]

I had a close friend, Jean, who lived through a difficult life. She said, "I guess God is too busy to intervene and handle my situation. He can't be everywhere at the same time. He has more important things to do." These statements were from a strong, life-long Christian who loved the Lord. She had given up hope. In her heart, she started believing the whispers of the enemy. Do you see the Accidental Agreements in these sentences? There are four Accidental Agreements.

1. God is too busy and can't multi-task.
2. God can't or won't intervene, implying He is uncaring towards her painful situation.
3. God can't be everywhere at one time, implying He is limited in His ability.
4. God has more important things to handle. She was not important enough to Him.

Ask, seek, and knock. If there is no clear answer, keep knocking until there is a clear answer. He is working things out behind the scenes. He may be asking you to move your position. Perhaps it is your job, a relationship, or your church. He may be trying to teach you about a generational curse which has been affecting you and your family. He may be asking you to truly forgive someone (including yourself), and you will not give it up. He may be discussing an inner vow you or your ancestors have made. Believe me, God will answer if you keep asking. He does not intend for you to sit idly doing nothing until your answer materializes. In Isaiah 40:31 the Lord says, "But they that wait upon the LORD shall renew their strength; they shall mount up with wings as eagles; they shall run, and not be weary; and they shall walk, and not faint."[22] The word "wait" means to seek counsel, to meditate on His word. Keep knocking!

Believe me, God will answer if you keep asking.

Remember, "For my thoughts are not your thoughts, neither are your ways my ways," declares the Lord. "As the heavens are higher than the earth, so are my ways higher than your ways and my thoughts than your thoughts." [23]

Mike Hutchings, a pastor and teacher with Global Awakening, has had excellent results helping heal PTSD. He says, "You can never trust your feelings. They will lie to you every time." Feelings do not usually speak the truth because we are riddled with soul wounds tainting our perceptions about people, situations or events. Feelings reflect what we believe, think or what we have experienced in the past. They are stored in our subconscious. While feelings are extremely important and should NOT be ignored, we must ask the Holy Spirit for His interpretation of a situation or person because He is the only one who knows the real truth. If you have a negative perception about something or someone, it probably does not line up with the word of God. If this is the case, you have just identified an Accidental Agreement with the enemy. Now, you have a clue and need to find the root cause of the problem which led to your AA. Study the Bible about the topic tied to your root problem and find a scripture which resonates within you. Meditate on the scripture and save it for the "Truth Statement" section at the end of this chapter.

Dr. Crandall says in his book, *Touching Heaven*,

> Right now, as you read these words, the army of God is advancing. The Word of God is active. The Spirit of God is moving. People are being saved and lives are being transformed. Broken, damaged bodies are being

> made well. Lost souls are receiving new life. Mental and emotional chains are being released and minds renewed. Hope is being restored.[24]

He wants to bless you! Jeremiah 33:3 "Call to me and I will answer you and tell you great and unsearchable things you do not know."[25]

JEANIE'S TESTIMONY

Jeanie rented a house, and the lease was expiring. She asked the Lord for a new rental house but heard nothing from Him. She started packing. Everything had to be boxed and put into storage. Jeanie started to feel abandoned and rejected by the Lord and believed God had forgotten about her and her kids. Jeanie's Accidental Agreements were:

1. I actively looked everywhere for a new rental house and could not find one. The answer must be no.
2. I determined God was not going to provide for me. Even though He was supposed to be my husband, I guess He forgot or didn't care much about me.
3. God must be too busy and my house need has fallen through the cracks.

Jeanie had a decision to make. Was she going to trust God or not? She had knocked on every door, answered many ads, checked new neighborhoods and worked hard to locate a suitable house. She worked hard at her job and took advantage of every opportunity provided to her. She was a good mother and provider. She had prayed about this issue for months with her prayer partners. Even though a house had not appeared, Jeanie decided she would start packing and trust God to provide.

The result when Jeanie decided to trust the Lord and the Accidental Agreements were broken:

When Jeanie was almost finished packing, a telephone call revealed a home owner who said they would rent their house to Jeanie. It would not be ready for a few weeks, so he provided free storage. It was better than her previous house. Jeanie had to pack everything and tell the Lord she trusted Him to provide. She thanked Him for His faithfulness and moved into the house a few weeks later.

The Lord expects us to work, be responsible, and step forward in faith. The Lord once told a friend of mine, "It's hard to move a parked car. I don't need to give you directions if you are not moving!"

LIES AND TRUTH STATEMENTS

Read through the following lies that are relevant to you and circle the top three. These are your Accidental Agreements, which we will use later in the book when implementing our AA Freedom Program.

Rather than waiting to begin the program at the end of the book, you can begin now if you prefer. However, when you read the rest of the book, you will find a common theme in the lies you are believing which may help you break the Accidental Agreement more quickly. In the Appendix, you will find the corresponding Truth Statements. Circle the Truth Statements and scriptures which resonate within you. Write the Lie and Truth Statements on a note card and put a mark by the lie each time you hear it, whether it's every minute or hour. Each time you hear the lie, repeat the Truth Statement and appropriate scripture out loud (dunamis power-Holy Spirit). Continue this for one week, and each day the number of lie whispers should diminish. You will be able to recognize the lies quickly because they are being moved out of your subconscious mind creating new brain patterns. The more consistently you practice this exercise, the more quickly the Accidental Agreements will be broken. Once broken, you will see movement in the heavenlies very quickly. Watch for the Lord's blessings! If you are not seeing blessings, read the rest of the book and check the Appendix for *Common Hindrances to Healing*. Ask the Holy Spirit which one applies to your situation. The Holy Spirit will highlight an issue very quickly because He wants to see you blessed!

1. LIE: I don't feel good about ________________(situation, person or circumstance).
2. LIE: I will always feel guilty about ________________.
3. LIE: I feel bad about myself when ________________ happens. It makes me sad and I get depressed.
4. LIE: I get mad when I think about ________________. (List a person or situation).
5. LIE: When I'm depressed or stressed, what brings me comfort/ happiness is ________________.
6. LIE: I'm an emotional person, so I can't help it when I get mad, upset, short tempered or say hurtful things to my family, husband, friend or coworker or ________________. I have a right to give someone a piece of my mind. What I say doesn't really matter. They'll get over it.
7. LIE: If I were married, I would be happy. If I weren't married,

I would be happy. If I were married to someone different, I would be happy.

8. Distrust keeps me safe.

Listed below are additional lies.
You may use different Truth Statements
for these from the Appendix.

9. LIE: I get overwhelmed and stressed when I _______________.

10. LIE: I am disappointed about ______________________________.

11. LIE: I have lost hope about ______________________________.

12. LIE: I don't have enough time to do everything, especially ______________________________.

13. LIE: Christians and others won't/don't like me because: ______ __________________________.

14. If I changed to____________________, they would like me more.

15. LIE: I feel like other people are more worthy of God's attention and deserve His love more than I do.

16. LIE: God can't heal me and my children from emotional problem.

---

[1] Proverbs 18:8 (NKJV)
[2] Luke 10:27 (NKJV)
[3] Proverbs 17:22 (NKJV)
[4] Proverbs 13:12 (NKJV)

[5] Leaf, 49
[6] Leaf
[7] Dr. Chauncey Crandall, *Raising the Dead* (New York: Faithwords) 2010. 180.
[8] Dr. Chauncey Crandall, *Touching Heaven* (New York: Faithwords) 2015. 89.
[9] Ephesians 6:12 (NIV)
[10] Matthew 18:3 (NIV)
[11] Crandall, *Touching Heaven*, 17.
[12] Matthew 19:14 (NLT)
[13] Dr. Henry Wright, www.beinhealth.com. 14 June 2017.
[14] Dr. Henry Wright, *A More Excellent Way to Be in Health* (New Kensington, PA: Whitaker), 2009. 59.
[15] Psalm 103:2–3 (NIV)
[16] Wright, 193–194.
[17] Wright, 113.
[18] 1 Thessalonians 5:23 (NLT)
[19] 2 Timothy 1:7 (NKVJ)
[20] Philippians 4:6 (NLT)
[21] 1 Thessalonians 5:23 (NLT)
[22] Isaiah 40:31 (NKJV)
[23] Isaiah 55:8–9 (NKJV)
[24] Crandall, *Touching Heaven*, 171.
[25] Jeremiah 33:3 (NIV)

CHAPTER 6
physical accidental agreements

Most people attribute physical sickness to physical causes. Did you know many hospital beds are filled with patients who literally THOUGHT themselves there? There is a tendency to separate the mind and body, inferring they are entirely separate from themselves and their spirit. A large majority of physical illness is a result of your thinking, which is aligned with Physical Accidental Agreements (AA). What is true in the spiritual world is true and manifests in the physical and emotional worlds. Whatever is true in the spiritual world is stronger than the other two. These realms mirror each other. Thus, when a person's spiritual life is out of alignment with God's will, the person's physical, mental, and emotional life are wide open to whatever the enemy throws their way. Stress is one of the main points of the enemy's access. Fear is usually the underlying root, and fear is the opposite of faith.

> **When a person's spiritual life is out of alignment with God's will, the person's physical, mental, and emotional life are wide open to whatever the enemy throws their way.**

The dictionary defines "stress" as a condition typically characterized by symptoms of mental and physical tension or strain, as depression or hypertension, resulting from a reaction to a situation in which a person feels threatened or pressured. Dr. Carolyn Leaf has made important discoveries regarding how the mind causes a person to become ill. Specifically, she discusses how our reaction to the events occurring around us often leads to the stress, not the event itself. In her book, *Switch on your Brain*, she says, "Reaction is the key word here. You cannot control the events or circumstances in your life, but you can control your reactions. And controlling those reactions is the difference between healthy minds and bodies and sick minds and bodies."[1]

In fact, take a look at a few of these alarming statistics about stress and our thinking:

1. A study by the American Medical Association found stress is a factor in 75% of all illnesses and diseases.
2. The World Health Organization estimates 80% of all cancer is directly related to lifestyle as opposed to genetics.
3. Dr. Bruce Lipton goes further, stating 98% of disease is related to lifestyle choices.
4. The American Institute of Health estimates 75–90% of all visits to primary care physicians are for stress related problems.

What we understand from these facts is many illnesses are a result of toxic thinking! Your brain is not something which controls you. In fact, it's the opposite. You control the brain through your thoughts and reactions to circumstances around you. Your ability to choose is what makes you human! This ability to choose literally affects the chemicals and wiring of the brain. As I mentioned in the Mental Accidental Agreements section, thinking shapes the neural pathways in the brain.

Dr. Leaf says,

> When you make a decision to focus and direct your brain correctly, you change physical matter in your brain and your body changes in a healthy way. Purposefully catching your thoughts can control the brain's sensory processing, the brain's rewiring, the neurotransmitters, the genetic expression and cellular activity in a positive or negative direction.[2]

In other words, you have the opportunity to choose whether or not to think and feel a certain way when something happens to you. How amazing and powerful is that? Instead of being a slave to what the world and the enemy throws your way, you get to choose how to react! In turn, this effectively means you have the ability to control your physical well-being. Through your decision of not thinking negatively from your Accidental Agreement, your stress level will decrease. Instead of viewing stressful circumstances in the physical realm, view them through the Lord's photo lens. If you view your Father in Heaven as a good Father who has no evil in Him, you must ask Jesus why you are feeling a negative emotion or why you are stressed.

What we are really talking about here, at its core, are Accidental Agreements. When your thoughts do not align with God (negative thoughts) you literally make yourself sick! When you come out of agreement with the enemy and into agreement with God and scripture, you heal. Negative thinking is and always will be contrary to what God thinks about you, meaning it's typically a strategy used by the devil to move you off track. If he can convince you to believe an Accidental

Agreement about your identity, he will have you trapped in a pit of negative, self-destructive thinking. This leads to physical sickness. Some healings require getting out of agreement with past generational bloodline covenants which you inherited at birth. Some of these issues are identified in the Curses Section.

Some healings require getting out of agreement with past generational bloodline covenants which you inherited at birth.

Dr. Henry Wright, founder of Be in Health Ministry and author of *A More Excellent Way To Be In Health* says, "Some people have disease resulting from their ancestor's sin issue. We carry the biological or spiritual results of our ancestors' participation with the enemy."[3] Exodus 20:5 says, "...for I the Lord thy God am a jealous God, visiting the iniquity of the fathers upon the children unto the third and fourth generation of them that hate me..."[4] Dr. Wright's ministry has amazing success healing "incurable" diseases and syndromes due to His commitment and revelation of the Word.

The Physical Section in the Appendix has prayers for specific medical conditions.

ANNA'S TESTIMONY

Let me give you an example of this in action. Anna, a highly-anointed Bible teacher, received amazing downloads from the Lord. She was always blessed with excellent health. Suddenly, she was rushed to the hospital due to severe blood and heart issues. The doctors had trouble stopping her bleeding and were forced to perform heart surgery to insert a stint. She was placed on blood thinner helping balance her blood issue.

She was praying shortly after this, asking the Lord what was going on and why this was happening. She had been in perfect health. The Lord spoke to her, "Anna, you made an Accidental Agreement about how you were going to die. You said, you wanted to die like your mother peacefully in her sleep." To Anna's knowledge, her mother had passed away eighteen years before in her sleep.

However, she began to talk with her brother about what the Lord had spoken to her. Much to her surprise, her brother straightened out a misunderstanding concerning how her mother passed away. Instead of passing away peacefully in her sleep, Anna's mother had suffered a massive heart attack. And what do you know, this was exactly where Anna's health was headed!

Some would call the issue genetics, but it was actually an Accidental Agreement. Just because a parent dies of one cause does NOT mean the child will die from the same issue. Anna immediately understood the gravity of what she had accidentally believed. What she had thought to be an innocent belief was on its way to killing her. She happily fell to her knees and repented for her agreement with the enemy, fully renouncing its power over her. Guess what? She is still alive and well today, freely sharing this story with all whom she comes into contact. Her story will save many lives!

God is very serious about the words we say. The word "bless(ed) and blessing(s)" is mentioned over 1000 times in the Bible. The word "curse(d)(ing)" is mentioned over 250 times in the Bible. Words have more power than we understand.

BOOMERANG CONCEPT

The definition of a boomerang is: a curved, flat piece of wood that can be thrown so as to return to the thrower, traditionally used by Australian Aborigines as a hunting weapon; or a plan or action that returns to the originator, often with negative consequences." Synonyms for a boomerang are: backfire, recoil, reverse rebound, ricochet; self-defeating; blow up in one's face.

Word curses are like a boomerang. When you speak unkind or negative words about someone, the words are thrown back at you like a boomerang, causing damage. These words actually cause spiritual damage to you and your family.

This word curse concept is identified as a COVENANT in Hosea 10:4. "They have spoken words, swearing falsely in making a covenant. Thus, judgment springs up like hemlock in the furrows of the field."[5] In the Bible, hemlock refers to a poison (poisonous plant) in the field or territory you have been praying for, seeding, planting, and cultivating! In Hosea's culture, the people's promises with each other were not kept. Instead they lied and stole from each other. Hosea is describing an Accidental Agreement word curse with the enemy! When you speak negative words, you have made a judgment about someone or a situation, which is a spiritual foul. God is the only one allowed to judge. If we judge, God will judge us in the same manner. Our judgment is tied to bitterness. We intend to harm someone else (even gossip counts) by speaking ill of them. Instead, the mean words boomerang back onto us like swallowing poison.

> "Today I have given you the choice between life and death, between blessings and curses. Now I call on heaven and earth to witness the choice you make. Oh, that you would choose life, so that you and your descendants might live!"[6]

> "Behold, I set before you today a blessing and a curse: the blessing, if you obey the commandments of the Lord your God which I command you today; and the curse, if you do not obey the commandments of the Lord your God, but turn aside from the way which I command you today, to go after other gods which you have not known."[7]

REMEMBER: BLESSINGS ALWAYS TRUMP CURSES. God's blessings are always more powerful than any trick Satan can devise. However, you must ***identify*** where you or your ancestors believed the lie and came into agreement with him. You must repent for yourself and all generations. It's that easy.

TRAUMA

Major trauma stores in your cells, heart, soul, and subconscious. Untreated, it leads to illness, disease, pain, immune system issues, depression and many other health problems. Major trauma can occur from events such as: a car accident, job loss, moving homes or cities, divorce, death, financial devastation, serious or debilitating injury, or other disturbing incidents. When the traumatic event occurs, fear enters the person's body and becomes an open door for the enemy to affect their life. Until the spirit of trauma is removed, complete healing will not happen.

The sooner the trauma and fear are removed, the sooner your body will begin to heal. Joan Hunter with Joan Hunter Ministries has some excellent books on healing trauma. *Healing the Whole Man* discusses trauma and how to remove it. Joan has interesting testimonials about heart transplant recipients experiencing memories from their heart donor. After prayer for trauma, the "trauma memory" in the heart recipient was erased. See Appendix for the Trauma Breaking Prayer.

REBECCA'S TESTIMONY

Rebecca hobbled into my home full of back pain. Her L4 and L5 documented dislocated discs and sciatic nerve pain shooting down her legs had her in full-blown discomfort mode. We began with a forgiveness prayer. We were silent and asked the Lord to download the names of people she and I were holding unforgiveness towards. God faithfully gave Rebecca the names of people. One by one, Rebecca repented in prayer for holding onto bitterness. She renounced the agreements with the enemy and asked the Lord to cleanse her with the blood of Jesus. We asked the Lord to fill the vacant places occupied by the enemy with His Shekinah glory light and His dunamis power.

However, the Lord said she had not forgiven herself. I asked Rebecca if she still held unforgiveness toward herself and she replied YES! The Accidental Agreements were: "God is not big enough to help her overcome her mistakes," and "this situation caught God by surprise." Rebecca asked for forgiveness from the Lord. She repented, renounced her agreement with the enemy, and asked the Lord to cleanse her with the blood of Jesus. She immediately stood up straight and walked out pain free! Just like that she was healed! Jesus is not complicated and He wants all of your heart!

KNEE TESTIMONY

Christy suddenly developed pain in her knee. She went to a counselor, who asked what Accidental Agreement she was holding onto in regard to her knee. Christy asked the Holy Spirit. He replied, "Christy, you think this battle is too hard for you, and it is too difficult to stand." The Holy Spirit told Christy, "The battle is not yours; it belongs to me (the Lord)." Christy asked for forgiveness, repented, and asked the Lord to cleanse her from this sin. She asked the dunamis power of the Lord to fill her soul wounds. Her knee immediately felt better!

A similar situation happened with her ankle. Her ankle was slightly twisted and painful. She asked the Lord what Accidental Agreement she had. He said, "You are trying to stand in your own strength in this battle instead of letting me handle it." Christy repented and surrendered her control. Her ankle felt better immediately, and her right leg straightened.

SUMMARY

God did not create you to live a fear or stress-filled life. He created you to be saturated with righteousness, love, peace, and joy. His desire is for you to be healthy and whole. He desires for you to be unmarred by Satan's opinions and lies. He wants you to be unhurt and unoffended by those who say unkind comments. God's opinion is the only opinion which matters. You are His child, a princess or prince of royal blood, created for His purpose. You enjoy a royal inheritance of blessings. Real blessings. By breaking the Accidental Agreements, you will be catapulted into your God-ordained destiny, full of miracles. However, you must choose to step away from believing the lies of the enemy. You must acknowledge and reject those agreements and begin to believe, speak, and live God's true opinion of who you are. See Appendix 2, the Lies and Truth Statements in the Physical Section, for Health Declarations and healing scriptures.

> **By breaking the Accidental Agreements, you will be catapulted into your God-ordained destiny, full of miracles.**

LIES AND TRUTH STATEMENTS

Read through the following lies that are relevant to you and circle the top three. These are your Accidental Agreements, which we will use later in the book when implementing our AA Freedom Program.

Rather than waiting to begin the program at the end of the book, you can begin now if you prefer. However, when you read the rest of the book, you will find a common theme in the lies you are believing which may help you break the Accidental Agreement more quickly. In the Appendix, you will find the corresponding Truth Statements. Circle the Truth Statements and scriptures which resonate within you. Write the Lie and Truth Statements on a note card and put a mark by the lie each time you hear it, whether it's every minute or hour. Each time you hear the lie, repeat the Truth Statement and appropriate scripture out loud (dunamis power-Holy Spirit). Continue this for one week, and each day the number of lie whispers should diminish. You will be able to recognize the lies quickly because they are being moved out of your subconscious mind creating new brain patterns. The more consistently you practice this exercise, the more quickly the Accidental Agreements will be broken. Once broken, you will see movement in the heavenlies very quickly. Watch for the Lord's blessings! If you are not seeing blessings, read the rest of the book and check the Appendix for Common Hindrances to Healing. Ask the Holy Spirit which one applies to your situation. The Holy Spirit will highlight an issue very quickly because He wants to see you blessed!

1.LIE: I will never get well. My doctor says I will always have this disease or limitation. This disease runs in my family, so I will just have to live with it; it's genetic. My doctor says there is no cure for this. I way born this way. I will always have…

See Appendix 1 for the Stronghold Breaking and Blessing Prayer, the Curse Breaking Prayers and Trauma Breaking Prayer. See Appendix 2 for Health Declarations.

Physical Appearance

2. LIE: My physical appearance matters more to people and God than my inner appearance. I don't need to exercise, stay in shape or eat healthy. God doesn't really care about that kind of stuff.

3. LIE: If I had a different ______________________ I would be happier/more effective for the kingdom. People would like me better. My life would be better. I wish I had a different: _________________, head, ears, nose, mouth, eyes, cheeks, neck, body, legs, arms, torso, feet, knees, fingers, etc.,

Listed below are additional lies. You may use different Truth Statements for these from the Appendix.

4. LIE: No one should ever have to go through what I went through when __________________________________happened.

5. LIE: God can't heal me and my children from physical problems.

6. LIE: I have lost hope about __________________________.

7. LIE: God doesn't care about my appearance or health. I don't have enough time to exercise.

---

1 Leaf, 37
2 Leaf, 73
3 Wright, 124
4 Exodus 20:5 (KJV)
5 Hosea 10:4 (NKJV)
6 Deuteronomy 30:19 (NLT)
7 Deuteronomy 11:26–28 (NKJV)

CHAPTER 7
financial accidental agreements

"Beloved, I pray that you may prosper in all things and be in health, just as your soul prospers." 3 John 1:2

"Let your character *or* moral disposition be free from love of money [including greed, avarice, lust, and craving for earthly possessions] and be satisfied with your present [circumstances and with what you have]; for He [God] Himself has said, I will not in any way fail you *nor* give you up *nor* leave you without support. [I will] not, [I will] not, [I will] not in **any** degree leave you helpless *nor* forsake *nor* let [you] down (relax My hold on you)! Assuredly not! So we take comfort *and* are encouraged *and* confidently *and* boldly say, The Lord is my Helper; I will not be seized with alarm [I will not fear or dread or be terrified]. What can man do to me?"[1] Hebrews 13:5 AMP

People love to discuss this topic! I have exciting testimonies to share with you about people prospering financially when they came out of Accidental Agreements (AA) with the enemy. However, this is NOT a teaching suggesting the Lord hands out blessings whenever we ask, regardless of whether we are sinning or have wrong heart motives. If greed or pride are involved with your financial prayers, creating a cord to the enemy, forget it. God cannot bless a heart motive of pride, greed, bitterness, or any other enemy motivated agenda. He is, however, a good Father who loves to bless His children and help them prosper in ALL things. But, He will not break His laws to do this. Bill Johnson has a book entitled, *God Is Good, He's Better Than You Think*. It is a clear explanation of how wonderful our Heavenly Father really is.

There is a misunderstanding about financial matters in mainstream Christianity today. Most people claim God is interested in all aspects of their lives, including their finances. But at the core, many believe money is the root of all evil. They believe being too wealthy is sinful; therefore, God limits His provision. Because an item or service may be greater than our "need," people assume anything in excess is contrary to God's will. This is just one financial example of the many lies perpetrated by the enemy we will cover in this chapter. Belief in these lies leads to Accidental Agreements which inhibit your ability to receive financial blessings from the Lord. I can assure you, if you believe God doesn't want you to have money, you won't. Where faith is lacking, blessing is lacking. Distress and unbelief often abound because of the hopelessness which develops because of Accidental Agreements.

Belief in these lies leads to Accidental Agreements
which inhibit your ability to receive
financial blessings from the Lord.

Let's set the record straight. We may be the one who "makes" the money, but the Lord is the one who provides and allows us to make money. The reality is, God wants to prosper you in ALL areas. He wants you to have provision, wealth, and abundance in this life, as well as wanting to prosper you in non-monetary ways. However, they are not mutually exclusive. The more you have, the more you can give. God is not blessing you with money to lavishly spend on yourself or others you randomly choose. He is also not blessing you with money to give to a cause or a person He does not ordain. He is God and we are not.

We are His servants and need to act accordingly. A cup overflowing has excess to share, but an empty cup has nothing to give. This is one way to show the light and love of Jesus. Jesus said THE LOVE of money is the root of all evil, not money itself. The Bible states materialism, greed, and the desire for money with the wrong intentions are what the Lord despises. Despises! God looks at the heart and the motives of why we have certain habits and behaviors. If the underlying motivation is to gain money and wealth for personal gain or pride or any other personal agenda, God will not endorse this. The Bible does not say anything about God promising us money. But, He does promise ABUNDANT blessings! Read Deuteronomy 28.

I don't know about you, but many Christians tend to have some guilt in their heart when one succeeds financially. It's as if we think it is sinful to be blessed in this area. Well, can I be blunt? That's an Accidental Agreement! To come out of agreement, it's imperative you understand God's truth about financial freedom in your life. God is fully capable of blessing everyone in all aspects of their lives. These blessings will abound spiritually, mentally, emotionally, physically, relationally, financially, and in your will. They are all interconnected. God may choose to bless you in an unexpected way, or He may choose to bless you through the marketplace with His power working through you.

One of the primary reasons many Christians believe money is evil is they see it spent incorrectly. Instead of using it as a tool to bless others, it's selfishly spent on materialistic possessions. Often people use it to gain higher status in society or to fill "holes" in their hearts. Material items temporarily help them feel better about themselves. Remember these holes are really "soul wounds," known as strongholds in the Bible, i.e., Accidental Agreements. Some people use their money as a signal to show others they are more important than those around them. Additionally, they can be intentionally benevolent by extravagantly spending money to show off their riches and gain attention. Something is out of balance in their lives. There is something unfulfilled they are longing to find. The answer is Jesus. They just don't know it yet.

Believe me, I understand why it can be easy to think this way. A great deal of "mixing" good intentions and God's intentions takes place in this world! The enemy is a master at mixing, disguising, or confusing the truth. But you can't let other people's sin or strongholds determine what you believe. You must go to the Bible and follow what it says. Listen to the Holy Spirit. Do not rely only on your personal life experiences. Just because some people are poor stewards over what they've been given does not mean the blessing is nullified. God will offer correction until they become good stewards.

How many times do we see the enemy distort something God meant as a blessing? Often, if you pay attention, you will find many areas in which people struggle most are the areas God has promised blessings! Satan sees this, creating a false belief system in that area, ultimately keeping people from pursuing God's original promise and blessing! After all, if you think something is wrong in the eyes of God, you won't pursue it. It's a demonic strategy set up to keep you from understanding God's true design and blessing for your life. It can ultimately delay you from achieving your God-ordained destiny. Don't settle for less than your FULL inheritance. God has tremendous, custom-designed blessings just for you.

God has given each one of us a skill set, which are God given talents and gifts. The information about the various "intelligences" as defined by educators is one such example. Keep in mind, there are thousands of unique gifts. When someone identifies and hones their God-ordained skill sets in their specialty areas, they are preparing for additional blessings. Ask the Holy Spirit to find a complimentary, gifted person who will take both of you to the next level in life. God prefers to work this way, as He does not want us walking alone on our journey. This partnership provides additional resources, protection and wisdom. God can and will activate and accelerate these gifts at any age in your life. He may be asking you to make a change. People develop at different speeds, so let's not judge.

Leviticus 26:8: "Five of you shall chase a hundred, and a hundred of you shall put ten thousand to flight; your enemies shall fall by the sword before you."[2]

Another way God loves to prosper us is in the area of creativity. God is a creative God who loves blessing His people with imaginative and innovative ideas. After all, He created the earth and everything in it. If you look around, you will realize how magnificently a flower is constructed; how a tree and its leaves are unique; how gorgeous the clouds appear, and the list goes on. God loves to drop inspired and artistic ideas into our minds to help us and others prosper. He loves blessing His kids with unique ideas which will delight their hearts.

I attended a conference led by Arthur Burk of the Sapphire Group. A lady sheepishly raised her hand and told the instructor she had always had a fascination with rocks. He encouraged her to pursue this dream as God had placed this passion for rocks and land inside of her from birth. He suggested she study rocks, research geological information, and join a rock club. Now, you may be thinking, a rock club sounds a little boring. But this proves God's amazing design all the more. You see, he gave this woman a passion for rocks, not you. He has given you other gifts and passions to pursue His design for YOUR life.

When the Lord gives you a creative idea, isn't it easy to sometimes dismiss it as a fleeting thought or a dumb, far-fetched idea? The truth is, great ideas are from Him. Instead of dismissing it, ask the Lord if the idea you heard was from Him. "Throw out your fleece" as Gideon did in the Old Testament.[3] Gideon was told to take his army to fight the Midianites. He questioned the Lord's request. In an effort to receive confirmation, he laid out a wool fleece overnight. He asked the Lord to wet the wool fleece with dew, and cause the ground to be completely dry. The Lord caused this to happen. Gideon prayed again for the Lord to give a second confirmation. This time he asked for the ground to be wet with dew, but the fleece to be dry. God also caused this to happen. Are you needing confirmation to pursue an idea? Throw out the fleece and see if it is the Lord speaking.

The Lord promises to answer prayer when you ask, believing in faith you will receive an answer. Many times, these ideas were given from God Himself in order to bless you. So take them seriously! If He clearly said to pursue the idea, do not stop until He says to stop. He may alter your direction, so listen carefully. It may be the beginning of a learning journey He wants you to explore. This journey will be filled with adventure, excitement, and tremendous blessing.

Recently, an idea for a new phone app was presented to me by my daughter. It sounded promising so I called my attorney asking if it had already been created. After researching the topic, he said a major corporation had patented something similar a few months earlier. Instead of continuing, I stopped. However, what should have occurred, was to prayerfully seek direction from the Lord. Should I stop? I even had a fleeting thought, should I still pursue it? But my reasoning and common-sense side said no, it's been created. The reality was, God wanted me to keep pursuing the app.

The truth is, had I pursued it further, I would have succeeded. One year later, another app developer came out with the same app but found an alternate use. Yes, I missed it, but it's okay. My Heavenly Father has many ideas. My lesson: He was training me to listen closer to His whispers. He has many more ideas. He is not a punitive Father. He knew I was going to make the mistake before I even made it! Everything we do is a training ground to know Him better and discover how He is incredibly loving and forgiving.

Often, your vocation may be an indicator or reflection of your God-ordained destiny within the Kingdom. When I worked in commercial real estate, God had already put inside of me a skill set to sell, lease and develop real estate, i.e. take territory. Now I work on reclaiming and restoring territory for the Lord. No matter what your current job, God will use these skills in your next career to influence the marketplace for Him. Learn as much as you can in your current job and take advantage of new opportunities. Think creatively.

Have you ever thought about there being only one tribe out of twelve called into ministry? If we're going by those numbers, this means less than 10% of believers are called to be in ministry. The rest of us are called to serve the Lord AND be in the marketplace taking care of family, working and reaching nonbelievers right where we are. In fact, many times marketplace believers have a much bigger podium to reach nonbelievers than even those in full-time ministry. Never feel as though you are inferior or somehow not living the life the Lord wanted you to live. Chances are, God has called you to be in the position you currently hold. Glorify Him in your work and let your life be a reflection of Jesus to those around you! He will arrange for you to go on mission trips or serve Him in other ministry capacities which will delight your heart!

Let's take a look at what the Bible says about work:

Colossians 3:23–24 "Whatever you do, work heartily, as for the Lord and not for men, knowing that from the Lord you will receive the inheritance as your reward. You are serving the Lord Christ."[4]

Proverbs 13:4 "The soul of the sluggard craves and gets nothing, while the soul of the diligent is richly supplied."[5]

Philippians 4:13 "I can do all things through him who strengthens me."[6]

2 Thessalonians 3:10–12 "For even when we were with you, we would give you this command: If anyone is not willing to work, let him not eat. For we hear that some among you walk in idleness, not busy at work, but busybodies. Now such persons we command and encourage in the Lord Jesus Christ to do their work quietly and to earn their own living."[7]

Proverbs 14:23 "In all toil there is profit, but mere talk tends only to poverty."[8]

Philippians 2:14–15 "Do all things without grumbling or questioning, that you may be blameless and innocent, children of God without blemish in the midst of a crooked and twisted generation, among whom you shine as lights in the world."[9]

Proverbs 16:3 "Commit your work to the Lord, and your plans will be established."[10]

For many of you, you may feel exhausted with your work. You may feel spiritually, emotionally, and physically drained every day. God calls you to work, and work hard, but He does not call you to work to exhaustion. If you are exhausted all the time, there may be something wrong or out of balance in your life. In fact, you may not be in the position where God wants you. The position where you will thrive with your God given skill set is what He desires. This is certainly an area in which you need to consult the Holy Spirit. He will never place you in a position where you will not thrive!

At other times, you may be in the right position, but there are minor personal changes needing to be made. Maybe it's a simple issue of time management. Ask the Lord to prioritize your time. This is exactly what I did years ago. He helped prioritize my tasks by having me write my "to do" list every morning for my day and week. I would submit the list to Jesus and asked Him to prioritize and bless the list. I was amazed how He took control of my day. The tasks I identified as high priority were sometimes not important to Him. He rearranged my day and I found myself rested at the end of each day. Many tasks miraculously were completed or eliminated without me. When this happened the first time, I was much more productive and thought it was a special day. The second time, I realized it was God. By the third day, it was a relief to know He was handling my schedule and the accompanying details. I would laugh out loud some days because my "to do" list was handled by God in such a way I had extra time! I had a demanding schedule and was triple booked most days with intense meetings. Yes, it only takes a few minutes in the morning, but allowing God to prioritize your day will save hours as well as make life more fun!

Here are a few exciting testimonies of God's goodness and attention to detail.

JILL'S HOUSE TESTIMONY

My friend Jill, understood God's financial economy. It seemed the harder she and her husband worked to get ahead, the bigger the hole in their "money bag." When her husband decided to get rid of bitterness once and for all, their "never getting ahead" cycle ended. The enemy was stopped from stealing their resources. The Lord immediately brought a full price offer on their home; provided a new home in the perfect area they never thought possible; helped discover furniture at ridiculously low prices (wonderful pieces at garage sale prices), and the list goes on. God knew her heart motivations were pure. She is opening her home to "pop up" Christian speakers and Bible studies, whatever God wants. Is she already busy? Yes. Does she have kids? Yes. Is God making a way where there seems to be no way? Yes. She kept thanking the Lord for what He wanted to give her. Obedience and thankfulness allowed her to be led by the Holy Spirit with each carefully purchased item. God wants to do this for everyone. That means you, the person reading this now!

MACY'S PANTS' TESTIMONY

My friend needed a pair of khaki work slacks for her husband. She went to Macy's, hoping they would have a reasonably priced pair. Unknown to her, Macy's had a sale. One pair of khaki pants remained in the back of the store, exactly his size. She ended up purchasing them for 75% off plus her coupon. This happens almost every time she buys him pants. Now, before she purchases any item, she asks the Lord about timing and pricing. This deep discount blessing also happens when she buys her niece clothes. She is frugal, led by the Holy Spirit, and generous.

Several other women I know ask the Lord for their work clothes, and He graciously honors them with the identical blessing. He gives them beautiful clothes at a fraction of the cost, sometimes free. However, if you have six dresses and you are asking for another, He may say "not now" because it is not needed. If your kids need clothes, ask your Heavenly Father.

Note: The Lord uses other major retailers besides Macy's to bless!

RUG TESTIMONY

My Oriental rug was stored at the cleaners for one year while I cared for my mother who had been diagnosed with cancer. When it was returned, the delivery personnel put it in my basement. I went downstairs a few weeks later to discover little mounds of dirt everywhere. I discovered moths had eaten the center of my rug, destroying it. The mounds were "leftovers" of my rug. The outside of the rug was untouched, as were the clothes nearby. The delivered rug was still tied with twine from the cleaners. Moth larvae were inside the rug, cross-contaminated at the cleaners. I knew it was unlikely the rug company would take responsibility because I could not confirm my belief. Turning a claim into the insurance company was not possible as I had several natural disaster claims already (all teaching me God's economy).

AA Lie: My first reaction was, "Oh no, I can't replace this rug. It's not fair, it's ruined. I didn't do anything wrong. Why is this happening to me?"

Truth Statement to Break the AA: "No, God knew it was contaminated before it came into my house. He sees everything and that includes moth eggs. He also knew it would not be discovered until the rug was damaged beyond repair. God, I don't know how and I don't know when, but I know you are going to replace it someday." Honestly, I said this half-heartedly.

The Result: Surprisingly, several months later, a letter from my mom's estate notified me I was to receive her Oriental rug. It was the same size, only better because it belonged to my mother. It is a cherished heirloom!

MICROBURST TESTIMONY

In 2012, I had a microburst (mini tornado) strike my backyard. Five huge trees fell on my house, impaling the chimney in my sunroom and pulling the chimney off the house. It also hit my daughter's and son's rooms. No one else in my neighborhood had damage except one neighbor a block away. My backyard looked like a war zone.

My Accidental Agreement:

1. Lie: I started to complain, "Oh poor me, not another devastating event. Why does this always happen to me?" These statements imply God isn't watching or protecting me.

Truth: God knows, sees and cares about every detail. He promises to turn everything for good.[11]

2. LIE: "The micro burst caught God by surprise."

Truth: He's omniscient, omnipresent, omnipotent.[12]

3. Lie: "God can't protect my property. I blessed my property, so I don't understand why this happened. Was God not paying attention?"

Truth: God can and does protect us and our property. He has a plan much bigger and better than we can imagine or dream up.[13]

4. Lie: "God can't handle the expenses or reconstruction. He can't manage the details."

Truth: God can handle the expenses and details to rebuild this mess. He built the entire world, so I think He can handle this construction job.[14]

Several months before this happened, God had begun teaching Accidental Agreements to me. Initially, I started to feel despair when this happened, but then switched my position. I broke the Accidental Agreement immediately. Standing in my dining room looking at destruction, I spoke out loud: "No God, you knew this was going to happen before it happened. I will not make an agreement with the enemy. God is in charge. He will take care of everything." Immediately, I felt a "shift" in the atmosphere.

Result After Breaking the AA:

A tree contractor suddenly appeared and hauled off the fallen trees for half the price. My previous contractor who remodeled the house was not available to rebuild. A new construction company bid the project. They turned out to be fast, inexpensive, and excellent quality. It was a seamless reconstruction.

Insurance coverage paid for everything except my $5,000.00 deductible. I started to make another Accidental Agreement. I thought, "Lord, I am still having to pay $5,000.00 for the insurance deductible. This is not fair. I didn't do anything wrong. I do not believe it was an act of God, because God is not destructive." I said out loud, "God, I don't know how or when, but I am trusting you to give back the $5,000.00 the enemy tried to steal."

One month later, I received a letter from my insurance company. I thought it was a cancellation letter. After two weeks, I finally opened the letter. I said, "God if they cancel me, you knew it was going to happen, so okay." Instead, I found a check for $5,000.00 to pay for a huge tree I had lost. I never claimed the tree on insurance. It repaid my deductible! That's God!

KATIE'S STUDENT LOAN TESTIMONY

Katie had $32,000 on a student loan left to pay off. Currently, she was in a difficult financial position from various hardships and was not able to make payments. She fell behind on her loan. She was toying with the idea of not tithing to have funds for her student loan. She began an intense time of prayer for the next two weeks. God led her to ask for forgiveness of sins from past generations and herself for not always handling money the right way. She also asked for forgiveness when she didn't tithe in the past. She repented for herself and past generations who "stole" the Biblical 10% tithe and for not trusting God's provision capability. She told God she was going to trust Him to meet all her needs. She decided she was not going to tell God how she thought He should handle the situation. God would provide the best way, however that might look.

After two weeks of prayer and releasing this burden to God, she received an unexpected call from a couple she knew. These people had no way of knowing she had a student loan or about her recent financial hardships. They said God had placed her on their heart and had instructed them to help. They asked her, "Do you have a student loan you are currently not able to pay off?" She was stunned at the question. Katie said she was in debt and not able to pay the loan. God revealed to the couple she needed a debt paid off. In obedience, the couple wanted to pay Katie's student loan debt, no matter the cost. The next day her student loan was paid in full. She was completely out of debt! Katie was diligent to hear from the Lord about her problem, asked for forgiveness, and repented on behalf of herself and past generations. These steps removed Accidental Agreements in the bloodline that were operating as curses. That is God's economy in action!

BETHANY'S LANDSCAPE TESTIMONY

Bethany and her husband purchased a home intending to tear it down and rebuild new. When construction was finished, they had huge mud pits in both back and front yards, void of any living plants other than trees. Wanting to be wise with their finances, they chose to delay purchasing grass and plants for landscaping the property. One morning, Bethany walked to the rear of their house, looked at the backyard and started speaking with God. She simply said, "Lord, I know the desires of my heart are important to you and I know You love me. Could you bless us with grass, plants, and flowers we could enjoy?" She listed all her favorite plants, even telling God the location she would like to plant them. She thought the yard would look beautiful. She thanked Him for what He would do and for listening to her heart. One week later, she received a call asking her to look at a model home. When she arrived, the owner said, "It is a shame the landscaping will go to waste as they are tearing it out." They asked if she knew anyone who might be interested. The owners even offered having their employees take out the grass, flowers, and plants. After they transplanted the landscaping, she realized every specific plant she mentioned to God (except one), including sod, had been planted in their yard. One week later she was thanking God for this amazing miracle. Five months later, their home won yard of the month!

Bethany did not come into agreement with the enemy suggesting God did not have enough resources to finish her landscaping. She also did not believe the lie that God did not care about her circumstances. In fact, Bethany expressed her innermost feelings by specifying which variety of plant, flower, and bush she would enjoy having if she had a choice. She thanked the Lord for His faithfulness. By repenting for her own and past generational financial curses, she came into alignment with God, removing her Accidental Agreements. This allowed her to become blessed! Can you imagine receiving from your Heavenly Father the exact rose bushes you desired?!

COMMON LIES ABOUT MONEY

I would like to discuss some of Satan's common money lies he uses to penetrate our minds and thoughts. Most of these lies are initiated by or related to Accidental Agreements. Money and possessions are the second most referenced topic in the Bible. Money is mentioned more than 800 times. Let's begin uncovering your lie!

A common lie is: "Money is evil and leads all people down a dark path. Therefore, having it would be sinful."

Did you know many of the Old Testament characters were extremely wealthy and blessed by God? Abraham, Isaac, Jacob, David, Solomon, and even Job were a few of the wealthiest people to have ever lived up to this point in time. In fact, Solomon is considered by many to be the wealthiest man of all time. The question becomes if God blessed them, how could money be inherently evil?

Most people hinge their belief system on Jesus's teaching in Matthew 19:16–23. He said it's harder for a rich man to enter the kingdom of God than for a camel to walk through the eye of a needle.[15] This teaching is taken out of context and is used by the enemy to keep people from pursuing God's financial blessing. Jesus is not saying money is bad. What He is saying is the rich man often trusts more in his materialistic goods and wealth than he does in the Lord. In other words, man is greedy. A person's dependence on worldly possessions is evidence of his underlying insecurity. This mindset is disbelief in God's ability to provide. Money and possessions become an idol. We know how God feels about idols! I repeat, the underlying belief is God cannot or will not provide for our needs. This is fear based.

How do we know this is what Jesus is saying? Because it's His answer to the young rich man who could not find it within himself to sell all he had and follow Jesus. The young ruler wasn't willing to sacrifice and surrender the very thing he was dependent upon, his money. Jesus said it's harder for the rich man to enter the kingdom. Men and women place their trust in the wrong source. The source, money, and their dependence upon it, becomes an idol.

The underlying belief is God cannot or will not provide for our needs. This is fear based.

Money is a tool. In our world, it carries the power to do both good and evil. Imagine for one second what our world would be like if the billionaires were God-fearing men and women. I believe much of the world's poverty, slavery, prostitution, and disease would be greatly minimized. God wants us all involved in the eradication of social injustice and disease.

Before you begin thinking "Well, they aren't God-fearing because the money made them greedy," I want you to look at this differently. Money does not change people; it simply enhances or accentuates who they are at their core, Accidental Agreements and all. Initially many wealthy people pursued wealth to live the "good life," or a better life for themselves and their family. However, some wanted to feel superior to others. Whichever road chosen, the individuals discovered they were unfulfilled when they reached their end goal.

They kept striving, hoping for fulfillment, never realizing monetary pursuit would not satisfy them. Some of the unhappiest people I know are very wealthy. They appear happy, but they continue searching for the "pot of gold" to make everything feel OK inside. This searching is really for Jesus and the peace, satisfaction, and soul healing He gives. Jesus is the only one who can provide this supernatural shalom peace. The "hole in their heart" existed before they ever began their money and intellectual pursuit. In fact, this hole is often the reason for their pursuit in the first place. Money did not change them, it simply made them more of who they were from the beginning.

What if we had more strong, passionate, and zealous Christians pursuing Jesus, believing the wealth blessing was intended to help change the world? If money truly is a tool, wouldn't it make sense to collect as many tools as possible to use in building the kingdom of God? I have personally met many wonderful Christians who walk in the blessing of wealth from God. Their humble work and influence for the kingdom is inspiring!

Let's be clear: there is no monetary wealth requirement to be influential in God's kingdom. In fact, I would hope your church places value on the obedient saints who hear from the Lord. These individuals are the real "movers and shakers" in God's kingdom. I have met many saintly Christians with very unique and valuable spiritual gifts. They have their own "God phone lines," receiving amazing heavenly downloads and revelation. Personally, they are my heroes. These Christians hear directly from the Lord and are obedient to His Word. With this said, I simply acknowledge money or provision helps advance God's work.

God will bless the work of our hands as long as it glorifies Him and is consistent with His Word. He provides all we need, recognizing needs are different for everyone. As an example, the needs for a single mom with three kids are inherently different than a married couple without kids. However, perhaps the childless couple running an orphanage with 100 kids requires greater provision. Realize, the needs may be very different in India, China, or North America.

The way God brings monetary or non-monetary wealth is entirely up to Him. His promise is to bless us with His riches. How He decides depends upon our circumstances and the provision we need to accomplish His will for our lives. He wants to prosper ALL of us. Read the scriptures and decide for yourself. There are many types of tools in the Kingdom which prosper us. Money is just one tool and a topic people love to discuss. Unfortunately, it is very misunderstood. This book is filled with testimonies of people who were monetarily blessed when they stepped out of agreement with the enemy. They were also blessed in other ways.

> 3 John 1:2 "Beloved, I pray that you may prosper in all things and be in health, just as your soul prospers."[16]

Let's revisit our wealthy Old Testament legends again. God prospered them beyond our imagination. In fact, God was fulfilling the promise He made to Abraham. Abraham's blessing is the promise God set forth in the book of Genesis, chapters 12 and 22. Chapter 12:1–3,7 says,

> The Lord had said to Abram, "Leave your native country, your relatives, and your father's family, and go to the land that I will show you. I will make you into a great nation. I will bless you and make you famous, and you will be a

> blessing to others. I will bless those who bless you and curse those who treat you with contempt. All the families on earth will be blessed through you." (7) Then the Lord appeared to Abram and said, "I will give this land to your descendants.[17]

Chapter 22:15–18 says,

> Then the angel of the Lord called again to Abraham from heaven. "This is what the Lord says: Because you have obeyed me and have not withheld even your son, your only son, I swear by my own name that I will certainly bless you. I will multiply your descendants beyond number, like the stars in the sky and the sand on the seashore. Your descendants will conquer the cities of their enemies. And through your descendants all the nations of the earth will be blessed-all because you have obeyed me.[18]

It is a multifaceted blessing, of which provision and wealth is only one segment. Abraham's blessing encompasses blessings for our family, land, and nation. Did you know the blessing of Abraham is alive and available for every believer today? Paul says in Romans, as believers in Jesus, we are grafted into this blessing. In Galatians 3:14 he says: "He redeemed us in order that the blessing given to Abraham might come to the Gentiles through Christ Jesus, so that by faith we might receive the promise of the Spirit."[19]

Believers, you have been grafted into receiving tremendous blessings from God. Your faith in Jesus Christ dying on the cross and rising three days later, defeating Satan's plan, qualifies you for blessing. How amazing?! It takes faith and courage to believe this. If you continue to let an Accidental Agreement convince you wealth is evil, this blessing will not supersede your unbelief. There are numerous times in scripture where unbelief, ties to the enemy, hindered God's promise. Don't believe the lie of the hidden

Accidental Agreement. Instead, understand God wants you to be blessed in the area of your finances! Remember, it is for your good and His glory.

COMMON LIES AND BELIEFS

1."Not everyone gets blessed with money and provision. Some do, some don't."

Essentially, this statement indicates God has favorites. Some people will be blessed and others will not. Do you believe provision and wealth is a calling for specific people, while poverty is a calling for others? Simply stated, God is very clear in His Word on this.

> In Romans 2:10, 11, it says, "But glory, honor, and peace for everyone who does good; first for the Jew, then for the Gentile. For God does not show favoritism."[20]

His unconditional love is for all people, and His blessing is for all who believe. As mentioned previously, Abraham's blessing is for everyone who has faith in Jesus. The idea that a blessing is only for certain people is simply a lie of the enemy. Can you clearly see the outcome the lie leads to? The lie is something similar to: God plays favorites and He just can't work with or through me because I'm not __________(fill in the blank). This lie will keep you from ever pursuing blessing in this area. Satan will effectively have taken you off the playing field.

> His unconditional love is for all people,
> and His blessing is for all who believe.

2. "It's too late for me to make money or have provision."

Abraham was 100 years old when Isaac was born. 100! How many people do you even know who have reached 100, let alone become a new parent? Not many. If there is breath in your lungs, God can still use you. If God can still use you, He will continue to bless you! His blessings are for you because He loves and trusts you to help build His kingdom on earth.

You may feel like you've blown all your chances. However, it may not be age holding you back, but past AA mistakes stored in your subconscious. Remember, if you have one string tied to the enemy and one string tied to the Lord, the area tied to the enemy cannot be blessed. Light and dark do not coexist. God is much bigger than your mistakes. He knew you were going to make mistakes before you made them. What is the Lord trying to teach you about this unholy alliance (string)? Ask Him. Did He ask you to move a position and you refused? Did He try to give you direction, but you did not make time to read the Bible and listen for His answer? Maybe you just blew it? It's okay. His promises can overcome even the darkest of times. The Israelites were pinned against the Red Sea with the Egyptians coming toward them in full attack mode. Truly, put yourself in that situation right now. You see an oncoming army on one side, and water as far as the eye can see on the other. There is no way out. What are you going to do, jump in the water and try to swim across? When all appeared lost, God parted the sea. He supernaturally intervened in their lives, giving them a path through the center of a massive body of water. He gave them a way out.

Why do you think God shared stories like these in the Bible? He wants you to understand Him and His gracious, patient nature. He intervenes. He blesses. He provides when all seems lost. Don't let this Accidental Agreement get the best of you. Believe God wants to bless your finances!

3."I don't have the right degree. I'm not smart enough to make money and receive provision."

The root of this wrong thinking is fear. Fear can cripple you into believing you're not good enough, smart enough, or gifted enough to reach elevated goals. Fear is probably the number one reason people don't pursue God's best for them. I'm not saying move forward irrationally without the Lord's leading. Make sure He is leading you. Just keep asking Him.

God's blessing is not a result of your skill or intelligence level. His blessing is supernatural. It overrides logic. It doesn't matter if you have a second-grade education or a PhD. God's blessing is for you. I have watched God give jobs to people who are not qualified by the world's standards. Yet, God said they were. I have observed God advance people in their jobs with on-the-job training they never could have afforded on their own. These people prayed in their office environment, blessed those in authority, and did not come into agreement with the enemy. They refused to accept the lies, such as they were too dumb; too old; passed over for promotion; could not be promoted; did not have enough time or money for training and the list goes on.

I have also seen Christians step forward and offer computer training to single moms reentering the workforce. What a gift! There is purpose in everything we do and experience. I have observed people getting sidetracked when refusing to move into a position. They either cannot or will not hear the Lord when He says it's time to move, advance, reposition, change their heart, rest, or leave. The other area where people experience setbacks is when they break their Accidental Agreements but fall back into believing the lies. Hence, they lose their freedom and reinstate their AA string with the enemy. The Lord helped me create an Accidental Agreement Freedom Program in chapter ten. It will help you permanently cut the strings and loosen the enemy's grip on your life.

Here's another example of the importance of checking with the Lord during every phase of your work. I worked on an exciting project, carrying the potential for huge blessings for many people. I received many insightful downloads from the Lord. I felt a nudge in my spirit to not move forward on a particular phase of the project. I questioned myself. I continued inching forward until finally, beyond a shadow of a doubt, the Lord shouted STOP. I stopped immediately. My Heavenly Father knows what is best and His timing is always correct. This is why you cannot rely on logical instincts.

4."That person got MY promotion, which clearly means God doesn't want me to succeed."

You can never let your personal experiences in life determine what you believe. God's blessing is not nullified just because one circumstance does not turn out the way you thought it should (your imagination). The Word is the final say. God says you will be blessed. You may not know how, when, or in what way, but His promises are true.

What I do know is jealousy and bitterness are major Accidental Agreements with the enemy. They will BLOCK your blessings. The underlying root lie for jealousy is that God doesn't have enough resources, jobs, or opportunities to prosper you. The next time you feel envious, ask God what is the root. Wait for the answer. The answer is the source of the root for your Accidental Agreement with the enemy. Once identified, loudly proclaim, "God has enough resources for me, and IS going to PROSPER me, so get behind me Satan! I choose to believe Jesus." Isaiah 54:13 has ministered to me. It says, "All your children will be taught by the Lord, and great will be their peace."

The other "blessing stopper" is bitterness, also known as unforgiveness. This causes your prayers to be blocked. This is addressed later in the forgiveness section. If you do not believe me, read the scriptures. It is very clear. Rodney Hogue, a minster and instructor with Global Awakening, has a short book entitled *Forgiveness*. It succinctly explains why it is not beneficial to hold onto bitterness.

In this life, we will never know why certain things happen and others don't. Sometimes, God may be protecting us, while at other times He may be holding out for an even greater blessing! There will always be times of questioning the occurrences in your life but never let it invalidate what the Bible says. God not giving you the blessing you desired in that moment, does not mean He will never bless you. It certainly doesn't mean He has changed His mind! He may be working on changing your heart or rearranging pieces. Right now, He is working on your behalf. That is what good Fathers do. Place your faith on His promise, fully trusting it will eventually come to pass. Stand strong! Remember, blessings trump curses(sin)!

STEWARDSHIP

How are you taking care of the things God has entrusted to you? Are you spending your money wisely? Are you purchasing things with the correct motives? You are called to be a good steward over your possessions. When blessings come, it's imperative to understand financial gain does not give you freedom to buy five purses or shoes, putting you in debt. Remember, financial blessing is meant to be a tool, nothing more.

> You are called to be a good steward over your possessions.

Maybe you find yourself in a state of "just getting by." You are left wondering why God's financial and provisional blessings have not appeared. Sometimes blessings take time. Occasionally, blessings do not happen because you are not taking care of possessions God has already given you. Are you praying for a new car when your current one is not being maintained? Is it full of trash and smelling like last week's dinner? Ask God for help maintaining mechanical functions of your car. There are many qualified mechanics affiliated with churches. Make sure to research your mechanic and car seller with several recommendations. Ask the Lord's blessing on your car each day!

Stewardship is an integral part of financial and provisional blessings. God wants to bless you, but if you are not acting mature enough, He won't give what He has in store, as it will ruin you. Take a step back and access the inventory of what you possess and how you are caring for it. Look at how you are spending your money. Ask the Lord what He thinks. Prayerfully ask the Lord each time you make an expenditure. You will be a better steward when you ask Him about your purchases.

My friend, Shirley, talks with the Lord each time she goes to the grocery store. She calls with the best "God stories!" Shirley is skillful at staying within her budget, even when entertaining guests. She found salmon on sale when she needed it; half price meat; a blueberry cobbler was given to her when entertaining a missionary whose favorite fruit was blueberries; and the list goes on! God is in the details.

If stewardship is an area you struggle with, Dave Ramsey has an excellent course to help you. I would highly recommend his books about financial freedom. Do not take this topic lightly. With every blessing comes great responsibility. Ask the Holy Spirit about your spending. Are your spending motives pure, or are they replacing God with some THING which gives you false comfort? Are they used to build up the kingdom and provide for your family, or are they to keep up with the neighbors?

> If you are not experiencing financial blessings right now, you may need to move a position or you may have a generational curse operating.

If you're not financially sound, are you somehow missing God's blessing? Absolutely not! This is not a prosperity Gospel message.

Does God want to bless you? Yes! God blesses in a variety of ways other than financial and provisional blessings. If you are not experiencing financial blessings right now, you may need to move into position, or you may have a generational curse operating. However, God is probably blessing you in other areas of your life. He wants to delight your heart. He may be trying to release an innovative concept into your spirit. He may be giving you inner promptings about ideas, songs, a new skill, a new talent, or a new business idea. God desires to bestow more blessings! That's His nature. He is excited and eager to promote and bless you!!

I believe the church is negligent in helping provide for widows and orphans, including single mothers and their children. I know of many non-profit organizations and churches with tens of thousands of dollars they refuse to donate. The Bible commands us to take care of widows and orphans. James 1:27 says, "Religion that God our Father accepts as pure and faultless is this: to look after orphans and widows in their distress and to keep oneself from being polluted by the world."[21] The Bible also discusses this in Exodus 22:22–27; Deut. 10:18–20; Zech. 7:10. If you do not have extra money to give, provide a meal, babysitting, companionship, clothes, or whatever is the need.

REASONS FOR NOT BEING ABUNDANTLY BLESSED (AS MUCH AS YOU SHOULD BE)

1. Repent. I believe many people are not blessed because they will not REPENT, meaning turn away from their sin. They keep repeating the sin instead of pressing into the Lord to help eliminate the stronghold (AA).

2. Believers don't know how to hear the voice of the Lord talking to them. He wants to communicate!

Here are two books I strongly recommend to help in this area of your life:

- *Four Keys To Hearing God's Voice* – Dr. Mark Virkler, President of Christian Leadership University
- *Discerning the Voice of God* – Priscilla Shirer

3. Believers can't or won't follow the Lord's leading in moving a position or making a change. They have sin traits and are not willing to get rid of their Accidental Agreements.

4. Believers have unidentified generational curses operating.

5. Believers have major fear issues.

6. Believers have a lack of gratitude, and have bitterness or unforgiveness.

I do not want you to think you're somehow missing God's blessings if you aren't financially blessed. Finances and provision are just one area of God's tremendous blessings.

Let's stop right now. Ask Holy Spirit if He is trying to tell you something. Let's begin by asking for forgiveness for holding a grudge against someone. Let's bind ourselves to Jesus and loose everything from the enemy (no strings attached!). "Father, is there something you want to tell me?" Write down what you hear right now. Just pick up your pen and start writing. Repeat this exercise every day for one week. Watch what happens!

MONEY SCRIPTURES

ORIGINAL SCRIPTURE: "With man this is impossible, but with God all things are possible." Matthew 19:26 [22]

PERSONALIZED SCRIPTURE: Thank You God that ALL things are possible. Matthew 19:26

PARAPHRASED SCRIPTURE: With man's ability, this situation is impossible but with my powerful God, ALL things are possible. Matthew 19:26

ORIGINAL SCRIPTURE: But remember the Lord your God, for it is he who gives you the ability to produce wealth, and so confirms his covenant, which he swore to your ancestors, as it is today. Deuteronomy 8:18 [23]

PERSONALIZED SCRIPTURE: You have given me power to get wealth, and this fulfills Your promise to my ancestors. Deuteronomy 8:18

PARAPHRASED SCRIPTURE: Thank You Lord, for giving me the power to obtain wealth by listening to Your wisdom. This fulfills Your promise to my ancestors. Deuteronomy 8:18

As you read the scriptures below, be sure to personalize or paraphrase them as I did in the examples above. There are more scriptures in the Appendix in the Financial Accidental Agreements Section.

Financial Scriptures: Luke 12:24, Psalm 37:25, Psalm 9:18, Psalm 22:26, Psalm 146:7, Amos 9:13–15

There are two financial prayers in this book. The first is the Money Declaration below. The long version is in Appendix 1. It is entitled, "The Prayer to Release You Into Financial Freedom."

MONEY DECLARATION

I decree and declare God does want to bless me now in my finances. The Lord wants to prosper me in all areas, and this includes even my smallest need. I ask You Lord to reveal where I have an Accidental Agreement. I ask Holy Spirit to help me remove it now. I decree I will have enough time and resources to fulfill the next step toward my God-ordained destiny. I am trusting You Lord, to give me wisdom, guidance and discernment as to what I am to do, what doors I am to knock on and which doors I am to walk through. Thank You Lord, for prospering me in everything I do according to Your will. Thank You for organizing my time and giving me the strength I need. With God's help: I do have time to balance my checkbook; I do have time to make a weekly and monthly budget; I do have time to find coupons; I do have time to research finance or lease options; I will have the right housing and ability to maintain it; I will be able to provide for my family; I can earn extra money; I believe God will give me ideas; I can improve my credit score; I can pay off debt; I can learn computer skills; I can complete continuing education; I can organize my schedule to be more efficient; I believe God will direct me. Thank you Lord for guiding me through this process.

CURSES

A curse may be operating in regard to your money, interfering with your ability to earn and keep money. This is similar to robbery in the spiritual world. Sometimes, a generational curse is passed down, affecting our lives and tainting our choices, uses and ability to maintain money. Failing to tithe can also cause financial disruptions.

Pablo Botari says in his book, *Free In Christ*, there are three reasons for Christians to stay in bondage, one of which is curses operating in the believer's life (Accidental Agreements).

1. Hatred - can be exhibited through bitterness, unforgiveness, anger, rage, judging, blaming, criticalness, violence, resentment, revenge, envy, fighting, assumptions, etc.

2 .Extreme Fear - can be exhibited through phobias, various fears such as fear of the unknown, fear of what's going to happen, fear of dying, fear of flying, fear of accidents, fear of abandonment, panic attacks, etc.

3. Unbroken Vows with the Enemy - This is an enormously

important area which needs exploring. This can take the form of intentional or unintentional agreements with the enemy and curses. Curses can be generational, self-imposed curses or inner vows, unintentional curses, or even curses put on you from another. There can even be objects or buildings which are cursed which can affect you. Words can be curses and are extremely powerful.

FEAR FINANCIAL BLOCKAGE

Fear is an underlying root for many of life's problems. Some common fears are: fear of man, the future, success, rejection, abandonment, poverty, being wrong, being abused, being a victim, dying, being unprotected, being alone, intimacy, sexual inadequacy, being controlled, losing control, being attacked, worry, anxiety, phobias, terror and trauma. If any of these resonate within you, it is an Accidental Agreement!

Overcoming fear is the greatest mindset challenge we face besides death.[24] Our society is based on fear motivated marketing. Whether it's fear of failure, fear of success, or any other fear, we're driven by fear! I have read up to 80% of our time is spent in fear-based decisions, which confirms the prevalence of our Accidental Agreements. This translates to 20% of our time living a fear-free life in alignment with scripture!

Paul says, "we have not been given a spirit of fear,"[25] yet we live in constant fear of punishment more than the reward of striving for the prize of doing God's will.[26] Since the majority of our decisions are based on our finances in some form or another, marketers, including Wall Street, use social media, news, commercials, movies, special interest groups and others, to get our attention and refocus through fear tactics. Greed and control are the motivational tools to move us at their will! Fear based advertising is worth billions of dollars. Ironically, fear is what drives us on to win the game and it's also what causes us to lose the game of life. Fear always produces adverse responses. As an example, anti-virus malware programs on our computers subconsciously warn us to always look for identity theft and fear-based predators or viruses in our lives. It puts us in a state of fear, wondering when, how, or if we will be attacked from an unknown predator.

I have read 95% of our decisions are made on a subconscious level. Only 5% of the decisions are influenced by the conscious level. Most individuals, according to neuroscientists, operate at 1% of their conscious choices. This confirms the vast majority of our daily choices are influenced and made by Accidental Agreements with the enemy. Looking back on my decisions and the decisions of people I counsel, Pablo Botari's simple explanation on why people stay in bondage due to hatred, fear and unbroken vows makes sense. The purpose of Accidental Agreements is to break the fear-based programming and reestablish Biblical order in our thinking. Botari's other two categories, bitterness and curses, require a deeper discussion. Please see the *Bitterness* discussion and *Common Hindrances to Healing* sections in the Appendix.

LIES AND TRUTH STATEMENTS

Read through the following lies that are relevant to you and circle the top three. These are your Accidental Agreements, which we will use later in the book when implementing our AA Freedom Program.

Rather than waiting to begin the program at the end of the book, you can begin now if you prefer. However, when you read the rest of the book, you will find a common theme in the lies you are believing, which may help you break the Accidental Agreement more quickly. In the Appendix, you will find the corresponding Truth Statements. Circle the Truth Statements and scriptures which resonate within you. Write the Lie and Truth Statements on a note card and put a mark by the lie each time you hear it, whether it's every minute or hour. Each time you hear the lie, repeat the Truth Statement and appropriate scripture out loud (dunamis power-Holy Spirit). Continue this for one week, and each day the number of lie whispers should diminish. You will be able to recognize the lies quickly because they are being moved out of your subconscious mind creating new brain patterns. The more consistently you practice this exercise, the more quickly the Accidental Agreements will be broken. Once broken, you will see movement in the heavenlies very quickly. Watch for the Lord's blessings! If you are not seeing blessings, read the rest of the book and check the Appendix for *Common Hindrances to Healing*. Ask the Holy Spirit which one applies to your situation. The Holy Spirit will highlight an issue very quickly because He wants to see you blessed!

1. LIE: I won't ever have enough________________. (fill in the blank)

2. LIE: I don't have enough time to ___________. (example: balance my checkbook, make a budget, find coupons, cook at home, research finance options to buy a house or rent to own, learn about my credit score, improve my credit score, pay off debt, earn extra money, learn new computer skills, do continuing education). God can't help me organize my time and schedule.

3. LIE: God can't or won't bless me financially, help me make money, provide for my needs or the needs of my children.

4. LIE: I have lost money or provision through fraud and theft. This lost or stolen money or provision can't be restored.

5. LIE: I don't know how to manage money or provision and I can't learn.

6. LIE: I can't possibly get out of debt. I must go into debt to succeed in life. I must borrow money my whole life. I must have debt on credit cards to live. It won't matter if I go into debt because I really want something.

7. LIE: I may have to compromise my integrity or biblical principles to get ahead.

8. LIE: God doesn't care or notice if I don't tithe. God won't withhold blessings if I don't tithe.

9. LIE: God doesn't care or notice if I don't give to others. God doesn't expect me to help other people I don't even know.

10. LIE: God isn't interested in my career or work. God can't help me advance my career. I don't have time to finish my work. God doesn't care if I'm sloppy in my work. God isn't interested in my work details.

Listed below are additional lies. You may use different Truth Statements for these from the Appendix.

11. LIE: I must always depend on other people to make me prosper.

Listed below are additional lies. You may use different Truth Statements for these from the Appendix.

12. LIE: I have mismanaged money through bad choices, investments or stealing so I won't get a second chance.

13. LIE: God doesn't care if I am frugal or not.

14. LIE: I love money and the things it buys. Possessions make me happy and I always want the newest and the best.

15. LIE: I can't earn enough money to ______________________ (fill in the blank). I can't imagine I would ever have enough money or provision to do __________________ (fill in the blank).

16. LIE: God isn't really interested in my finances.

17. LIE: God can't download creative ideas to help me at work. God can't give me favor with coworkers, my boss, clients or other people. God can't give me wisdom, revelation and guidance in the workplace. God can't help me do well at work.

18. LIE: God can't provide another job for me.

19. LIE: God can't help me in school or continuing education for training. God can't help me study for tests. I don't have time to finish my work so it's okay if I'm sloppy. God isn't interested in school or education details.

20. LIE: I have lost hope about _______________ (fill in the blank).

---

[1] Hebrews 13:5–6 (AMPC)
[2] Leviticus 26:8 (NKJV)
[3] Judges 6:36–40 (NKJV)
[4] Colossians 3:23–24 (NKJV)
[5] Proverbs 13:4 (NKJV)
[6] Philippians 4:13 (NKJV)
[7] 2 Thessalonians 3:10–12 (NKJV)
[8] Proverbs 14:23 (NKJV)9 Philippians 14:23 (NKJV)
[10] Proverbs 16:3 (NKJV)
[11] Psalm 37:23, Romans 8:28 (NKJV)

[12] 1 John 3:20 (NKJV)
[13] Psalm 91, Jeremiah 29:11 (NKJV)
[14] 2 Samuel 23:5, Philippians 4:67 (NLT)
[15] Matthew 19:16–23 (NKJV)
[16] 3 John 1:2 (NKJV)
[17] Genesis 12:1–3, 7 (NLT)
[18] Genesis 22: 15–18 (NLT)
[19] Galatians 3:14 (NIV)
[20] Romans 2:10–11 (NIV)
[21] James 1:27 (NIV)
[22] Matthew 19:26 (NKJV)
[23] Deuteronomy 8:18 (NIV)
[24] Hebrews 2:15 (NKJV)
[25] 2 Timothy 1:7 (NKVJ)
[26] Philippians 3:14 (NKJV)

CHAPTER 8

relational accidental agreements

The Bible says, "Bad company corrupts good character."[1] The people we spend the most time around will often have a profound effect on us, both positively and negatively. Did you know hurt often comes as a result of a Relational Accidental Agreement (AA). Some wounds are due to everyday relationships exhibiting non-healthy conflict resolution. Through hurtful and broken relationships, these Accidental Agreements can cause you to live under clouds of disappointment, defeat, distrust, and oppression. They will cripple and damage you, or at the very least causing mediocre, unsatisfying relationships. They may cause you to justify reasons to stay in unhealthy relationships, allowing you to disconnect and shut down emotionally and mentally. Serious illnesses result. If left untreated, the following may result: bruised and broken friendships and marriages; manipulation by overly dominant individuals; chronic physical or emotional abuse; inability to have faith and confidence in people; and other consequences.

A Relational Accidental Agreement with the enemy evolves over time, beginning at birth, and is affected by all interactions from birth until today. It can occur through some subtle acceptance of mistrust, negativity, abandonment, rejection, moral compromise, or sinful behavior by someone close. It is usually a friend, parent, relative, sibling, or coworker. While other persons of influence can affect your thinking such as ministers, motivational speakers, reality shows, celebrity personalities or great leaders, they are not truly relational. However, they can have significant influence on your perception of relational reality. Relationally generated Accidental Agreements with the enemy are those we accept because of our closeness and familiarity with people. We agree to compromise and overlook or accept certain behaviors, conclusions, and circumstances as "the way things are or should be." In other words, it is because of the relationship itself or our perception of what is acceptable. This is often why it hurts more when people close to you make offensive comments rather than an acquaintance. You value your loved one's opinions more. Therefore, they often have greater emotional power in your life because you have a stronger tie to this person. Remember, ties can be good or bad. It is important to make sure the comments are uplifting, positive, and loving, even with correction. There is a distinct difference between loving correction from a God-ordained person and condemnation which is intended to tear you down.

Dr. Henry Wright, author of *A More Excellent Way to Be In Health*, says:

> Disease follows relationship breakdown. Relationship breakdown involves separation on three levels. 1) Separation from the Godhead. Many of you don't have your peace with God the Father. 2) Separation from yourself. Many people don't like themselves." Dr. Wright says, "Remember the woman with face cancer? When she dealt with self-hatred, the curse was broken and healing came. 3) Separation from others. This could be due to

> bitterness, envy and jealousy, or it could be anger or fear of another. Healing begins with reconciliation. If 80% of all disease involves separation, then 80% of all healings begin with reconciliation to God, the Father, the Son and the Holy Spirit, to yourself and to others.[2]

The power you give others over yourself will often be the root of how a Relational Accidental Agreement forms. No man or woman should ever have the power to negatively change the way you see yourself or see God. Not even your husband, wife, mother, father or best friend should have that kind of power. If they are able through their words or actions to negatively alter your identity in some fashion, it means you have given a human too much power over your life. Soul wounds occur from inherited DNA, childhood experiences, repeated negative interactions, or any situation or person whose actions create a trauma to your soul. God's opinion of you should be what drives you, nothing else.

This misdirected power has nothing to do with the amount of love or admiration you feel for this person. Giving God the ultimate power to reveal the truth about the relational AA is going to alter the relationship. You'll find it will usually improve (unless you are dealing with abuse) after eliminating the relational AA and giving God the power back. Compromise should not be made if it is against what the Bible says, or abuse is involved.

My point is: you must have relationships in proper alignment with God in the first position. If you place others above the relationship with your Heavenly Father, you cannot truly be surrendered to the Lord. It is not possible to have two number one places in your heart! Nobody else should occupy the throne of your life other than God himself. However, the Bible should not be used as an excuse for behaving badly.

The reality is, most of us have Relational Accidental Agreements in some form. If you had parents who argued while a baby in the womb, this had and has an effect on you. As a child, if you were not hugged, nurtured or encouraged there are negative implications with your ability to connect in a healthy way. Fortunately, this can be relearned. Healing comes through the love of Jesus. By identifying the relational lies and replacing them with Biblical truth, it changes your perspective about God, others, and yourself. You will be able to properly assess whether a situation requires love, grace, boundaries, forgiveness, or even termination of the relationship.

For example, perhaps you found yourself in a relationship with a loved one where you found it impossible to stand up for yourself and your beliefs. You have tried to resist before, but the reaction from this person has proven to be too painful due to verbal or emotional attacks or silence. You choose to not resist in an effort to make peace. However, on the inside you have suffered a soul wound, a breakdown of your own sense of self-worth and importance. The result can be either guilt, unforgiveness, anger, sadness, self-pity, or all of these. They all lead to bitterness of spirit. An agreement like this is poison to the soul. It intensifies with every aggravating episode, driving the pain deeper. It builds a wedge of destruction. Unresolved, it destroys the relationship and slowly erodes you spiritually, mentally, emotionally, physically, and financially. Recovery is hard. The deeper the wound, the longer the recovery seems to be. Good news: Jesus can fix this!

This is just example of how Accidental Agreements may result in deeper wounds should you not deal with these issues early. You will save yourself a great deal of unhappiness by facing a bad agreement head on and eradicating it from your life, sooner rather than later. Do not think you must address all of the relational issues at once. This is not how the Lord works. He starts one at a time and carefully peels the Accidental Agreements layer by layer. However, the process does not have to be prolonged for months. Let's talk about how to face these relational agreements.

The first part is recognizing you have a problem with a relationship. Do you find yourself thinking unhealthy thoughts toward another person? Do you react in unhealthy ways to comments made by an individual? Do you feel bitterness, anger, or hatred toward a certain individual or possibly a certain stereotype? Are you irritated when you hear their voice or name? Does the hair on the back of your neck raise when you see them? These are all indications of a soul wound which has formed because of a past experience. This has resulted in a Relational Accidental Agreement with the enemy.

Dr. Henry Wright says in a marriage argument, females lose emotionally because it takes longer for them to recover than a male. He says:

> The damage to the immune system in a female who comes from strife in the home is incredible. In America, 85 to 90% of the people who have MCS/EI (Multiple Chemical Sensitivity/ Environmental Illness) are female. The reason why the female is the one who gets sick is because she is more susceptible to the spiritual and emotional damage. God created the female to be a responder to good, strong spiritual leadership, not to abuse. My finding in thousands of cases across America over the years is that MCS or EI is the result of a breakup in the human relationship between the person who has the disease and someone else. The other person is usually a close family member and one or more of four life circumstances is involved. I have found this in every person I have ministered to without exception." Dr. Wright says, "Here are the four life circumstances that exist collectively or singly in MCS/EI:
>
> 1. Verbal and/or emotional abuse
> 2. Physical abuse

3. Sexual abuse
4. Drive to meet the expectations of a parent in order to receive love.[3]

Dr. Wright continues:

> I believe this is true with many additional illnesses where there has been a disruptive situation in the home whether in childhood or adulthood. This causes an entry for fear, anxiety, stress, shame control, victimization, abandonment and sexual dysfunction. God's intent is for us to experience peace not dis-ease. One Thessalonians 5:23 says, "May God himself, the God of peace, sanctify you through and through. May your whole spirit, soul and body be kept blameless at the coming of our Lord Jesus Christ.[4]

John 14:27 says, "Peace I leave with you; my peace I give you. I do not give to you as the world gives. Do not let your hearts be troubled and do not be afraid."[5]

Let's talk about how to heal it.

FORGIVENESS

Often, the main hindrance in relational agreements is unforgiveness. You are rarely conscious of your unforgiveness toward someone or toward a group of people. It isn't fun to think about, so you often bury the feelings and try not to open up the issue again. The problem is, resentment, if not dealt with, will build and multiply. Unforgiveness is like a poisonous weed, growing and taking over different pieces of your heart and mind. It causes reaction to certain people with irritation, anger, hatred, or criticism. Sometimes, you may surprise yourself with your reaction! Why? Because the unforgiveness is buried deep within your subconscious. God wants to clean out every part of your body holding onto bitterness. Bitterness is especially dangerous because it is an alliance of numerous strongholds rendering it lethal. Bitterness must be removed for God to fully bless you. The way to repair and restore your soul is to forgive! See the Appendix for the Bitterness discussion.

Forgiveness is perhaps one of the hardest decisions to carry out in life. Everything in you wants to "give them what they deserve" because of how you were treated or what they did. Perhaps, they hurt you so deeply you simply cannot see them the same way. The thought of what they did to you won't go away. You may think it's wrong to forgive because it feels as though you are downplaying what happened to you. It's like you are admitting you overreacted, or it's not a big deal. If you're honest with yourself, it almost feels like you are letting them win. Not at all! Forgiveness does not work like this.

Forgiveness is the ability to acknowledge the depths of what was done, but releasing the person into God's hands instead. Not because what they did was OK, but because of the love and mercy your Heavenly Father shows you. His love allows you to have the same love and mercy toward another. In the Lord's Prayer it states "...forgive us our debts as we forgive others." Forgiveness is understanding the other person's human and sinful nature. Sometimes it is acknowledging your own nature, seeing you have hurt others at times as well. Nobody is perfect. In this broken world, hurt comes from all angles. Regardless of whose fault it was, our mandate is to forgive. It becomes your choice to hold onto resentment and bitterness. You should release the person into the hands of our loving Father. He is the only one allowed to judge-we are not. Rather, we are judged by God as we judge others. Yikes!

> Forgiveness is the ability to acknowledge the depths of what was done, but releasing the person into God's hands instead.

UNFORGIVENESS MANURE PIT

In addition, when we choose not to forgive, we are actually spiritually tied to the very person we do not like. It is as though you are both lassoed face to face together in a dung-filled corral. How's that for a visual? We don't want to be stuck in an unforgiveness manure pit. Forgiveness will give you freedom like you have never experienced before!

Once unforgiveness is broken, freedom has a chance to take hold. How do you deal with repeat offenders, a person who continues to act the same way? Well, I do not have a perfect solution. Sometimes seeing a counselor may be your best option. Every circumstance is unique, and every person is different. I am not going to recommend a specific course of action, but rather give you a framework to help you intentionally deal with this directly.

BOUNDARIES

The other common sign of an unhealthy Relational Accidental Agreement is dealing with someone who exhibits inappropriate boundaries.

First, if physical, sexual, verbal or emotional abuse is occurring within the relationship, seek immediate help. The lies the devil will place in your mind are: to keep the abuse to yourself; it's too embarrassing to admit to myself or someone else; if I am patient they will stop this behavior; if I make them go to church more, they will change; if I give them self-help books, they will change; if I place them by other healthy couples, they will get the picture and change; if I try harder, they will change; if I have children, he will change; and the excuse list goes on. If you related to any of these comments, you need to seek help from a counselor to learn how to set a healthy boundary. Quit imagining you can change the person. God is the only one who can change them, and He will do it His way in His timing. He wants you to become healthy FIRST. He does not intend for you to remain in an abusive relationship or marriage.

Fear may set in, keeping you from seeking outside help. Use wisdom, but please talk to someone. DO NOT STAY in an abusive relationship. It is NOT biblical and should NEVER be tolerated. If abuse has happened once, it will happen again. The pattern is repeated 95% of the time. It is usually a hereditary stronghold. If your counselor suggests staying in an abusive marriage, get a new counselor.

Secondly, if emotional or verbal abuse is occurring, really understand whether or not their words are meant to be hurtful. If they are truly emotionally and verbally abusive, seek help immediately from a counselor who understands abuse. Do not tolerate any abuse at all. Zero tolerance! Unfortunately, I have found many counselors say they understand abuse but do not. Again, this pattern is repeated 95% of the time. The abuser doesn't have any boundaries and does not want them, no matter what they say. Actions speak louder than words. If they are truly attempting to emotionally wound you, then again, I would encourage you to seek Christian counsel on how to deal with your specific situation. Not setting a firm boundary with a repeat offender is NOT going to solve this problem. If your friend or spouse is wounded, pray for them, bless them, and honor them, but set a good boundary. A good boundary does not mean letting the abuse offense occur again and again. It's like a child throwing a temper tantrum. If you allow the tantrum to continue, it will get louder, longer, stronger, and more offensive…out of control. As with an out-of-control child, you set your boundary, and if it is ignored, there is a consequence. The consequence is immediate, severe, and non-negotiable. If there has been physical or verbal abuse, and it is repeated, someone has to leave until the tantrum is permanently halted. The love you show them by setting a firm boundary of respect, kindness, and love can often be the power to help them overcome their own Relational Accidental Agreement! It is not your responsibility to change them. That is God's assignment. It is your job to pray and set a firm boundary.

> A good boundary does not mean letting the abuse offense occur again and again.

In conclusion, Relational Accidental Agreements are primarily based upon hurts from past issues and past generational issues, as well as bitterness and resentment in your relationships. You might believe a lie about them or about God, causing you to react in unhealthy emotional ways. Thankfully, you have a powerful and loving God who is able to heal your wounds. It first requires your willingness to forgive the person and release them into God's hands. He first forgave you, so in turn, you must be willing to forgive another. Forgiveness is not accepting what was done as being okay. You are simply releasing the bitterness and anger **to** God. When forgiveness comes, the healing of a soul wound will result. If repeat offenses continue to erupt, and showing love to a person doesn't change the situation, I recommend seeking outside help. God is your Father. He loves you and gives you a heart to love others. Don't let a relational AA hold you back from God's healthy design for the relationships in your life. He wants you free, so be free!

SUSAN'S FAMILY DYNAMICS

Here is an example of three siblings in a Christian family and how they individually interpreted their family's dynamics growing up. Susan was raised in a loving Christian family who attended church on Sunday. Her father worked long hours providing for the family. Her mother worked part-time outside the home. Susan knew she was loved, but the family was always in a hurry. They kept busy with school, sports, work, and life. A great deal of emphasis was placed on performance. Expectations were to excel in all activities. However, the subtle underlying message accidentally conveyed to the kids was, "If you do not excel, you are not valuable. You must try harder to get the most love and be lovable." In other words, conditional love. The parents were involved in the kids' lives and truly loved their children. However, Susan's life perspective was she had to be excellent in every activity or situation in which she was involved, or she was a failure and unlovable.

Susan's younger sister was artistic and creative. In her home, this gift was not nurtured or valued. Her younger sister tried very hard to excel at areas outside of her God-given talents. It resulted in disappointing and unfulfilling jobs, relationships, and stress. She was given the gift of creativity, born to be involved in the arts. However, she was forced, or forced herself, to operate in areas which weren't her gifts and were not God-ordained.

Susan's older brother was an achiever but never felt like he could live up to his father's standards. Thus, he felt inferior and angry, trying desperately to prove he was successful in order to be worthy of love.

Here is an example of three wonderfully different children within the same family—three different results with Relational Accidental Agreements based upon their family experiences not valuing their God given talents. All three had love and trust issues because they were desperately seeking unconditional love. All three married abusive spouses with no boundaries, trying to be loved no matter the cost. Once Susan broke her AA's, she was able to receive unconditional love from her Heavenly Father, love others more freely, and have healthier personal relationships.

Once this unconditional, performance driven Accidental Agreement with the enemy was identified, it was dealt with layer by layer. When Holy Spirit identifies and reveals information about an AA, He wants to deal with it now. A Truth Statement can be identified from scripture, when the Lord's Word resonates within your heart. Repeating this "God-ordained scripture statement" out loud, as it goes deep within your soul, breaks the agreement with Satan. Your heart and soul wounds will be healed relationally, allowing them to love more fully in other areas. This will open you to love, trust, and nurture in a healthy manner. Our Heavenly Father is the only one who can give us unconditional love and peace. He wants us free of these relational wounds so we can be blessed beyond our wildest dreams! This is why the Bible says to emulate the love of Jesus. For you scientists, the sound frequency for love is healing to the body and soul!

PAIGE'S FORGIVENESS TESTIMONY

Paige is a lovely woman who attends church three times per week, goes to Bible studies, helps with projects in church, and loves the Lord. She is a wonderful Christian woman. Her son married a woman who would not allow her to see the grandchildren. It was a control issue by the daughter-in-law. As you might imagine, it grieved Paige. She tried her best to hide her disappointment, but silently it was eating away at her. The Lord had been nudging Paige to go to a different church. The new church had in-depth understanding of intercessory prayer and believed the gifts of the Spirit operate today. God even provided a ride for her to the new church with several acquaintances who attended. Paige tried the new church, but found her previous church more comfortable.

Paige began to not feel well. Her health deteriorated. She prayed for years concerning this split-family situation. She diligently kept seeking the Lord for answers. The Lord placed a new friend, Jean, in her path. She was trained to hear from the Holy Spirit and had a phone line directly to the Lord! A family member asked Paige about harboring unforgiveness towards her daughter in-law. She also suggested the family stress was hurting her health. Paige said, "No, I have already forgiven her." However, the Holy Spirit kept nudging her about this unforgiveness issue. Paige asked Jean if she thought she was harboring unforgiveness, and if it could be hurting her health. Before Paige could tell who she had an issue with, Jean said, "You're harboring unforgiveness against your daughter-in-law. It is now time to forgive her completely because it is injuring your health."

Paige was shocked and quickly asked the Lord for forgiveness repenting for this sin. She asked to have the sin covered with the blood of Jesus. Paige felt like a huge burden had been lifted from her shoulders. She said she had never felt so good!

The lies Paige was believing:

1. I have forgiven her once, so I do not have to do it again.
2. My family split is not affecting my spiritual, physical, emotional, mental, or relational health.
3. My prayers are unable to solve this problem.
4. God can't be everywhere all of the time. He must have forgotten about me.
5. My church is fine. God didn't really mean what He said when He was nudging me to attend the new church.

Paige's results after cutting the tie to the enemy:

Paige was immediately invited to her son and daughter-in-law's home three times in the next six weeks. Previously, she had not been invited three times in the last ten years.

The reuniting of her family was being blocked due to her unforgiveness tied to her relational AA. This was the very desire of her heart.

LIES AND TRUTH STATEMENTS

Read through the following lies that are relevant to you and circle the top three. These are your Accidental Agreements, which we will use later in the book when implementing our AA Freedom Program.

Rather than waiting to begin the program at the end of the book, you can begin now if you prefer. However, when you read the rest of the book, you will find a common theme in the lies you are believing which may help you break the Accidental Agreement more quickly. In the Appendix, you will find the corresponding Truth Statements. Circle the Truth Statements and scriptures that resonate within you. Write the Lie and Truth Statements on a note card and put a mark by the lie each time you hear it, whether it's every minute or every hour. Each time you hear the lie, repeat the Truth Statement and appropriate scripture out loud (dunamis power-Holy Spirit). Continue this for one week, and each day the number of lie whispers should diminish. You will be able to recognize the lies quickly because they are being moved out of your subconscious mind creating new brain patterns. The more consistently you practice this exercise, the more quickly the Accidental Agreements will be broken. Once broken, you will see movement in the heavenlies very quickly.

Watch for the Lord's blessings! If you are not seeing blessings, read the rest of the book and check the Appendix for *Common Hindrances to Healing*. Ask the Holy Spirit which one applies to your situation. The Holy Spirit will highlight an issue very quickly because He wants to see you blessed!

1. LIE: I don't have enough time to _________ (relationships).
2. LIE: Why do I keep dating or marrying the same type of guy who doesn't care and love me the way I deserve to be loved? Am I stupid? What's wrong with me?
3. LIE: I enjoy the excitement of romance novels, reality shows, pornography, and R rated movies with sex and violence. There's nothing wrong with masturbation. It helps me relax and gives me pleasure.
4. LIE: The media says I have to be prettier, thinner, and sexier than I am in order to be more attractive to men and more lovable.
5. LIE: Waiting to have sex until I get married is totally unnecessary and outdated. There's no harm in not waiting. Everyone does it; and the guys expect it. We love each other and will probably get married. We are already engaged. It doesn't matter if I want to have sex for one night and "give him or her my love."
6. LIE: As a divorced or widowed person, the Bible says Jesus is my husband and cares for widows and orphans. I don't get it. I'm not seeing blessings and I feel abandoned by Jesus, my church, and even my church friends. This is too hard, so there must be something wrong.

7. LIE: My marriage is beyond repair. My spouse won't change. He or she will never be as religious as I am. My marriage will be disappointing at best. If my spouse would change, everything would be okay.

8. LIE: My family is so messed up You can't straighten them out. You can't help my children learn or grow so I have to take charge. I have to fix my family or they won't get to Heaven. My children/family run from you. I don't know how you will get their attention to save them. I'm too far away physically and emotionally to be able to fix, help, or save my family.

9. LIE: My family/extended family is too messed up to fix. They suffer from stress, anxiety, disorders, depression, and other mental health issues. They are addicted to alcohol, pills, drugs or pornography, etc. I don't know how this unhealthy cycle will get broken. I don't know if they will ever get free from bondage and find You.

10. LIE: My children lack maturity, guidance, and wisdom. I'm never going to get them out of my house. They are never going to be able to stand on their own. My children are never going to hold a job, connect with others in a healthy manner, or make a living for themselves.

11. LIE: I need a good friend, but You can't help me heal my broken relationships. You can't help me have godly friends. I will always have to hang out with people who are a bad influence on me or I will be alone and lonely. You can't help my children quit hanging around bad influencers and form godly, healthy relationships.

12. LIE: I'm too old, and it's too late to see my family restored. My children and siblings are adults who aren't serving You.

Listed below are additional lies. You may use different Truth Statements for these from the Appendix.

13. LIE: God can't help me with______________. It's just too: big, complicated and too hard.

14. LIE: I have lost hope about ________________________.

15. LIE: Jesus, you're supposed to be my husband while I'm waiting for a godly spouse to come along, but I feel lonely, abandoned, and hopeless. I'm tired of waiting. I think I could find satisfaction and be happy even if I had to compromise my standards.

16. LIE: Just because I'm married doesn't mean I can't fantasize or look at other men. My spouse and I have grown apart. If no one finds out about my emotional or physical affair, then no one gets hurt and I feel better.

17. LIE: It's okay for me to be gay and Christian because I was born this way. The Bible is mistranslated, doesn't mean what it says, and is not relevant for today. God made a mistake when He made me. He made me the wrong sex. It's okay for me to be bisexual because I love everyone.

18. LIE: My children constantly waste their time. They are always on their computer; they play too many video games, watch too many movies—even inappropriate content. They are obsessed with social media, texting, and talking on the phone. They hang out in questionable places like bars. They don't spend enough time with their family or You.

I don't know how they will get free of these habits and/or addictions.

19. LIE: You can't help my children heal. They need to grow spiritually, mentally, emotionally, physically, financially, in their relationships and in their will. You can't really help my children in all these areas. There are just too many details.

20. LIE: Why don't You care about my family? Watching my children suffer, even if it's a result of their bad choices, is more than I can take. Why don't You heal me or my children from the diseases or injuries we endure? It just seems like You don't care about us.

21. LIE: I have too much to take care of. I don't have time to take care of myself and my family and complete my work. I can't effectively organize my time or my kid's time! I can't help my children study, get to activities, or a church youth group. I just don't have enough time.

22. LIE: I know You care about me and my children, family, and extended family, but I also know You are very busy. You can't be everywhere all the time trying to straighten out my family. You aren't able to help us to the extent we need. I guess that's just the way it will be for us.

---

1 1 Corinthians 15:33 (NIV)
2 Wright, 125.
3 Wright, 180.
4 Wright, 180.
5 John 14:27 (NIV)

CHAPTER 9

willful accidental agreements

Some Accidental Agreements are unintentional, while others are intentional agreements. Some AA's are very deliberate and premeditated. However, the majority of Accidental Agreements are unintentional agreements spurred by soul wounds unconsciously controlling you. You think you are reacting to situations logically (reasoning) or repeating these habits because you desire to do them. However, your actions are based upon your skewed thinking from soul wounds. Accidental Agreements are guiding your behavior in what you deem as an acceptable standard. You are still operating in a manner not consistent with your true identity and your God-ordained destiny.

Remember, the level of agreement you have with the enemy will reflect the health of your spirit, soul (mind, imagination, will, and emotions) and body. When we allow the Holy Spirit to completely control our lives, He becomes dominant over our mind, will, emotions, desires, passions, and our body. The unintentional AA usually begins as something small and seemingly harmless, but with the passing of time and the increase of pain, they turn into much more than just thoughts.

In fact, you start becoming very conscious of your choice to act upon these thoughts. What began accidentally quickly becomes a focal point of reference, defeating or delaying God's purposes for you. An Accidental Agreement never stays stagnant. It either increases or decreases depending upon your level of commitment to eradicate the AA with the enemy. When the enemy gains a foothold in the territory of your heart and soul, he is not going to give it back easily. He's a squatter with a legal right to be there. As long as you have given him a legal right, he does not have to leave. He has created a structure, if you will, inside your heart and soul. You gave it to him. Now, it's time to take it back.

A willful agreement is an alliance with the enemy in which he convinces you to fully believe an all-out lie. It is an unrecognized, unacknowledged alliance, a tie and covenant with Satan. It is an explicit choice to desire, propose, or develop a course of action inconsistent with the word. It can be motivated by the following: gaining an advantage in a situation; avoiding what you perceive to be harmful (fear); attempting to conceal something, motivated by guilt or shame; masking disappointment or hopelessness; finding a substitute for love; controlling a situation or person; manifesting pride; performance, jealousy, or revenge to name a few.

A willful agreement is an alliance with the enemy in which he convinces you to fully believe an all-out lie.

Here's an example. A habit begins as something as benign as shopping for pleasure. Then, the shopping, in a store or on the internet becomes excessive. Another example can be any obsession: an obsession with work, eating, drinking, gambling, smoking, caffeine, parties, pills, exercising, television, computer games, sex, education, sports, or your appearance. Anything that becomes something you think about nonstop is an obsession. While there is nothing wrong with some of these activities, when they become the first thing you think about in the morning, plan your day around, and end the evening thinking about, you need to examine the underlying motive.

Yes, work is important. Yes, physical exercise is important. After all, our body is a temple belonging to the Lord. The problem arises when the conduct or thinking pattern evolves into something which overtakes your will, and you are unable to stop. The Lord may ask you to fast from a certain food, activity or habit. I know someone whom the Lord asked to fast from the news for a few days. She was obsessed with the media, and it was harming her. There was a great deal of negative news, and she became agitated. Stress had become an issue.

Another example is if the Lord asks you to fast from coffee or tea for a month. Can you do this? Do you argue with the Lord? This may be a habitual sin pattern. This is sinful behavior you do not have clear control over. Ask the Lord right now if there is something He wants you to abstain from for a period of time. He will tell you what to fast from, what kind of fast to do, how long, and give you the strength to do it. There are many kinds of fasts. An accountability partner also helps.

Now, I know what you're thinking. That sounds intense. What kind of person would desire to fast?! Well, unfortunately, many of us have these Willful agreements within ourselves and choose to either ignore them or mask them with something else. As unintentional as the Willful agreement may sound, it can still fly under the radar for many of us.

Let me give you an example. Nancy loved to drink her daily coffee. This may be fine for some people, but the Lord was nudging her to not drink any coffee. She started by eliminating coffee in the morning. She continued her tea at noon. Then the Lord nudged her to eliminate drinking tea, but she waivered. Eventually, she substituted a green tea.

After a few weeks, she started drinking a half glass of black tea, thinking it was okay. One half glass led to one glass which led to a "taste" of coffee in the morning. You can see the pattern slipping back into her daily routine. This may not sound like a big issue to you, but it was to the Lord. He had a reason for it.

The lies she was subconsciously believing were: God doesn't know what is best for me. God doesn't really care about caffeine or coffee that much. God can't fix my problems through this type of fasting. God has other ways to help me rather than giving this up. She had at least four Accidental Agreements tied to this Willful Agreement.

When she finally quit completely, she received important breakthroughs in her life—breakthroughs she had waited to receive for years. In this case, it had to do with Numbers 5:26–27. You may be thinking, really? God made each of us, each cell in our bodies. He only wants the best for us. He knows our DNA weaknesses. He alone knows what we need. Don't argue with Him. When you argue, you are revealing you have a Willful Accidental Agreement. This is disobedience.

Willful AA's are perhaps the easiest to spot, but sometimes the hardest to heal. Keep this in mind: If you willfully got yourself into an agreement, you can willfully get yourself out with the help of the Holy Spirit! Maybe it feels too powerful, too burdensome, or too damaging. Let me express something to you. You have a very powerful, loving Heavenly Father who wants to help you. Remember, He is much more powerful than the devil. Often it simply takes your willingness to give up and surrender. Ask the Holy Spirit to help you defeat this stronghold. Let Him do what He does best. Let Him be the God in charge of your life. The three-week Accidental Agreement Freedom Program will help guide you into freedom from these Willful Accidental Agreements. You will be much happier and filled with peace.

> **Willful AA's are perhaps the easiest to spot, but sometimes the hardest to heal.**

LIES AND TRUTH STATEMENTS

Read through the following lies that are relevant to you and circle the top three. These are your Accidental Agreements, which we will use later in the book when implementing our AA Freedom Program.

Rather than waiting to begin the program at the end of the book, you can begin now if you prefer. However, when you read the rest of the book, you will find a common theme in the lies you are believing which may help you break the Accidental Agreement more quickly. In the Appendix, you will find the corresponding Truth Statements. Circle the Truth Statements and scriptures which resonate within you. Write the Lie and Truth Statements on a note card and put a mark by the lie each time you hear it, whether it's every minute or hour. Each time you hear the lie, repeat the Truth Statement and appropriate scripture out loud (dunamis power-Holy Spirit). Continue this for one week, and each day the number of lie whispers should diminish. You will be able to recognize the lies quickly because they are being moved out of your subconscious mind creating new brain patterns. The more consistently you practice this exercise, the more quickly the Accidental Agreements will be broken. Once broken, you will see movement in the heavenlies very quickly. Watch for the Lord's blessings! If you are not seeing blessings, read the rest of the book and check the Appendix for *Common Hindrances to Healing*. Ask the Holy Spirit which one applies to your situation. The Holy Spirit will highlight an issue very quickly because He wants to see you blessed!

1. LIE: I can't break the habit of ______________________. Every time I try to stop this habit it seems to sneak back into my life. I've asked the Lord to help but He's not helping enough.

2. LIE: I can't stand up to ____________________. My voice isn't heard when I'm speaking to ____________________.

Listed below are additional lies. You may use different Truth Statements for these from the Appendix.

3. LIE: I can't __________________________________ (Fill in the blank).

4. LIE: I can't forgive _________________and ______________________for _________________________ (Fill in the blank).

5. LIE: God can't heal me and my children from ______________ (an activity) due to their choices and will.

6. LIE: I have lost hope about ______________________.

7. LIE: I don't have enough time to _________________________. (Fill in the blank.)

CHAPTER 10

accidental agreements freedom program

BREAKING LIES AND TIES

Are you ready to be blessed? You have learned about the seven types of Accidental Agreements: spiritual, mental, emotional, physical, financial, relational and your will. You know about the enemy strings with their adverse effects on your life. Now, you are ready to deal with these subconscious issues and eliminate them. It's time to receive your God given blessings!

This AA Freedom Program (AAFP) requires your effort and prayers. You will experience blessings, breakthroughs, and healing beyond what you can imagine. Isaiah 55:8–9 says, "My thoughts are nothing like your thoughts," says the Lord. "And My ways are far beyond anything you could imagine. For just as the heavens are higher than the earth, so My ways are higher than your ways and My thoughts higher than your thoughts."[1] Remember, when the results look otherwise than you imagined, God is reconstructing your life and the lives of the people around you. He is removing the web of strings created by these ungodly alliances, bringing you into alignment with God's purpose. Continue pressing in, relying on the Lord. Don't stop praying, as this is just what the enemy wants you to do. Let the Holy Spirit help you break the lies and strings. God will bless you with the gifts He has waiting!

Let's begin breaking AA lies and cutting their ties.

At the end of chapters 3–9, you were asked to circle three lies which resonated. This was the Holy Spirit prompting you to pay attention. Summarize all circled items from chapters 3–9 at the end of this chapter. You will have 21 lies, three from each of the chapters. Read your summarized list, circling the top three lies. Therefore, you have selected the top three Rotten lies! Find their matching Truth Statements. You may shorten your AA Truth Statements, but do not leave out the scriptural basis or the scripture itself. Scripture, God's Word, permeated into your heart, soul and gut is what will change your life.

Write the three Rotten lies and their Truth Statements on separate 3 x 5 notecards. If a different AA Truth Statement resonates more strongly, use that one. This will allow you to have one in the kitchen, car, work, or where ever you go. You have just identified your personal Accidental Agreements setting the stage for freedom. You are ready to begin breaking every barrier holding back your blessings!

You will begin with Rotten lie #1. For the first three days, count each time you hear Rotten lie #1. When you hear the whisper, make a notation on your notecard and repeat, out loud, your Truth Statement. Repeat this AA Truth Statement several times, out loud, until it starts to "take hold" of you. It is important to say it aloud because scripture creates dunamis power in the atmosphere. The word base of dunamis is derived from the word dynamite. It's as though scripture is rippling through the room, dropping spiritual bombs. Often, you can "feel" the difference. Notice if there is an activity or time of day when you have more AA's lies whispered in your ear. Unless this truth comes from your gut, it is still "head knowledge" and will not break the AA. Head knowledge is liturgy, something memorized, which has not penetrated into your heart and soul.

At the end of day one, you should be keenly aware of the enemy's whispers. The Rotten lie count should decrease daily. Continue tallying your notecard for the remainder of the week. Don't worry if you feel the AA Lie is no longer a whisper, but becoming louder and stronger. Temporarily, the enemy is attempting to bully you to back down. He knows you are almost free. He is squealing because he is desperate to keep his gained territory. The enemy doesn't want you to understand how much your Heavenly Father loves you and wants to bless you! Tell Satan to "back off. Your lies are busted" or "I'm fed up with your lies and I'm not going to be harassed anymore." "Be quiet, I don't believe your ridiculous lies." Remember, the enemy will harass you as much as you allow. Exercise your authority through Christ.[2]

> The enemy doesn't want you to understand how much your Heavenly Father loves you and wants to bless you!

This completes one week of the AA Freedom Program. You will soon be alert to hearing the lies, quick to dispute them and your Truth Statement will roll off your tongue immediately. If you are willing to do the work and are serious about getting blessed, be faithful to follow the program. Some of you have lost hope and do not believe a program this easy will solve your problems. God is not complicated. He said we are to have childlike faith. Following this program for three weeks is not hard work, especially when you consider how long this problem has been pestering you. Each three-week segment will release a previously hidden AA or a layer off of a more complicated agreement. This positions you for blessings.

The women and men who have pursued this Accidental Agreement Freedom Program and understand God's economy of blessings are the majority of testimonies you read about in the book. There are so many testimonies it astounds me! We will put more of these on the web site to encourage you. God blessed these women and men within weeks because they permanently broke their Accidental Agreements. The blessings keep happening as they have stayed in agreement with the Word of God. He will do the same for you!

DON'T BE EMBARRASSED. DON'T QUIT.
IT REALLY IS THIS EASY!

God is excited to bless you. Cut the tie to the enemy and watch God's blessings flow in the very area in which you believed the lie.

Everyone has some type of Accidental Agreement, everyone. Clearing away all of them is a lifelong process. Today you can and will, if you persist, remove the dark lies holding you back and stealing your blessings! This process brings the lie out of your subconscious and moves it into the conscious part of your brain where you can deal with it properly.

Are you ready to get blessed? Are you really ready to get blessed? Then, let's go! Once you free yourself of Rotten lie #1, you will be excited to launch into Rotten lie #2. Three weeks are required to break Rotten lie #1. However, do not jump ahead to lie #2 until lie #1 is solidly trampled under your feet. I want your brain retrained so you do not regress and lose your freedom. Do you remember the neuroplasticity and grooves we learned about earlier in the book? This is why we have the Accidental Agreement Freedom Program. We are literally reshaping the way your brain behaves, thinks, reasons, and operates. We are bringing negative thinking into alignment with God's positive thoughts, scriptures, and patterns heading towards love. There is no down side to this! Everyone wins! (Except Satan of course).

We are bringing negative thinking into alignment with God's positive thoughts, scriptures, and patterns heading towards love.

If the lie whispers are not decreasing, there is probably a blockage. Some of these can be identified in the "Hindrances to Healing and Blockages Section." Ask Holy Spirit to reveal which blockage on the list is a problem. Once revealed, open your Bible and conduct a word search on this topic. If you are unsure this is the issue but suspect it might be, *pursue it!* Write down the scriptures on this topic and pick the top three which resonate. Meditate upon these scriptures until Holy Spirit reveals truth. Once Holy Spirit identifies the blockage, look for a Lie and Truth Statement which fits the topic. Once the curse is identified, repent and ask for forgiveness for the sin for yourself, your ancestors and your descendants back to the beginning of time. Ask the Lord to cover it with the blood of Jesus and break the power of the sin by simply commanding it to leave your bloodline permanently. Ask the Lord to fill the vacated areas with the glory light of Jesus Christ. This would be a good time to read the Renouncing Prayer. I also recommend Robert Henderson's teachings on the *Courts of Heaven* and *Unlocking Your Destiny in the Courts of Heaven.* They are life changing in understanding how to receive justice in the Courts of Heaven and how God works.

Many Christians have been stuck for years, reciting and recycling scriptures weekly. I share this because if you truly want freedom, you MUST personalize the scriptures. There is a major difference between hoping God's word is true and believing God's word is true. This is why personalizing scripture and speaking out loud from your gut changes the spiritual dynamics. Some of the most anointed pastors meditate on one scripture for several days until the Lord reveals His supernatural wisdom. Julie Meyer, a gifted Christian singer, said she sings the scripture, sings it to God by personalizing it, and then sings it as though God is singing it to her. Check out Julie's interview on Sid Roth's, *It's Supernatural* television and internet program to see her archived segment.[3] She has many breakthroughs combining personalized praise and scripture.

Personalizing scriptures appropriate for your problem are highly effective. The personalized and paraphrased scriptures in the Appendix are powerful because you are appropriating them for yourself and your individual situation. I learned to pray this way through a powerful little book by Ruth Shinness. It is entitled, *Unlocking the Heavens, Prayer Strategy Resource Book.*

BLESSINGS

Now for the fun part. After you feel you have eliminated the whispers from AA Rotten lie #1, you will begin to experience blessings. Be alert. Expect to see God's goodness. Before you receive blessings, thank the Lord out loud for the specific ways you believe He will move. When you see His blessing, no matter how big or small, write it down and thank the Lord out loud. Begin thanking Him for everything. Continue looking for blessings in the category where you were accidentally tied to the enemy. Sometimes, you receive blessings in what may appear to be an area totally unrelated to the lie. After Holy Spirit insight, you will realize the areas were tied with an Accidental Agreement.

If for example, you receive blessings in the area of your job, look for small movement at first such as favor, time off, training, pay increase, or a new assignment. If the lie was tied to a specific need such as the "Macy's Pants' Story", ask Holy Spirit for guidance and watch! Record the blessings you see and give thanks continuously. The Lord values gratitude. Remember the story about the lepers who were healed, and only one came back to thank Him in Luke 17:11–19? This must be very significant for it to be mentioned. There are numerous scriptures about thankfulness and prayer. For example, Philippians 4:6: "Don't worry about anything; instead, pray about everything. Tell God what you need, and thank him for all he has done."

Please keep a journal of the blessings you receive after getting out of agreement with the enemy. I would love to hear your story. It encourages others to pursue breaking their lies and ties. I love to rejoice when a Christian gets blessed! Our Heavenly Father is truly better than we think! Keep praising and thanking Him even before you receive your blessings! This is a powerful act of faith which pleases God!

SUMMARY OF LIES AND TIES

Record the lies you circled at the end of each chapter here.

Spiritual Lies Pages 46–49

1.____

2.____

3.____

Mental Lies Pages 58–59

1.____

2.____

3.____

Emotional Lies Pages 74–75

1.________________________________

2.________________________________

3.________________________________

Physical Lies Pages 87–88

1.________________________________

2.________________________________

3.________________________________

Financial Lies Pages 121–123

1.________________________________

2.________________________________

3.________________________________

Relational Lies Pages 139–142

1.________________________________

2.________________________________

3.________________________________

Lies of the Will Page 150

1.______________________________

2.______________________________

3.______________________________

TOP THREE ROTTEN LIES

1.______________________________

2.______________________________

3.______________________________

---

[1] Isaiah 55:8–9 (NLT)
[2] Luke 10:19 (NKJV)
[3] "Julie Meyer." *It's Supernatural.* Nov. 17, 2014. Television.
[4] Philippians 4:6 (NLT)

APPENDIX I

I. DAILY PRAYER FOCUS

I am assuming you have already prayed to break any operating curses, whether brought in by you or your ancestors, and said the renouncing statements for your Accidental Agreement lies. I am also assuming you have read the *Hindrances to Healing* section, praying for removal of any hindrance or blockage that resonates within you.

1. FORGIVENESS

Ask the Lord to download who you are holding unforgiveness toward. He will give you their names within a few seconds to a few minutes. This is how badly He wants you to forgive! Write down every name He gives you. Don't argue with God that you have already forgiven them. He knows if you have or haven't. Pray the *Forgiveness Prayer* in the *Bitterness* section, inserting all of the names. Harboring unforgiveness blocks prayers. If you are unwilling to forgive, you are choosing to remain stuck.

2. THE LORD'S PRAYER

Matthew 6:9–13

In this manner, therefore, pray: Our Father in heaven, Hallowed be Your name. Your kingdom come. Your will be done on earth as it is in heaven. Give us this day our daily bread. And forgive us our debts, as we forgive our debtors. And do not lead us into temptation, but deliver us from the evil one. For Yours is the kingdom and the power and the glory forever. Amen.

3.ARMOR OF GOD

VERY IMPORTANT – Say daily. Memorize.

Ephesians 6:10–18

[10] Finally, be strong in the Lord and in his mighty power.[11]Put on the full armor of God, so that you can take your stand against the devil's schemes. [12]For our struggle is not against flesh and blood, but against the rulers, against the authorities, against the powers of this dark world and against the spiritual forces of evil in the heavenly realms.[13]Therefore put on the full armor of God, so that when the day of evil comes, you may be able to stand your ground, and after you have done everything, to stand. [14] Stand firm then, with the belt of truth buckled around your waist, with the breastplate of righteousness in place, [15] and with your feet fitted with the readiness that comes from the gospel of peace. [16] In addition to all this, take up the shield of faith, with which you can extinguish all the flaming arrows of the evil one. [17] Take the helmet of salvation and the sword of the Spirit, which is the word of God. [18] And pray in the Spirit on all occasions with all kinds of prayers and requests. With this in mind, be alert and always keep on praying for all the Lord's people.[2]

4. PSALM 91 PRAYER OF PROTECTION – Memorize this!!

"Those who live in the shelter of the Most High will find rest in the shadow of the Almighty. This I declare about the Lord: He alone is my refuge, my place of safety; he is my God, and I trust him. For he will rescue you from every trap and protect you from deadly disease. He will cover you with his feathers. He will shelter you with his wings. His faithful promises are your armor and protection. Do not be afraid of the terrors of the night, nor the arrow that flies in the day. Do not dread the disease that stalks in darkness, nor the disaster that strikes at midday. Though a thousand fall at your side, though ten thousand are dying around you, these evils will not touch you. Just open your eyes, and see how the wicked are punished. If you make the Lord your refuge, if you make the Most High your shelter, no evil will conquer you; no plague will come near your home. For he will order his angels to protect you wherever you go. They will hold you up with their hands so you won't even hurt your foot on a stone. You will trample upon lions and cobras; you will crush fierce lions and serpents under your feet! The Lord says, "I will rescue those who love me. I will protect those who trust in my name. When they call on me, I will answer; I will be with them in trouble. I will rescue and honor them. I will reward them with a long life and give them my salvation."[3]

5. PRAYER OF JABEZ

1 Chronicles 4:9–10

"Now Jabez was more honorable than his brothers, and his mother called his name Jabez, saying, 'Because I bore *him* in pain.' And Jabez called on the God of Israel saying, 'Oh, that You would bless me indeed, and enlarge my territory, that Your hand would be with me, and that You would keep *me* from evil, that I may not cause pain!' So God granted him what he requested."[4]

1 Chronicles 4:9–10

"There was a man named Jabez who was more honorable than any of his brothers. His mother named him Jabez because his birth had been so painful. He was the one who prayed to the God of Israel, 'Oh, that you would bless me and expand my territory! Please be with me in all that I do, and keep me from all trouble and pain!' And God granted him his request."[5]

6. DAILY PRAYER

"In the name of Jesus of Nazareth, I ask for us to be covered with the blood of Jesus Christ. I pray against all accidents, disease, sickness and harm for me, my family, and all that concerns me. I break all demonic hexes, vexes, spells, curses, incantations, vows, all black magic and white magic sent against me or my descendants. I cancel all demonic assignments and contracts, demonic spiritual bonds or covenants, future rights and communication by the enemy against me, my family and all that concerns me and declare them permanently null and void. I break their power from operating in my life or the lives of my family. I ask this be ruled upon in my favor, and my descendants, in the Courts of Heaven and these sins be erased from my book of life. Blind the eyes of the enemy to protect us. Holy Spirit fire burn up all shield, seals, devices, and anything affecting us which is not from You. I bind my body, soul (mind, will, emotions, and imagination) and spirit to Jesus and loose anything not from the Lord. I consecrate my body, soul, spirit, and imagination to You, Lord Jesus. I ask You to cleanse me with Your blood. I ask You to break any ungodly covenants made with anyone or anything affecting my body, soul, or spirit and realign all boundaries with God's intended boundaries for my life. I ask You to bring the earthly reality to align with Your spiritual reality. I pray Your will be done on earth as it is in heaven. I take authority over anything the enemy would try to do to kill, steal, or destroy and command it to go to Jesus. Father in Heaven, release Your mighty angels to minister and protect me, my family, and all that concerns me."

7. NAMES OF GOD

Here is a partial list of the names, titles, descriptors, and metaphors of God from the book, *Names and Titles of God*, by Dr. Ralph F. Wilson. It is important to memorize some of the names of God so it soaks into your soul! I play a game where I memorize the names of God using the ABC's. I try to list as many as I can remember for each letter. It's a great way to focus on God!

- ABBA
- ALMIGHTY GOD (EL SHADDAI)
- AVENGER
- BRIDEGROOM
- BUILDER
- COMMANDER OF THE ARMY OF THE LORD
- COMPASSIONATE
- CREATOR (OF HEAVEN AND EARTH) (OF THE ENDS OF THE EARTH)
- DELIVERER
- DWELLING PLACE
- EL-ELOHE ISRAEL
- ELOHIM
- ETERNAL KING
- EVERLASTING FATHER
- EVERLASTING GOD
- ETERNAL GOD (EL 'OLAM)
- EVERLASTING LIGHT
- FAITHFUL CREATOR
- FAITHFUL GOD
- FATHER
- FATHER IN HEAVEN
- FATHER OF COMPASSION
- FATHER OF GLORY

- FATHER OF LIGHTS
- FATHER OF THE FATHERLESS/ORPHANS
- FORGIVING GOD
- FORTRESS
- GLORIOUS FATHER
- GLORY OF ISRAEL
- GOD ('EL, 'ELOHIM)
- GOD AND FATHER
- GOD AND FATHER OF OUR LORD JESUS CHRIST
- GOD OF ABRAHAM, ISAAC AND JACOB
- GOD OF ALL COMFORT
- GOD OF ALL GRACE
- GOD OF ALL THE EARTH
- GOD OF BETHEL
- GOD OF HEAVEN AND EARTH
- GOD OF HOPE
- GOD OF ISRAEL
- GOD OF LOVE AND PEACE
- GOD OF PEACE
- GOD OF SEEING (EL ROI)
- GOD OF TRUTH
- GODHEAD/DEITY/DIVINITY
- GRACIOUS GOD AND MERCIFUL
- GREAT AND AWESOME GOD
- HEALER
- HELP/STRENGTH
- HELPER
- HIDING PLACE
- HIGH AND LOFTY ONE
- HIGH TOWER
- HOLY FATHER
- HOLY LORD

- HOLY ONE
- HOLY ONE OF ISRAEL
- HOPE/HOPE OF ISRAEL
- HUSBAND
- I AM THAT I AM
- ISRAEL'S CREATOR
- JEALOUS AND AVENGING GOD
- JUDGE
- JUDGE OF THE EARTH
- JUST AND MIGHTY ONE
- KING
- KING AND GOD
- KING ETERNAL
- KING OF GLORY
- KING OF HEAVEN
- KING OF ISRAEL
- KING OF KINGS
- KING OF THE NATIONS
- KING OF THE SAINTS
- KING, THE LORD OF HOSTS
- LAWGIVER
- LIFTER UP OF MY HEAD
- LIGHT
- LIGHT OF ISRAEL
- LIVING GOD
- LORD (YAHWEH)
- LORD (ADONAI) LORD AND FATHER
- LORD GOD, SOVEREIGN GOD
- LORD OF ALL THE EARTH (HEAVEN AND EARTH)
- LORD MY SAVIOR
- LORD OF LORDS
- LOVING GOD

- MAKER
- MAKER OF HEAVEN AND EARTH
- MAN OF WAR (WARRIOR)
- MOST HIGH GOD (‘EL ‘ELYON)
- MY GLORY
- MY GOD
- MY SONG
- MY STRENGTH
- PORTION
- PORTION OF MY INHERITANCE
- POTTER
- PRINCE
- PRINCE OF PEACE
- PROTECTOR/DEFENDER OF WIDOWS
- REDEEMER
- REFUGE
- RIGHTEOUS FATHER
- RIGHTEOUS JUDGE
- RIGHTEOUS ONE
- ROCK
- ROCK OF ISRAEL
- ROCK OF MY SALVATION
- RULER OF ALL THINGS
- RULER, SOVEREIGN
- SAVIOR
- SAVIOR OF ALL MEN
- SAVIOR OF ISRAEL
- SHADE
- SHELTER
- SHEPHERD
- SHIELD
- SONG

- SOVEREIGN LORD
- SPRING OF LIVING WATER, FOUNTAIN OF LIVING WATER
- STRONG DELIVERER
- STRONG FORTRESS
- STRONG REFUGE
- STRONG TOWER
- STRONGHOLD
- SUN
- SUSTAINER OF MY SOUL
- THE ALMIGHTY (SHADDAI)
- THE ALPHA AND OMEGA
- THE FIRST AND THE LAST
- THE LORD IS PEACE (JEHOVAH-SHALOM, YAHWEH-SHALOM
- THE LORD OF HOSTS (JEHOVAH-SABAOTH, YAHWEH-SABAOTH)
- THE LORD OUR RIGHTEOUSNESS (JEHOVAH-TSIDKENU, YAHWEH-TSIDKENU)
- TRUE GOD
- UPRIGHT ONE
- WHO IS AND WHO WAS AND WHO IS TO COME
- WONDERFUL
- YAH
- YAHWEH (OLDER PRONUNCIATION JEHOVAH)
- YAHWEH PROVIDES (YAHWEH-YIR'EH, JEHOVAH-JIREH)[6]

The book, *Names and Titles of God*, by Dr. Ralph F. Wilson is a comprehensive 234-page book that examines the names, titles, descriptors, and metaphors of God. It includes about 120 core names, with 219 variations. You can purchase it online in e-book or printed book format. www.jesuswalk.com/ebooks/names

II. STRONGHOLD BREAKING AND BLESSING PRAYERS

Introduction

The Stronghold Breaking Prayer is powerful! I have witnessed miraculous results with this prayer. Jesus has literally moved governments in 15 minutes. He wants to bless everyone and has a God-ordained destiny for every person on this earth.

After the Stronghold Breaking Prayer, be sure to pray the Stronghold Blessing Prayer. Remember, blessings always trump curses. God's blessings always supersede anything the enemy can do. The enemy tries to convince us he is strong and in charge, which is a big fat lie. The Lord is the Creator of heaven and earth, and the enemy is a tiny speck in comparison. Isaiah 40:12 asks the questions, "Who else has held the oceans in his hand? Who has measured off the heavens with his fingers?" There is no comparison to the Lord, God Almighty.

God's blessings always supersede anything the enemy can do.

The 16 strongholds to be broken are:

1. Antichrist
2. Bondage
3. Deaf and Dumb
4. Death
5. Divination
6. Error
7. Fear
8. Harlotry
9. Haughtiness
10. Heaviness
11. Infirmity
12. Jealousy
13. Lying
14. Perversion
15. Seduction
16. Stupor

Bitterness is a major stronghold and is a powerful enemy alliance, a secret web linking most or all of these 16 strongholds. Another name for bitterness is unforgiveness. Unforgiveness is one of the deadliest poisons a person can take. The enemy loves to use it against us. We feel so justified in clinging to it because we feel we have been *legitimately* wronged. I heard someone say if you are clinging to unforgiveness, "it is like giving the enemy the keys to your house." This is a sobering thought, and is too high a price to pay to hold a grudge. Unforgiveness blocks prayers, ends relationships and causes a variety of mental and physical problems. Unfortunately, the only one wounded is the person who refuses to forgive. See the *Forgiveness* section and pray the prayer if you are not 100% sure you have forgiven *everyone* including yourself.

STRONGHOLD BREAKING PRAYER

Father, in the name of Jesus, I ask You to break the power of these strongholds[1] in my life and in ____________ (people's names) lives and any affiliated or unaffiliated parties, governments[2] and laws.

LORD, Your word says we have powerful weapons of warfare.[3] On behalf of me and______________ (name), in Jesus' name, I ask You to pull down every stronghold,[4] belief, thought, and philosophy that we see as truth but are lies[5] from the enemy keeping us in bondage.[6]

Your Word says, "You shall know the Truth and the Truth shall set you free."[7] I ask You, Jesus of Nazareth, to illuminate the truth[8] of Your Word[9] and take every thought captive to the obedience of Christ,[10] even into our innermost being. Shine Your light[11] in our body, soul, and spirit. I also pray this for ____________ (his or her influencers, work, friends, family, media, affiliated, unaffiliated parties, government, and laws). Lord, shut the original doors of disobedience opened by me or my ancestors flowing to my descendants allowing the enemy into our lives. I ask You, Jesus, to be set up as the permanent doorkeeper. I ask for forgiveness, I repent and renounce any agreements[12] or covenants I, or my ancestors have made with the enemy. I ask You to cleanse and cover us with the blood[13] of Jesus, His dunamis* power and His glory light.[14] Fill us with Your Holy Spirit. In Jesus' name, I ask for each of our God-ordained destinies[15] to come forth, for us and our descendants. I ask that no weapon formed against us will prosper[16] and we will receive all of the Deuteronomy 28 blessings You have planned for us and our descendants to a thousand generations.[17] Amen.

Francis Frangipane said, "Each of us has thinking processes, strongholds in our minds, which have been shaded and conditioned by the spirit of antichrist."[18] Yikes! He said do not defend them, but instead, expose them as sin.

STRONGHOLD BLESSING PRAYER

Father God, in the name of Jesus of Nazareth, I have asked You to break every stronghold because You say, "You shall know the Truth and the Truth shall set you free" (John 8:32, NKJV). Thank You for breaking every ungodly stronghold, structure, and covenant with the enemy.

I come before You, Lord, in the courts of heaven and ask You to reinstate me into good standing in full covenant with You. I ask You to call forth every blessing belonging to me and my family and all that concerns me, which was stolen by the enemy. Thank You the enemy's power is now cut off. The blood of Jesus Christ who died on the cross, rose again three days later, and sits at the right hand of God has set me free.

Thank You for filling my life with freedom, my spirit, body, heart, and soul, (mind, will, emotions, and imagination) with:

- The fruit of the Spirit—love, joy, peace, patience, kindness, goodness, gentleness, faithfulness, and self-control.
- The fullness of Jesus Christ living inside of you
- A full understanding of Your truth
- Godly wisdom
- A sound mind filled with love and power
- Godly humility
- The glory and light of Jesus
- Perfect health and wholeness in body, soul, and spirit
- A new infilling of the Holy Spirit, the Spirit of Truth, in every soul wound and opening vacated by the enemy.

Thank You, Jesus, for Your promise given years ago to Abraham, our ancestor and seed, that You will lead and take us into our Promised Land (Galatians 3:29). Thank you for reestablishing our God-ordained boundaries for me, my family and all that concerns me.

III. FORGIVENESS

BITTERNESS–SPIRITUAL ALLIANCES EXPLANATION

Bitterness is a major blockage toward freedom and healing as it is tied to many strongholds. It is literally a woven web of stronghold alliances. Bitterness is usually a combination of the 16 strongholds, making it a key blockage to answered prayer. Thus it creates a legal right for the enemy to harass you. This is why the Bible is very clear about the importance of not staying offended! Bitterness is mentioned 64 times in the Bible! Bitterness creates an alliance between evil spirits.

Here are some terms that relate to bitterness: resentment, anger, retaliation, animosity, hostility, cynicism, negativity, indignation, irritation, fury, infuriate, annoy, provoke, rage, temper, rant, explode, destructive, belligerent, antagonistic, revenge, retribution, cruelty, brutality, heartlessness, hardhearted, callousness, meanness, nastiness, spitefulness, vindictive, viciousness, malice, unsympathetic, uncaring, pitiless, stony, unemotional, unfeeling, hard, cold.

Remember the childhood game, Red Rover? The bitterness alliance is the same concept. Red Rover is a game divided between two teams. Each team's members are holding hands tightly to create a strong, impenetrable wall. Their enemy, the other team, invites someone from the opposing team to run toward them trying to "break" through their "hand shake alliance," or human wall. Similarly, the enemy attempts to create a strong wall dividing us from God through the bitterness spirit alliance. This keeps you from achieving your freedom and God-ordained destiny. Just as in Red Rover, when the enemy breaks through your spiritual wall causing you to believe lies and align with the enemy, you are taken captive to the enemy's team.

Fortunately, God is awesome in power and promises a way of escape! Why do we hang on to bitterness? Pride. We believe we have been wronged. We have made a judgment what has happened is unjust and we want vengeance. You may tell yourself there is a different reason other than vengeance, but the truth is, it is retaliation, prompted by pride. Unforgiveness gives the enemy the right to move boundaries which is your territory!

Why do we hang on to bitterness? Pride.

Bitterness is usually tied to some or all of the 16 strongholds:

1. Anti-Christ: These strongholds all lead to an Anti-Christ spirit. They are opposed to Jesus Christ fully living in all of you. Our mandate is to "Love the Lord Your God with all your heart and with all your soul and with all your mind and with all your strength." Mark 12:30

2. Bondage: Bitterness makes an agreement with the enemy, creating bondage. You believe a lie, imagining something should happen a certain way to correct the situation or person about which you are bitter. You have made a judgment. God is the only one allowed to judge. You have a belief which doesn't line up with scripture.

3. Deaf and Dumb Spirit: Bitterness leads to an agreement with deaf and dumb spirits, inhibiting your ability to hear, speak, and see the Holy Spirit.

4. Death Spirit: Bitterness can eventually lead to death, whether it's physically, mentally, spiritually, or emotionally.

5. Divination: When bitterness enters your soul, divination attempts to destroy and manipulate the situation.

6. Error: Bitterness leads to error in your thinking, due to soul wounds.

7. Fear: Bitterness leads to fear because someone feels they are being slighted. They are afraid there will not be justice unless they interfere.

8. Haughtiness: Bitterness is based upon a belief you have been harmed and something unfair has happened. This is pride manifesting in your imagination. Fear is created when you feel you are entitled to receive something and are afraid it will not happen.

9. Heaviness: Bitterness creates heaviness of heart. You begin to feel hopeless or angry the situation will not be resolved to your satisfaction. Heaviness invites divination, leading to manipulation.

10. Harlotry: means to commit idolatry. Bitterness is prompted by a hidden idol. Therefore, any other "love" desired more than the Lord creates an idol.

11. Infirmity: Infirmity, or illness, becomes the physical manifestation of bitterness. It will manifest through stress related illnesses such as kidney disease, gall bladder disease, inflammation and arthritis to name a few. See Dr. Henry Wright, Be In Health Ministry, for more information about this.

12. Jealousy and Envy: Bitterness leads to jealousy and envy because you believe or imagine you are supposed to have something that the other person has instead of you. That's pride. False expectations.

13. Lying Spirit: Bitterness misleads us into believing a lie about who God is, who we are (and God's plans for us) and what God thinks about others.

14. Perversion: The word of God and truth become twisted and perverted due to bitterness and the alliance of ungodly strongholds.

15. Seduction: Bitterness opens the door for the seduction stronghold to enter. Manipulation attempts to control or seduce the outcome. An example of seduction is gossiping to destroy the other person you are bitter towards in an attempt to manipulate the outcome.

16. Stupor: Bitterness creates an inability to hear and speak correctly from the Holy Spirit. This leads to a stupor because the word of God is unable to be thoroughly understood.

The Bible says when two or three are gathered to pray He is present. It also says a three-cord strand is hard to break. (Ecclesiastes 4:12)

This is exactly why the enemy loves to bring buddies or other spirits, to fortify His legal position.

The reverse is true also. God is much greater than the enemy. The Lord loves for believers to pray as a group, in unity and oneness. God knows unity creates a strong, unbreakable alliance in the spiritual world, defeating every area of darkness.

Becoming aware of the enemy's strategies is important to help us learn how to pray effectively. We will focus on God, our Redeemer and Savior. Call a friend and begin praying for the permanent breakage of the spirits of bitterness.

If any of the bitterness synonyms or a stronghold category jumped off the page at you, go to the *Forgiveness* section and pray the prayer, followed by the Stronghold-Breaking and Blessing Prayers.

FORGIVENESS PRAYER

Father, Your desire is for my soul to be restored and whole. I declare Jesus defeated Satan and His demons by His shed blood on the cross and His resurrection. God has given me weapons empowered by the Holy Spirit to tear down the lies, agreements, and all thoughts that have been raised up against the knowledge of Him, keeping me in bondage. I confess I have given the enemy a legal right to build a stronghold of bitterness in my soul. I ask for forgiveness and repent for agreeing with bitterness and allowing it into my life. I renounce my agreements with the enemy and command any ungodly spirits, demonic residue, and structures to be removed from me right now. I cut off any attachments or strings I have to my offender or anyone else which are ungodly. I command them to leave me in the name of Jesus Christ. I ask You to cover me with the blood of Jesus. I ask You, Father, to heal my soul wounds and tongue with Your dunamis power and the shekinah glory light of Jesus. I ask you to reinstate me in full covenant with You. I permanently surrender my right to hang onto unforgiveness or my right to stay bitter at anyone, including myself. I ask for forgiveness for self-condemnation and self-judgment because I am already forgiven. You remember my sins no more!

I declare Jesus is my defender and righteous judge and it's His job to judge, not mine. I place my offender into the hands of Jesus, who will judge them. I declare God will help me overcome all bitterness, His love for me and the working of the Holy Spirit will enable me to have greater love and compassion. Luke 10:19 says, "Look, I have given you authority over ALL the power of the enemy, and you can walk among snakes and scorpions and crush them. Nothing will injure you."

Father, I acknowledge I have held resentment and bitterness against ________________. I confess this as sin and ask you to forgive me and cover me with the blood of Jesus. I forgive and bless (name)__________________. Remind me, Lord, to not hold any more resentment, but rather to love this person and ask their God-ordained destiny come forth. I acknowledge and declare You have great plans for all of us. Thank you for hearing and answering my prayer. In Jesus' name, Amen.

IV. PRAYER TO RELEASE YOU INTO FINANCIAL FREEDOM

By: Jolene McCord, Hearts of Forgiveness Ministry
www.heartofforgiveness.org

Father, I come boldly before Your throne of grace, thanking and praising You for Your blessings and prosperity upon my life, and upon the lives of my family. Father, You said that You desire above all things that we would prosper and be in good health as we prosper. Therefore, I know that it is Your will for me to prosper. I thank You first of all, Father, that my soul prospers in You. I thank You that I prosper daily in the knowledge and the understanding of Your Word, and that I become rooted, grounded, settled and established in Christ Jesus. I thank You Father, that according to Your Word, You have established us as kings and priests unto the Most High King, Jesus Christ. Father, You said in Your Word, that "when a king shall decree a thing, it shall be established." Therefore, I decree and declare, according to Your Word, that I am blessed in the city and blessed in the field; I am above only, and not beneath; I am the head and not the tail; I am blessed coming in, and blessed going out, and my marriage is blessed with peace, harmony, happiness, unity and love.

I am blessed Father, upon my job, and blessed in my home; and I confess according to Your Word, that all of my children are blessed and prosperous all the days of their lives.

I thank you Father, that I am blessed in my mind with the peace of God that passes all understanding, and I am blessed in my body with good health, as You desire for us. I thank You Father, that according to Your Word, You make me to lie down in green pastures, which are the abundance of Your blessings, and these blessings are constantly upon me and overtaking me. I thank You Father, that the windows of heaven are upon me, and You are constantly pouring out the abundance of Your blessings upon my life spiritually, physically, financially, and in every other aspect of my life, whereby I do not have room enough to contain them.

I thank You Father, that You are the one who opens doors of prosperity and success for me, which no man can shut; and You close every door of failure and defeat in my life, which no man can open; and I pray that You anoint the work of my hands, whereby I may prosper in everything that I do.

I repent that I have not treated and valued the kingdom of heaven as I should and that I have exchanged the value of the kingdom of heaven for the desires of my heart in the form of an earthly kingdom. Lord I repent for worrying about life, food and clothing.

I repent for robbing the Lord and not freely and cheerfully giving my tithes and offerings to You out of a heart of love and allowing the spirit of fear to keep me from giving freely.

I repent of the belief that money is the answer to everything in life. I repent for choosing to serve mammon in preference to You and thereby filling my life with darkness. I renounce on behalf of my ancestors and myself for every agreement made with mammon by using money in ungodly ways and for ungodly purposes. I repent for being double-minded with money and unstable in all of my ways. I repent for making money my defender, security and protection. I repent for believing that chants, spells, fate, superstition and luck will provide the money I need.

I repent for making money the center of the universe and not You, Lord. I ask for forgiveness for living outside of my means. I repent for myself and my family line for not exercising our responsibility to pay money that was owed to the government agencies. I also repent for a begrudging and bitter attitude in paying my taxes.

I repent on behalf of myself and my ancestors for believing in a poverty mindset and being stingy with the body of Christ and stealing the tithe from You Father. I declare that Jesus came to give us abundant life. Father, in your mercy, free me and my future generations of the consequences of this. I repent for being disconnected from the river of life of God's endless supply. I choose to be connected to the river of life where God will grant me the ability to acquire wealth for His kingdom. I repent for spending money on that which does not satisfy and not coming to Your loving waters to drink. I repent for myself and my generational line for hardening my heart and shutting my hand against my poorer brothers in their needs. I ask for forgiveness for not feeding the poor nor taking care of the widows and orphans.

I repent for myself and my family line for not receiving our inheritance, and I choose to receive the inheritance, abundance and gifts that You have for us. I ask that it come in such abundance that we will be able to leave an inheritance for our children and grandchildren.

Lord, I ask You to disconnect my ancestors from me, and my ancestors from money that was tied to freemasonry, secret societies, secret agendas, covert operations, ungodly funding of churches and institutions and for the building of ungodly altars and for funding prostitutes and abortionists, including Freedom of Choice Act.

Lord, connect me to You alone. I choose not to hold on to anything but You. I give everything I have to You. I repent for myself and my family line for the judgment that the gifts of the Holy Spirit could be purchased or sold. I repent for my wickedness and my generational wickedness and ask that my heart would be restored into a right relationship with You.

Lord, I ask for forgiveness for making my giving an obligation to You and not a free act of love. Lord remove the yoke of obligation from me. Remove the canopy of law and obligation from me. Lord allow me to live in Your grace and Your provision. I ask You Lord to send the Holy Spirit to direct me what to give. Lord make my giving come from an attitude of gratitude and of love. I choose to seek and follow Your guidance in my giving.

Lord, I repent for not trusting You and not trusting You to provide.

On behalf of my ancestors and myself and for future generations, I choose to forgive those who have swindled me, especially banks, financial institutions, and government agencies as well as those who have charged me usury and those who have tried to keep me in poverty and have disinherited my children.

I take authority over every hindering spirit of the enemy. I bind them from my life, and I render them helpless, powerless, inoperative and ineffective to hinder my life in any way, by the authority of the name of Jesus Christ. I pull down every stronghold of the enemy, and I cast down every wicked spirit that Satan would attempt to use against me.

Father, according to Your Word, if an enemy is caught stealing; he must return sevenfold of that which he has stolen. Father, I have caught the enemy. For Your Word has revealed and exposed Satan as the thief, who comes to steal, kill, and destroy. Satan, by the authority of the name of Christ Jesus, I command you to return sevenfold of everything that you have stolen from every area of my life.

I thank You Father, that this is a prosperous day, week, month, and year for me, and the doors of success have been opened. I confess that I shall succeed in everything in Christ Jesus, because every door of failure has been closed, and I shall not know defeat. I am fully persuaded, that what You have promised in Your Word, You are able to perform in and through my life. I declare I will be content in You and in my wages in whatever financial state I am in.

I declare that Your Word says: You will go before us and make the crooked places straight; You also said in Your Word, that Your

Word shall not return to You void, but it shall accomplish that in which You sent it to perform; and even as I have prayed Your Word, I thank You that it is performed and accomplished in my life, and in the lives of my family.

In the name of Jesus Christ, I pray, Amen.

V. Common Hindrances to Healing

This is an educational tool to assist in identifying blockages to healing. However, the Lord, God Almighty trumps any work of the enemy. God's light overcomes any darkness in your life. Once you renounce the curse, focus on the Lord, His Word and His positive attributes. See the Appendix for *The Names of God* and memorize many of them. Read Deuteronomy 28:1–14 to comprehend all the blessings the Lord has planned for you!

There is only ONE Holy Spirit. All others are demonic masquerading as the Holy Spirit. To determine if the spirit is the Holy Spirit, use the test mentioned in the Bible in 1 John 4:1–3 (ESV). It says, "Beloved, do not believe every spirit, but test the spirits to see whether they are from God, for many false prophets have gone out into the world. By this you know the Spirit of God: every spirit that confesses that Jesus Christ has come in the flesh is from God and every spirit that does not confess Jesus is not from God. This is the spirit of the antichrist, which you heard was coming and now is in the world already."

"By this you know the Spirit of God: every spirit that confesses that Jesus Christ has come in the flesh is from God and every spirit that does not confess Jesus is not from God."

COMMON BLOCKAGES:

1. Unforgiveness, anger, rage, resentment, bitterness, revenge
2. Disobedience, sin, habitual sin, iniquitous sin
3. Fear
4. Unbroken vows; Example: 1) A child vows to never let her harsh father hurt her or her siblings again, 2) "I will never forgive myself if _______ happens." "I will never speak to______again." "I'm stupid." "I'm not going to grow up."
5. An operating curse versus a dormant curse
6. Ungodly soul ties or covenants
7. Guilt
8. Generational problems
9. Soul wounds needing inner healing
10. Difficulty believing Christ heals today (the false belief that sickness is sent from God to develop character)
11. False belief God doesn't or won't talk to me.
12. Occult involvement: By self or bloodline-relative involvement: witchcraft, satanic rituals, songs glorifying sin and death, obsessions or skulls (depicting death), hexes, spells, potions, curses, black magic, white magic.
13. Fortune telling: Ouija boards, levitation, horoscopes, tarot cards, palm reading, voodoo, talking to the dead (mediums),

psychics, ghost hunting, heavy metal music promoting violence or perversion, television or movies promoting violence or perversion, crystals, reading tea leaves, crystal balls. Anything in the media that references witchcraft. Anything which creates ties to the enemy.

Definition of Curse

Curses are words spoken against another person intended to directly or indirectly harm them or their family. Curses are one of Satan's favorite tricks. He exploits our vulnerabilities through deception.

Word Curses are not harmless. They are real and carry power in the spiritual realm. What is true in the spiritual realm is more powerful than anything in the physical realm. Proverbs 18:21 states, "Death and life are in the power of the tongue, and those who love it will eat its fruit." When you speak ill of someone, you are creating an opportunity for Satan to attack not only the person, but yourself also! Christians speak many curses through critical, judgmental words. Sarcasm is negativity which can even be a curse. Speaking against a pastor, church, fellow members or nonbelievers is a serious sin. It's the opposite of what God has intended for that person's life and *yours*!

SCRIPTURES ADDRESSING CURSES

Proverbs 26:2 (NJKV) tells us "A curse without cause shall not alight." This means a curse cannot affect you unless you have a legal opening allowing the enemy access to your soul.

Psalm 139:23–24 (NIV) says "Search me, God, and know my heart, test me and know my anxious thoughts. See if there is any offensive way in me, and lead me in the way everlasting."

Word curse references: Proverbs 18:21, Proverbs 6:2, Psalm 34:13, Matthew 12:36–37

EFFECTS OF A CURSE

When you or your ancestors have cursed someone or something, it gave a legal right to the demonic realm to exercise influence over people. It opened a legal door to your soul for the enemy to touch both you and the recipient. Having engaged in this practice, you have submitted to the enemy's authority. Therefore, you have also *opened a door* to allow the enemy to continue harassing you.

TYPES OF CURSES

Curses can be intentional or unintentional. Curses can be conditional or unconditional. Curses can be written or oral. These include our careless statements that create word curses.

Curses can be placed by anyone, even ordinary people. They may also be intentionally placed by a witch, shaman, warlock, medicine man, or someone involved with satanic practices calling upon any spirit other than the Holy Spirit. They place curses by using hexes, vexes, spells, voodoo dolls, personal pictures, potions, charms, black magic, and white magic to intentionally hurt and negatively affect and control someone or something. Some New Age practices invite demonic spirits to attach to your body. These curses are placed on people, generations, dates, animals, objects, land, areas, cities, and countries. These satanic practices are calling up spirits, unclean spirits which intend harm.

Example: A shaman *blessed* a farmer's land, offering protection and prosperity by inviting his god, the demonic realm, to be in charge of this property. This may seem like it's working for a short time, but will eventually explode in disastrous results for the people involved, their family members, and the land. It will also affect future generations and future land owners.

These curses continue in operation until they are permanently broken.

Curses can affect your health, work, finances, family issues, property and many other areas. Generally, anything which concerns you is a target. They will affect you and your family members spiritually, mentally, physically, emotionally, financially, relationally and willfully. This opens the door and gives legal rights to the enemy creating soul wounds. This allows him to harass you and influence your thoughts, beliefs, philosophies and actions.

Curses *will* result from joining secret societies such as Freemasons, Scottish Rites, York Rites, Elks, Woodsmen, Odd Fellows, DeMolay, Shriners, and others. Female versions of secret societies are Rainbow Girls, Rebekah Lodge, Daughters of the Eastern Star and others.

These secret societies require oaths, vows, or covenants to their organization. They also include beliefs in other gods and other religions, although the members are usually unaware of this. The curses continue from the organization to you and your descendants until you resign from the organization and *repent and renounce all involvement* in the organization on behalf of you and your ancestors. This includes renouncing all specific vows you or your ancestors have ever made as well as asking the Lord to break the power of these oaths and closing demonic doors. (Luke 10:19) All automatic renewal rights must be permanently broken and hidden shields, seals, and devices must be removed. Remember the first commandment? "Thou shall have no other gods before me" Exodus 20:3. I suggest you read Robert Henderson's books, *Courts of Heaven* and *Unlocking Destinies from the Courts of Heaven*. Watch him on YouTube to assist you in understanding how to complete this curse termination with the power available in the courts of heaven.

FREEMASONS

"Freemasonry involves taking oaths each time a member passes to a new level. Each promotion takes place at a ceremony where the member recites a new set of vows and covenants repeating certain goofy sounding words. In reality, the ritual includes words which are combinations of carefully planned vows, pledging their loyalty to foreign gods. These vows are primarily based upon Egyptian and Hindu gods and literally, Satan himself. When confronted with the truth, the unsuspecting member always says, "But, I joined for business and they seem to do good works. I didn't think those silly words meant anything." Most of the members don't have any idea what the words mean until they are promoted to Level 33 or above in the organization.

The Freemason vows call for worshipping other gods. Peter Horrobin, author of *Healing Through Deliverance,* says:

> I have no difficulty in including Freemasonry among false religions (Freemasons worship a god whose very name, Jahbulon, incorporates the names of Baal and the fertility goddess of Egypt)[19]. The practice of Freemasonry is idolatry. Idolatry is an anathema to the Lord. The commandments warn us that the sins of the fathers in this respect will be visited on the children for three or four generations (Exodus 20:4–5). If during those four generations there is further idolatry, a new line of demonic control is established.[20]

If you or ancestors have ever been involved in Freemasonry or a secret society, ask for forgiveness and repent and renounce all agreements with the enemy, including *all* specific vows. Breaking Freemasonry vows require a specific renunciation prayer. This is necessary due to the number of oaths taken, the layers of vows, the corresponding soul wounds, and the seriousness of the covenants. However, I know many people who have prayed the Freemason Curse-Breaking Prayer numerous times, and the curse effects are still in place. Everett Cox with Deliverance Ministries.org in Oklahoma City, OK, is very skillful at dealing with curses. Everett may be reached at: www.delmin.org or (405)842–5509. His website has an excellent 26-page prayer to break freemasonry curses. You will need to pray the prayer with a partner. You will need to pray it several times until the Lord says you are released from this strong curse. Specific forgiveness brings greater release and freedom from the offense than general forgiveness prayers.

When leaving Freemasonry, repent and renounce *all* involvement and remove possession of all objects or artifacts. You must completely break your Freemasonry bond or ties by destroying all artifacts. *Do not keep any artifacts,* and do not give them away. Belief in these objects carrying sentimental value is deception from the enemy. There is no sentimental value with an object bringing curses intending to harm you, your family, and your descendants. The best legacy one can leave is a clean bloodline.

Selwyn Stevens and Larry Kunk, of Jubilee Resources, have an excellent book entitled, *Unmasking Freemasonry—Removing the Hoodwink* [21]. It explains Freemasonry and offers repentance prayers. Another good book, with a Freemasonry explanation and breaking prayer, is entitled, *Deliverance, Rescuing God's People*[22] by Pat Legako and Cyndi Gribble.

Signs of Freemason or Secret Society Curses

Freemason initiates are required to take oaths which are acted out prophetically and physically. The first-degree oath involves a hoodwink, which means to mislead, blindfold, and deceive. It involves a noose around the neck and choking. Physical symptoms are passed down to future generations following the oath. These curses and oaths manifest as throat and tongue problems, breathing and chest issues, blindness and eye issues, fear of choking, fear of light, and many other related issues. Curses manifest in various ways and are different for every family. A partial list of physical curse symptoms includes: barrenness, premature death, miscarriages, repeated illness, weird illnesses, weird accidents, and plantar fascia. Curses also pass down to future generations emotional, mental, financial, and spiritual issues.

The negative spiritual impact of these oaths, which means curses, are passed down four generations in your family bloodline. The Masonic Bible is different than the Holy Bible because it contains selected biblical passages. Masons are never allowed to openly examine their altered Bible.

Breaking Satanic Agreements

Pray the Freemason breaking prayer on behalf of you, your ancestors, and your descendants. It should contain the following components: ask for forgiveness; repent; renounce the organization; renounce all individual vows; renounce all contracts, past, present, and future; renounce all involvement with other gods or idols; break the agreement with Satan out loud; close the door opened to the enemy. Ask for the blood of Jesus to cleanse your sin, the sin of your ancestors, and your descendants. Ask the Holy Spirit to heal soul wounds. Ask the glory light of Jesus and His dunamis power within your spirit to heal your body and soul. Decree and declare, out loud, "My soul is healed. I am excellent of soul." See the references mentioned above for complete Freemasonry curse-breaking prayers. Replace these curses with family blessings from Deuteronomy 28:1–14 and other blessings you desire. Ask the Lord to reestablish your possession of God-ordained boundaries and territories, including all blessings hijacked. These are comprised of: spiritual, mental, emotional, physical, financial, relational, and willful areas plus your gifts and talents to name a few. The list is limitless so do not think small!

The following Curse-Breaking Prayers are for general use. The Freemason Breaking Prayer is a separate prayer found in the references above. Let the Holy Spirit lead you in these Curse-Breaking Prayers. There will be specific sins He will want you to repent for on behalf of your bloodline. It will be important to complete this process by praying in the courts of heaven. Ask your Heavenly Father to cleanse your sin record. (Psalm 103:12)

CURSE BREAKING PRAYER–LONG

FATHER GOD, IN THE NAME OF JESUS OF NAZARETH, I ask for forgiveness and repent and renounce my agreement with the enemy for the curse of________________. I take responsibility for all of these sins and inequities in my life and generation, past generations and future generations on both sides of my family lineage, back to the beginning of time for the curse of ___________(name of sin/disease).

I ask You to forgive me for coming into agreement with the enemy and allowing him to manifest through me and my family. I ask You Lord, that the power of this curse_________________ (sin/disease) in my life, or inherited through my family tree be permanently broken. I release myself from this sin including thoughts and behavior. I take authority on the basis of my asking forgiveness and I break this curse in the name of Yeshua off of my children, myself, and my ancestors. I take a stand that this _________(sin) and/or _______(disease) which is the effect of this curse will be broken off of our lives. (Luke 10:19)

By the authority of the Father, through Jesus Christ of Nazareth and by the power of the Holy Spirit, I take authority over any spirit associated with ____________(sin) and I command it to leave me. I send it to Jesus to dispose of how He chooses (or send it to the dry places) now, never to return again.

Lord, I ask for our family line to be restored to the correct godly order and alignment under God. Lord, we ask You fill us with Your life-giving power. Bring my body, soul, and spirit back into their proper God-ordained alignment to fulfill our God-ordained destiny. Thank you, Father, for your forgiveness and restoration, and my covering with the blood of Jesus Christ.

This part of my being, the pineal gland, belongs to Yeshua and no one else. Lord, I ask You to forgive my ancestors for opening the psychic door. I ask You to forgive us and cleanse us from 1000 generations back all the way to the beginning of time. I ask You to consecrate, sanctify, Redeem, and bless my ability to see what You want me to see in the name of Yeshua. God, we ask You to open the family books, the book of life, and bring before Your throne every covenant in force in my life. If they are right and just and holy, then let them stand. Every covenant not in conformity with righteousness and justice, let them be annulled according to Isaiah 28:14. Lord, annul every covenant my ancestors or I made which was unholy, unjust, and unrighteous and was inconsistent with Your Word. Every curse and its power is now broken in Yeshua's name and by the power of His blood. Lord, we ask You to release punitive damages to the demons. Lord, we ask You to go back in history and bring forward all of the prayers, all of the inherited territory with the correct boundaries which are part of our Promised Land, all of the missed blessings. all that You have for me my family, and all that concerns and belongs to me as Your child. Thank You for restoration to me, my family, and all that concerns me, including blessing of body, soul, and spirit. Thank You for doing this in the name of Yeshua.

BREAKING CURSES PRAYER-SHORT

Breaking Word Curses, Pacts with the Devil, Hexes, etc.

In the name of Jesus, I sever every spiritual bond and break every covenant made by me or on my behalf, knowingly or unknowingly. I also break any word curses, hexes, and incantations I have spoken over myself or which have been spoken over me. Satan, I declare that you have no hold over me. Jesus is my Lord, and I sever every spiritual tie, every spiritual covenant that I have ever had with you, or made on my behalf in the name of Jesus. I specifically bind and break the power of the spirits of (Name the specific spirits involved. See the Stronghold-Breaking Prayer, i.e. spirits of divination, fear, etc.) from operating in my life or the lives of my family. I cancel your assignment against me in the name of Jesus Christ.

PARTIAL LIST OF CAUSES OF CURSES

- Breaking curses prayer (general)
- Word curses,
- Soul ties (covenants)
- Breaking witchcraft
- Breaking spirit of rejection
- Generational spirits
- Personal spirits-especially fear
- Trauma
- Freemasons and secret societies
- Covenant breaks
- Illegitimacy (Deut.23:2)
- Idoltry (Deut. 27:15)
- *Moving boundaries (Deut. 27:17) Very important
- Misleading the blind (Deut. 27:18)
- Honoring mother and father (Deut. 6:4–5); Ten commandments
- Peverting justice(Deut.27:19)
- Perversion (Deut. 27:20)
- Rebellion (I samuel 15:23)
- Slaying a neighbor (even with words) (Deut. 27:24)
- Slaying an innocent person (Deut. 27:25)
- Not agreeing with the law (Deut. 27:26)

TRAUMA BREAKING PRAYER

Lord, I ask that you bring to (the person's name) remembrance or to his/her conscious level any part of the trauma which needs to be healed. In Jesus name, I break their power and cast out the spirits of trauma and fear.

I cast out the spirit(s) of (name the spirits the Lord shows you) that entered at the time of the trauma.

Lord, I ask You to heal the spirit and the soul that were broken, crushed, or damaged in any way during the trauma.

Lord, I ask You to show (the person's name) where you were when this trauma happened and what you thought about it.

Lord, I ask that You bring that healed spirit and soul (including cellular memory, DNA damage or imbalance, muscle memory) through the years to the present day and mature that part which was damaged to the level of maturity of today.

Lord, I ask that You bring the body in line with the healed spirit and soul and heal the body as well.

Lord, I ask that You divinely integrate the body, soul and spirit together into perfect strength and healing.

I ask their God-ordained destiny come forth in the name of Jesus.

If there are multiple traumas, it may be necessary to repeat this prayer.

[1] 2 Corinthians 10:3–5
[2] Isaiah 9:6, Isaiah 22:21, 1 Corinthians 12:28
[3] 2 Corinthians 10:4–5, Ephesians 6:10–20
[4] 2 Corinthians 10:3–5
[5] John 10:10, John 8:44
[6] Galatians 5:1, 2 Peter 2:19, Romans 8:15
[7] John 8:32
[8] John 14:6, John 16:13
[9] John 1:14
[10] 2 Corinthians 10:5
[11] John 3:21, John 9:5, James 1:17, 1 John 1:5
[12] Exodus 23:32, Acts 14:15, John 4:21–23, 1 Timothy 2:5, James 2:19 1, Corinthians 8:6–7, Hebrew 8:6, Acts 3:25, Matthew 26:28, Romans 11:27
[13] Matthew 26:28, Luke 22:20
[14] 2 Corinthians 4:4,6, Revelations 21:23
[15] Jeremiah 29:11, Psalm 73:24, NLT, James 4:11–12, MSG
[16] Isaiah 54:17
[17] Deuteronomy 7:9, 1 Chronicles 16:15, Psalm 105:8
[18] Frangipane, F. (2011). *The Three Battlegrounds*. Cedar Rapids, IA: Arrow Publications, Inc. *dunamis–Strong's 1411
[19] Horrobin, P.J. & Prince, D. (2008). Healing through Deliverance: The Foundation and Practice of Deliverance Ministry. Ada, MI: Chosen Books. p. 113.
[20] Horrobin, P.J. & Prince, D. (2008). Healing through Deliverance: The Foundation and Practice of Deliverance Ministry. Ada, MI: Chosen Books. p. 363.
[21] *Unmasking Freemasonry – Removing the Hoodwink*, Jubilee Publishers, 2007.
[22] *Deliverance: Rescuing God's People: Developing and Operating the Ministry,* Tate Publishing & Enterprises, 2007

APPENDIX 2

VI. LIES AND TRUTH STATEMENTS

This section is to be used as a guide to coming out of agreement with the enemy by explicitly stating each lie, one by one, and replacing it with truth. For each lie, say the renouncing statement out loud first, followed by each specific prayer.

Many people like to use the name Yeshua instead of Jesus, because Jesus is a common first name in several cultures. If you prefer, use Yeshua, Jesus Christ, or Jesus of Nazareth.

Spiritual Accidental Agreements

NOTE: Before beginning, let's ask Holy Spirit if you have any hidden unforgiveness. Remember, unforgiveness blocks prayers! Unforgiveness manifests as these attitudes and feelings: bitterness, anger, resentment, hatred, accusation, retaliation, fighting, rage, passive aggressive behavior, indignation, violence, criticism, judgment, cynicism, and negativity. See *Forgiveness* section for prayer.

Take a moment of silence and ask the Lord to download the names of people you have unforgiveness towards. Ask for forgiveness and repent to remove any unforgiveness or bitterness.

Next, renounce your specific agreement (the lie) with the enemy listed below. First, speak the renouncing statement followed by the Truth Statement." Read the personalized scriptures out loud (Dunamis power).

Read the renouncing statement before all Truth Statements.

Renouncing Statement: "Lord, on behalf of me, my ancestors and my descendants, I ask for forgiveness, and repent and renounce my agreements with the enemy in regard to lie number _______. I submit my body, soul and spirit to the Lord and ask You to align me with Your Will. Cleanse my sin and cover me with the blood of Jesus. Fill my soul wounds with Your resurrection power and the Shekinah glory light of Jesus in my innermost being.

I ask You to silence the enemy. Thank You the power and legal rights of the enemy are broken. (Luke 10:19) I ask to be restored in full covenant with You. As I am in covenant with You, I enjoy the benefits and blessings of being Your royal child. Lord, You are the Sovereign Judge in the courts of heaven and also the Judge on earth. Lord, I ask You to rule in my favor in the courts of heaven and ask You to release the angels to enforce this judgment.

I ask Your will be done on earth as it is in heaven. You have given me the legal right to trample on the enemy (Psalm 91). I reclaim everything the enemy has stolen from me, my family and all that concerns me. Thank you for restoring the generational blessings and liberating our DNA in alignment with Your original plan for our lives which is our godly inheritance. I ask that our God-ordained blessings come forth in the name of Jesus. I ask You to activate our DNA correction and blessings. These blessings include wisdom, knowledge, understanding, discernment, gifts, talents, and all other godly generational blessings. Lord, I ask specifically for You to bless me with the talents of ________________________. (Fill in the blank with your God aligned desires. Examples: music, languages, artistic ability, dance, writing, or business).

1. LIE: God can't possibly hear everyone's prayers much less answer them! God is too busy to care about the details in my life. God would never talk to little old me. He is busy with more important things than me and my problems. Besides, God can't really help me now because He's in heaven. This problem is unsolvable. I will have to deal with it the rest of my life.

TRUTH: *Read renouncing statement at the beginning of this section.* I decree and declare You care about every part of my life. I am Your special child. You want to talk with me about everything and I will listen for Your voice throughout the day. You want to discuss every detail I think about and all I do. You love to talk with me and bless me, even today! I will not worry about anything but ask You about everything! Thank You Lord for strengthening me. Even though You are in heaven, you sent Your helper, the Holy Spirit, who lives in me. He is alive and active today and every day. I choose to believe You want to help me prosper in all areas of my life, my family's lives, and everything which concerns me. You will speak to me through scriptures and provide wisdom and revelation for each area I'm concerned about. I choose to not believe my lying emotions but trust in God's Word. You hear every one of my prayers and are working on the answers right now! You created the whole earth. I believe You when You promised in Romans 8:28, You would work everything out for good! You always want what is best for me. Because You always tell the truth, I choose to believe You, God.

ORIGINAL SCRIPTURE: "Don't worry about anything; instead, pray about everything. Tell God what you need, and thank him for all he has done. Then you will experience God's peace, which exceeds anything we can understand. His peace will guard your hearts and minds as you live in Christ Jesus." Philippians 4:6–7, NLT

PERSONALIZED SCRIPTURE: **Lord I refuse to worry about anything, but I will pray about it. I will tell You what I need and thank You for what You have done and will do. I will experience Your peace, which exceeds my ability to understand. Your peace guards my heart and mind as I meditate on Christ Jesus.** Philippians 4:6–7

PARAPHRASED SCRIPTURE: **Lord I will not worry about anything in my life. Instead, I will pray, tell You my needs, and thank You even before Your answers come. Your peace is so amazing. It's greater than I can even imagine. As I meditate on and believe Your promises, Your peace envelops my heart and mind.** Philippians 4:6–7

ORIGINAL SCRIPTURE: "My sheep listen to my voice; I know them, and they follow me." John 10:27

PERSONALIZED SCRIPTURE: **Thank You that I listen to Your voice and You know me. I will follow You**. John 10:27

PARAPHRASED SCRIPTURE: **Thank You, Lord, that when You speak to me I hear Your voice. I belong to You and I will follow You wherever You lead me.** John 10:27

ORIGINAL SCRIPTURE: "And we are confident that he hears us whenever we ask for anything that pleases him. And since we know he hears us when we make our requests, we also know that he will give us what we ask for." I John 5:14–15, NLT

PERSONALIZED SCRIPTURE: **Lord I am confident You hear me when I ask for anything, which pleases You. I know You**

hear me when I make my requests and I also know You will give me what I ask for within Your will for my life. I John 5:14–15

PARAPHRASED SCRIPTURE: **Lord I am thankful You always listen when I ask for anything according to Your will. I know You hear my requests and I am certain You will answer me.** I John 5:14–15

ORIGINAL SCRIPTURE: "God is not human, that he should lie, not a human being, that he should change his mind. Does he speak and then not act? Does he promise and not fulfil?" Numbers 23:19

PERSONALIZED SCRIPTURE: **God is not human, so He does not lie; He is not human, so He does not change his mind. He does what He says. Thank You for fulfilling what You promise.** Numbers 23:19

PARAPHRASED SCRIPTURE: **Lord, many people have disappointed me. I'm so glad You are not like humans. Because You are divine, I know I can always trust You. You follow through on what You say. You always fulfill Your promises to me. You are a trustworthy God.** Numbers 23:19

As you read the scriptures below, be sure to personalize or paraphrase them as I did in the example above.

Additional Scripture: Jeremiah 33:3, Isaiah 30:21, John 16:13, John 14:16–17, Psalm 121:3, Psalm 115:12, Psalm 147:3, Psalm 8:4, Psalm 103:13–14, Isaiah 49:15, Psalm 23:1, Psalm115:12, 1 Peter 5:7, Psalm 55:22, Isaiah 41:10, Luke 12:6–7

2. LIE: God can't heal me and my children from our spiritual issues, when we try but fail or are rebellious.

TRUTH: *Read renouncing statement at the beginning of this section.*

I decree and declare I will not wrestle control from You by running ahead of Your perfect plan for me and my children. I acknowledge You are the Author of our faith and You've written the script for our lives. I acknowledge Your plan is good for us and Your timing will be perfect, but not as I imagined. I give You my frustrated plans and I surrender the situation to You. When I become anxious and want to see immediate results, I will cooperate by praying, "My children are taught of the Lord and great is their peace." I know You love my children more than I do. I ask for help trusting You with our wonderful God-ordained destiny.

ORIGINAL SCRIPTURE: "All your children will be taught by the LORD, and great will be their peace." Isaiah 54:13 (This includes spiritual children.)

PERSONALIZED SCRIPTURE: **Thank You, Lord, that all my children will be taught by You and their Shalom peace will be great. Thank you they will experience Your Shalom peace. This Shalom peace includes wholeness (body, soul, spirit, mind, will and emotions), soundness, welfare, safety, health, prosperity, tranquility, contentment and a stronger covenant relationship with God. Thank You as I align with Your Word, You shower me with greater blessings!** Isaiah 54:13

PARAPHRASED SCRIPTURE: **Lord, being a parent is a challenging job and I need Your help. I am grateful for Your promises to teach my children and they will experience great peace. The next time I'm upset I will remember Your promise to me.** Isaiah 54:13

ORIGINAL SCRIPTURE: "For he has rescued us from the dominion of darkness and brought us into the kingdom of the Son he loves," Colossians 1:13

PERSONALIZED SCRIPTURE: **Thank You for rescuing me from the enemy and bringing me into Jesus' Kingdom of light and love.** Colossians 1:13

PARAPHRASED SCRIPTURE: **Thank You for Your goodness in my life. You snatched me from the Devil's kingdom and from an eternity in Hell. You placed me firmly into Jesus' Kingdom, a Kingdom filled with light and life.** Colossians 1:13

As you read the scriptures below be sure to personalize or paraphrase them as I did in the example above.

Additional Scriptures: Ephesians 6:11–17, Hebrews 12:1–2, Psalm 16:11, Colossians 2:15, Matthew 11:28–30, John 14:27, Psalm 29:11, John 16:33, 1 Peter 2:24

3. LIE: The way I speak and the words I use don't really matter. They are just figures of speech and everyone says them. It's just the way I am. It's the way I was raised.

TRUTH: *Read renouncing statement at the beginning of this section.* Lord, I decree and declare I am leaning on You to help me know when to speak and when to be silent and pray. I will not offer advice unless I am asked but will rely on the Holy Spirit to work in their hearts. I thank You for helping me control my tongue, temper and emotions. I choose to allow You to be the only judge and I will align with Your perspective. I choose to bless people with my words and to speak life, blessings, hope and love to everyone. Thank You for prompting me to choose Your words of life, hope and only positive comments!

ORIGINAL SCRIPTURE: "This day I call the heavens and the earth as witnesses against you that I have set before you life and death, blessings and curses. Now choose life, so that you and your children may live." Deuteronomy 30:19

PERSONALIZED SCRIPTURE: **Today, Lord You have set before me life and death, blessings and curses. As Heaven and earth are my witnesses, I choose life so my children and I will live abundantly.** Deuteronomy 30:19

PARAPHRASED SCRIPTURE: **You have graciously allowed me to choose between life and death and blessings and curses. Today, with Heaven and earth as my witnesses, I solemnly choose life so my children and I will receive Your daily blessings and eternal blessings.** Deuteronomy 30:19

ORIGINAL SCRIPTURE: "Finally, brothers and sisters, whatever is true, whatever is noble, whatever is right, whatever is pure, whatever is lovely, whatever is admirable—if anything is excellent or praiseworthy—think about such things." Philippians 4:8

PERSONALIZED SCRIPTURE: **Lord, I choose to only think about whatever is noble, right, pure, lovely, admirable, excellent or praiseworthy.** Philippians 4:8

PARAPHRASED SCRIPTURE: **Lord, I want my thoughts to be pleasing to You and beneficial for me. I renounce worry; it is not my friend. Thank You for helping me keep my mind focused on whatever is noble, right, pure, lovely, admirable, excellent or praiseworthy. I choose to only focus my attention on what is positive.** Philippians 4:8

As you read the scriptures below be sure to personalize or paraphrase them as I did in the example above.

Additional Scriptures: Matthew 5:44, KJV, Luke 6:37, NLT, Ephesians 4:29, ESV, Proverbs 15:2, ESV, James 3:9–11, James 1:19–20, Proverbs 12:18, ESV, Proverbs 15:1, ESV, I Peter

3:11, NLT, Proverbs 25:11, ESV, Proverbs 16:23, NLT, Proverbs 16:24, NLT

4. LIE: God is a God of grace so it doesn't matter if I sin a little or a lot.

TRUTH: *Read renouncing statement at the beginning of this section.* I decree and declare You are a God of grace by forgiving my sins. You have given me commandments by which to live my life to help me, not to harm me. You do care if I sin, whether it's a little white lie or a major problem. Sin is sin in Your book, and You are the only Judge. When I am tempted to break one or more, of Your precepts, I will seek Your guidance and counsel as to the correct path and steps to take. When unsure of what to do, I will use the motto "If in doubt—don't." I ask You to give me self-control, Holy Spirit led discernment, and a way out to escape sin. I choose to trust Your perspective on this issue.

ORIGINAL SCRIPTURE: "But the fruit of the Spirit is love, joy, peace, forbearance, kindness, goodness, faithfulness gentleness, and self-control. Against such things there is no law." Galatians 5:22–23

PERSONALIZED SCRIPTURE: **Thank You I am filled with the fruit of the Spirit which is love, joy, peace, patience, kindness, goodness, faithfulness, gentleness, and self-control. There are no laws against these.** Galatians 5:22–23

PARAPHRASED SCRIPTURE: **Lord, I love being filled with the fruit of the Spirit because it makes me more like You. I have love, joy, peace, patience, kindness, goodness, faithfulness, gentleness, and self-control working inside of me. I want these attributes always working in my life.** Galatians 5:22–23

ORIGINAL SCRIPTURE: "To open their eyes so that they may

turn from darkness to light and from the dominion of Satan to God, that they may receive forgiveness of sins and an inheritance among those who have been sanctified by faith in Me." Acts 26:18, NASB

PERSONALIZED SCRIPTURE: **Thank You for opening my eyes from darkness to light and from Satan's power to God's power. Thank You that I am a child of God and You have forgiven my sins. I have an inheritance in Heaven along with those who have been sanctified by faith in Christ**.

PARAPHRASED SCRIPTURE: **Thank You, Lord, for opening my spiritual eyes so that I can discern and turn from Satan's dark kingdom to Your kingdom of Light and life. Thank You for giving me forgiveness and an eternal inheritance along with those who are saved by faith in Christ.**

As you read the scriptures below be sure to personalize or paraphrase them as I did in the example above. Additional Scriptures: Romans 6:1–2, Ezekiel 18:4b, Matthew 25:46, John 4:36, Romans 6:23, IJohn3:4, Ehesians 5:8, NASB, I Peter 2:9, Isaiah 9:2, NASB

5. LIE: If I work harder and smarter, God will love me more.

TRUTH: Read the renouncing statement at the beginning of this section. I decree and declare I don't have to perform for You to love me. Your love for me is not dependent upon my worldly successes and failures, as You love me unconditionally. Father, when I accepted Your son, Jesus Christ, as my savior, You promised to love me no matter what and nothing can separate us. Your love is so gigantic I can't imagine how much You love me! I will ask Holy Spirit to show me what I need to know for my journey, whether in work, play, or other decisions. Your plans for me include a fun and satisfying journey for my good. I want to be taught by the Lord to have great peace and to fulfill my God-ordained destiny.

ORIGINAL SCRIPTURE: "For your unfailing love is higher than the heavens. Your faithfulness reaches to the clouds." Psalm 108:4, NLT

PERSONALIZED SCRIPTURE: **God, thank You that Your unfailing love for me is higher than the heavens. Your faithfulness reaches to the clouds.** Psalm 108:4

PARAPHRASED SCRIPTURE: **God, Your love for me is sky high! Your love for me couldn't even be contained in all the galaxies You created. And Your faithfulness? It reaches to the top of the atmosphere! Thank You for helping me understand how much You love me.** Psalm 108:4

ORIGINAL SCRIPTURE: "For I am convinced that neither death, nor life, nor angels, nor principalities, nor things present, nor things to come, nor powers, nor height, nor depth, nor any other created thing, will be able to separate us from the love of God, which is in Christ Jesus our Lord." Romans 8:38–39

PERSONALIZED SCRIPTURE: **Thank You, Lord, that death, or life, or angels, or principalities, or things present, or things to come, or powers, or height, or depth, or any other created thing, will not be able to separate me from Your love which is in Christ Jesus.** Romans 8:38–39

PARAPHRASED SCRIPTURE: **Lord You promise nothing in the world can separate me from Your love. Whether I encounter: death, life, angels, principalities, things present, things to come, unclean powers, height, depth, or any other created thing—none of these can separate Your love from me.** Romans 8:38–39

As you read the scriptures below, be sure to personalize or paraphrase them as I did in the example above.

Additional Scriptures: Isaiah 55:8–9, Psalm 104:33–34, Romans 3:28, Galatians 2:16, Romans 3:23–24, Romans 8:38–39, John 3:16–17, NLT, John 15:9

6. LIE: It doesn't really matter if I fast and pray. Fasting and prayer won't really move God's hand or make a difference in my problems or my family's lives. Fasting is just too hard. I have to fast completely from all food to please God. Fasting is not for today and it doesn't make a difference.

FASTING: This concept is very important for spiritual breakthrough during difficult periods. Jesus told His disciples "But this kind does not go out except by prayer and fasting" Matthew 17:21. Some versions of the Bible no longer include this verse in the body of the text and instead is footnoted. Jesus is very clear about the importance of fasting and demonstrated its power by spending forty days in the wilderness and resisting three temptations by the enemy. Then angels came and ministered to Him. Matthew 4:1–11. If you are trapped in a difficult problem, you should consider denying yourself something you love, even it's for half a day.

TRUTH: *Read renouncing statement at the beginning of this section.* I decree and declare fasting and prayer helps move God's hand because You say in Matthew 17:21 "this kind only comes out through prayer and fasting." Your Son found it important to fast, so I will follow His lead. I will remember, God delights in rewarding me, He loves to bless me! You promise to openly bless me when I forgive, pray, tithe, and fast. You are pleased when I eliminate habits or food from my life and sacrifice to make You the priority, even if only for a little while. You see everything I am doing. You know my motivations, my heart's desire, and what truly needs to happen in this situation. You are pleased with me, even if I break down and eat a few chips (I'll try harder next time.) You still want to bless me. I choose to believe You will honor my prayers and fasting! I look with expectation to see Your generous blessings!

NOTE: Fasting and praying with two or more people in unison, corporate fasting, causes major movement in the spiritual realm. Leviticus 26:8

"Five of you shall chase a hundred, and a hundred of you shall chase ten thousand, and your enemies shall fall before you by the sword." "Though one may be overpowered, two can defend themselves. A cord of three strands is not quickly broken." Ecclesiastes 4:12

ORIGINAL SCRIPTURE: "That is why the LORD says, "Turn to me now, while there is time. Give me your hearts. Come with fasting, weeping, and mourning." Joel 2:12

PERSONALIZED SCRIPTURE: **Lord, I give You my heart now and come to You with fasting, weeping, and mourning.** Joel 2:12

PARAPHRASED SCRIPTURE: **Lord, I am turning from my ways to Yours, which are so much better. I give you my heart and my spirit, soul and body. With Your help, I will fast so my heart will be tenderized before You.** Joel 2:12

ORIGINAL SCRIPTURE: "So we fasted and petitioned our God about this, and he answered our prayer." Ezra 8:23

PERSONALIZED SCRIPTURE: **Thank You God, when I fast and petition You in prayer You answer me.** Ezra 8:23

PARAPHRASED SCRIPTURE: **When I fast and pray, I can count on You, Lord, to answer my prayers in a miraculous way. You delight me with Your answers every time.** Ezra 8:23

As you read the scriptures below be sure to personalize or paraphrase them as I did in the example above.

Additional Scriptures: Matthew 17:18–21, Deuteronomy 32:30, Matthew 6:16, Joel 2:12–13, Luke 4:2–4,

Joel 2:15, Acts 14:23, Acts 13:2

7. LIE: I don't have time for daily prayer. If I pray once per day, that's enough because my little prayers bother God. I don't have time to read the Bible daily. God won't speak to me through the Bible—that's just for preachers.

TRUTH: *Read renouncing statement at the beginning of this section.* I decree and declare God loves me and wants to talk with me about my life's details. I will make time to listen to Holy Spirit speaking to my heart and through the Scriptures, which is how I stay connected to You. Give me a thankful heart. Teach me how to mediate and soak in Your Word, day and night. I will pray without ceasing. Thank You for helping me believe in small, daily miracles such as preferred parking spots, as well as large concerns such as miracles needed in work and family. You are still in the miracle business today because You are the same yesterday, today, and tomorrow. You promise You never change in Your love or commitment to me. I choose to believe You will guide me in all matters when I seek your face, humble myself, and repent for my sins. Thank You Jesus.

ORIGINAL SCRIPTURE: "Devote yourselves to prayer, being watchful and thankful," Colossians 4:2

PERSONALIZED SCRIPTURE: **Lord, I will devote myself to You in prayer, always being watchful and thankful.** Colossians 4:2

PARAPHRASED SCRIPTURE: **Lord, thank You for meeting me when I spend time with You in prayer. I know You always hear my request. I will be watchful and have an attitude of thanksgiving for the many blessings You are sending me.** Colossians 4:2

ORIGINAL SCRIPTURE: "Therefore, confess your sins to one another, and pray for one another so that you may be healed. The effective prayer of a righteous man can accomplish much." James 5:16 NASB

PERSONALIZED SCRIPTURE: **I will confess my sins to trustworthy people, and we will pray and petition You for healing. Thank You the prayers of a righteous person are effective and accomplish much.** James 5:16

PARAPHRASED SCRIPTURE: **Lord, when I sin, I will confess my specific sins to a trustworthy Christian. We will pray for each other's physical, spiritual, and emotional healing. I am grateful You are faithful to answer a righteous person's prayers.** James 5:16

ORIGINAL SCRIPTURE: "All Scripture is God-breathed and is useful for teaching, rebuking, correcting, and training in righteousness, so that the servant of God may be thoroughly equipped for every good work." 2 Timothy 3:16–17

PERSONALIZED SCRIPTURE: **Thank You for giving me a Bible that is God-breathed. It helps me learn, rebuke, correct, and train myself in righteousness so I can be thoroughly equipped for every good work.** 2 Timothy 3:16–17

PARAPHRASED SCRIPTURE: **Your word is precious to me, and I will study it day and night. It is breathed out from Your very mouth. It helps me grow in the areas of teaching, rebuking, correcting, and training in righteousness. Then I will be closer to reflecting Your image. These principles help equip me for every situation and opportunity to succeed.** 2 Timothy 3:16–17

As you read the scriptures below, be sure to personalize or paraphrase them as I did in the example above.

Additional Scriptures: Luke 18:1, James 5:13–15, Psalm 5:2, Psalm 102:17, Psalm 143:1, Psalm 119:105, John 17:17, Hebrews 4:12, ERV

8. LIE: Surely God doesn't expect me to follow His guidelines in the Bible in everyday life. God doesn't really mean what He says in the Bible.

TRUTH: Read the renouncing statement at the beginning of this section. I decree and declare You have given me godly instructions on the best way to live and prosper. I choose to believe You want to protect and love me. You provide truth, wisdom, guidance, and correction only found in Your living guidebook, the Bible. I acknowledge You are not being restrictive or punitive, but simply trying to assist me in avoiding pitfalls and disasters when I ignore Your commands. Teach me to quickly obey, removing displeasing behavior or speech to You. I choose to show my love for You through obeying Your Word, seeking Your opinion, and loving You with all of my heart, soul, mind, and strength. You promise when I am taught of the Lord, great will be my peace. This shalom peace includes wholeness of body, soul, spirit, mind, will and emotions, soundness, welfare, safety, health, prosperity, tranquility, contentment and a stronger covenant relationship with God. Thank You that as I align with Your word, You will shower me with greater blessings!

ORIGINAL SCRIPTURE: "If You fully obey the Lord your God and carefully follow all his commands I give you today, the Lord your God will set You high above all the nations on earth." Deuteronomy 28:1

PERSONALIZED SCRIPTURE: **I will fully obey You, Lord, and carefully follow all Your commands. You will set me high above all the nations of the earth.** Deuteronomy 28:1

PARAPHRASED SCRIPTURE: **Thank You for helping me carefully walk in obedience to Your word. You have amazing blessings in store for me because I follow Your commandments. You are setting me high above all of the nations. I will capture my Promised Land and fulfill my God-ordained destiny.** Deuteronomy 28:1

ORIGINAL SCRIPTURE: "And observe what the LORD your God requires: Walk in obedience to him, and keep his decrees and commands, his laws and regulations, as written in the Law of Moses. Do this so that you may prosper in all you do and wherever you go." I Kings 2:3

PERSONALIZED SCRIPTURE: **I am walking in obedience to You; keeping Your decrees and commands; and keeping Your laws and regulations as written in Your Word. I will prosper in everything I attempt and everywhere I go.** I Kings 2:3

PARAPHRASED SCRIPTURE: **God, I choose to obey all Your decrees, commands, laws and regulations. I know Your commands bring life, health, prosperity and wisdom. Teach me to meditate, understand, and love Your word.** I Kings 2:3

As you read the scriptures below, be sure to personalize or paraphrase them as I did in the example above.

Additional Scriptures: John 14:23, Deuteronomy 5:33, James 1:22, 1 Corinthians 15:58, Psalm 119:147, Psalm 130:5, Luke 9:23, Psalm 119:30, ESV

Mental Accidental Agreements

NOTE: Before beginning, let's ask Holy Spirit if you have any hidden unforgiveness. Remember, unforgiveness blocks prayers! Unforgiveness manifests as these attitudes and feelings: bitterness, anger, resentment, hatred, accusation, retaliation, fighting, rage, passive aggressive behavior, indignation, violence, criticism, judgment, cynicism, and negativity. See *Forgiveness* section prayer.

Take a moment of silence and ask the Lord to download the names of people you have unforgiveness towards. Ask for forgiveness and repent to remove any unforgiveness or bitterness.

Next, renounce your specific agreement (the lie) with the enemy listed below. First, speak the renouncing statement followed by the Truth Statement. Read the personalized scriptures out loud (dunamis power).

Read the renouncing statement before all Truth Statements.

Renouncing Statement: "Lord, on behalf of me, my ancestors and my descendants, I ask for forgiveness, and repent and renounce my agreements with the enemy with regard to lie number _______. I submit my body, soul and spirit to the Lord and ask You to align me with Your will. Cleanse my sin, and cover me with the blood of Jesus. Fill my soul wounds with Your resurrection power and the shekinah glory light of Jesus in my innermost being.

I ask You to silence the enemy. Thank You the power and legal rights of the enemy are broken. (Luke 10:19) I ask to be restored in full covenant with You. As I am in covenant with You, I enjoy the benefits and blessings of being Your royal child. Lord, You are the Sovereign Judge in the courts of heaven and also the judge on earth. Lord, I ask you to judge in my favor. I ask Your will be done on earth as it is in heaven. You have given me the legal right to trample on the enemy (Psalm 91). I reclaim everything the enemy has stolen from me, my family and all that concerns me. Thank you for restoring the generational blessings and liberating our DNA in alignment with Your original plan for our lives, which is our godly inheritance. I ask that our God-ordained blessings come forth in the name of Jesus. I ask You to activate our DNA correction and blessings. These blessings include wisdom, knowledge, understanding, discernment, gifts, talents, and all other godly generational blessings. Lord, I ask specifically for You to bless me with the talents of ________________________. (Fill in the blank with your God-aligned desires. Examples: music, languages, artistic ability, dance, writing, or business.)

1. LIE: There's no way for God to correct the mistakes and bad choices I've made. There's no way for God to work everything out for my good.

TRUTH: *Read renouncing statement at the beginning of this section.* I decree and declare God knew I would make these mistakes before I made them because You know all things, and You still love me. Your instruction and guidance is training me to be aligned with You and for my benefit to prosper. You never get mad at me for making mistakes but still love me unconditionally. With Holy Spirit help, I will listen and obey all You are teaching me believing You are for me. I can't wait to see how great this will end because You promised to work everything for my good. I choose to believe You, God, over the lies. I choose You Jesus.

ORIGINAL SCRIPTURE: "And we know that in all things God works for the good of those who love him, who have been called according to his purpose." Romans 8:28

PERSONALIZED SCRIPTURE: **I'm grateful You work everything for good for me because I love You and am called according to Your purpose.** Romans 8:28

PARAPHRASED SCRIPTURE: **Lord, I am so relieved to know**

it's impossible for me to make a mistake big enough You can't correct it. Thank You for working everything out for good for my life because I love and respect You. Romans 8:28

ORIGINAL SCRIPTURE: "And he said, 'The things which are impossible with men are possible with God.'" Luke 18:27

PERSONALIZED SCRIPTURE: **I'm grateful that things which are impossible for me are ALL possible for You.** Luke 18:27

PARAPHRASED SCRIPTURE: **Lord, as a human, there are many things which are impossible for me, but I am grateful to know that there is nothing that's impossible for You—absolutely nothing!** Luke 18:27

As you read the scriptures below be sure to personalize or paraphrase them as I did in the example above.

Additional Scriptures: Psalm 103:8–11, I Thessalonians 5:9, Lamentations 3:22–25, Proverbs 24:16

2. LIE: I'm too tired to continue this battle. This battle is too hard. My whole life is too hard.

TRUTH: *Read renouncing statement at the beginning of this section.* I decree and declare the battle is not mine, it's yours, Lord. Strengthen my knees and body to stand firm while You fight for me. I will live in peace because I am taught of the Lord and great is my peace. I will put on the armor of God daily for me and my family to stand and be victorious against the plans of the enemy. I will meditate on Your word day and night, and I will live to declare the works of the Lord in the land of the living. I choose to trust You, Jesus.

ORIGINAL SCRIPTURE: "You will not have to fight this battle. Take up your positions; stand firm and see the deliverance the Lord will give you, Judah and Jerusalem. Do not be afraid; do not be discouraged. Go out to face them tomorrow, and the Lord will be with you.'" 2 Chronicles 20:17

PERSONALIZED SCRIPTURE: **Thank You, Lord, for fighting this battle. I will take up my position and stand firm ON YOUR WORD, and I will see the deliverance the Lord will give me. I will not be afraid or discouraged. I will face tomorrow, and I know the Lord will be with me.** 2 Chronicles 20:17

PARAPHRASED SCRIPTURE: **Lord, I'm so relieved to know You promised to fight my battles for me if I stand firm and believe in You. I reject fear, and I reject discouragement. I will face them head-on, and You will be with me.** 2 Chronicles 20:17

ORIGINAL SCRIPTURE: "For the Lord your God is the one who goes with you to fight for you against your enemies, to give you victory." Deuteronomy 20:4

PERSONALIZED SCRIPTURE: **Thank You, God, for going with me into battle and giving me victory over my enemy.** Deuteronomy 20:4

PARAPHRASED SCRIPTURE: **Thank You, Lord, victory is assured because You always go with me when I battle my enemies.** Deuteronomy 20:4

As you read the scriptures below be sure to personalize or paraphrase them as I did in the example above.

Additional Scriptures: Isaiah 40:31, Deuteronomy 1:30, Deuteronomy 3:22, Galatians 6:9

3. LIE: I can't accomplish or do ____________________. I'm not smart enough, capable enough and I lack the resources.

TRUTH: *Read renouncing statement at the beginning of this section.* I decree and declare if You say I can do it, Jesus, I can because You will help and guide me. You will make me capable to complete this assignment. I look only to You for each step on the path You custom-designed for me. I will not worry about anything but pray about everything, tell You what I need and thank God. I take a physical step forward. (Take a physical step forward with your foot right now as an act of faith and intention to follow You.) Thank You for preparing me for the next job or divine appointment waiting for me. God, You have all resources because You created the earth and everything in it. I choose to believe You are in control. Thank You for providing and promoting me to the next level You want to bless me with.

ORIGINAL SCRIPTURE: "I can do all this through him who gives me strength." Philippians 4:13

PERSONALIZED SCRIPTURE: **I can do/accomplish all things through You, Lord, who gives me strength.** Philippians 4:13

PARAPHRASED SCRIPTURE: **Thank You, Lord, I don't have to rely on my strength, skills, or wit. Your strength enables me to do everything I need.** Philippians 4:13

ORIGINAL SCRIPTURE: "Commit to the Lord whatever you do, and he will establish your plans." Proverbs 16:3

PERSONALIZED SCRIPTURE: **Lord I commit whatever I do to You. I will watch as You complete Your plans.** Proverbs 16:3

PARAPHRASED SCRIPTURE: **Lord I can relax in knowing when I commit my to do lists and problems to You, that You are always there for me and You complete Your plans.** Proverbs 16:3

As you read the scriptures below be sure to personalize or paraphrase them as I did in the example above.

Additional Scriptures: Ephesians 2:10, Psalm 37:23, NLT, Philippians 2:13, HCSB,

4. LIE: I'm never going to get ahead. I'm going to be stuck in this situation, place or position forever.

TRUTH: *Read renouncing statement at the beginning of this section.* I decree and declare I am going to get ahead of this circumstance, situation or problem with Your help, Lord. I will break free of this bondage because You promised You are always with me and for me. You promised a way out of my difficult situation. I believe Your promises and trust You, Jesus. Lord show me where my personal Accidental Agreements are so I can rid myself of them and move forward and prosper. Thank You for prospering me because I declare You want to bless me, Your child You love unconditionally. You promise to delight my heart so I choose to believe You.

ORIGINAL SCRIPTURE: "No temptation has overtaken you except what is common to mankind. And God is faithful; he will not let you be tempted beyond what you can bear. But when you are tempted, he will also provide a way out so that you can endure it." I Corinthians 10:13

PERSONALIZED SCRIPTURE: **Lord thank You no temptations come against me except the ones common to everyone. You are faithful and will not allow me to be tempted more than I can bear. Thank You when I am tempted You will also provide a way out so I can endure it.** I Corinthians 10:13

PARAPHRASED SCRIPTURE: **Lord sometimes it seems like every time I turn around the enemy is flinging another temptation at me. But You are so faithful because You will not allow me to be tempted beyond what I can stand up to. I'm so glad You always provide a way for me to overcome.** I Corinthians 10:13

ORIGINAL SCRIPTURE: "It is God Who is all the while effectually at work in you [energizing and creating in you the power and desire], both to will and to work for His good pleasure and satisfaction and delight." Philippians 2:13, AMP

PERSONALIZED SCRIPTURE: **Thank You for effectually working in me by energizing and creating the power and desire for me to will and work for Your good pleasure, satisfaction and delight.** Philippians 2:13

PARAPHRASED SCRIPTURE: **Lord thank You for being the One who is giving me the desire to do Your will. Goodness doesn't begin with me; it comes from Your work in my life. Thank You, Lord, for taking great pleasure in helping me.** Philippians 2:13

As you read the scriptures below be sure to personalize or paraphrase them as I did in the example above.

Additional Scriptures: Psalm 55:16–17, Jeremiah 29:11, Philippians 4:13, KJV, Psalm 103:5, NLT, Luke 18:27

5. LIE: God doesn't have time for me. God is too busy to bother with the details in my life. God can't be everywhere all the time. God has bigger things to worry about than me.

TRUTH: *Read renouncing statement at the beginning of this section.* I decree and declare God has plenty of time for me because He loves and cares for me. You love Your children all the same. You are All-Powerful watching me everywhere at all times. Thank You for caring about all that concerns me. You tell me not to worry but to pray about everything so I will leave the worrying to You. You are always in charge, working through the difficulties of my life for good and to prosper me. Thank You for caring about every hair on my head and every cell in my body. I will be taught by the Lord and great will be my peace. I choose to trust Jesus.

ORIGINAL SCRIPTURE: "The LORD remembers us and will bless us: He will bless his people Israel, he will bless the house of Aaron," Psalm115:12

PERSONALIZED SCRIPTURE: **Thank You, Lord, for remembering me and blessing me. Thank You for blessing my house.** Psalm115:12

PARAPHRASED SCRIPTURE: **Lord You never forget me. Thank You for the abundant blessings You give me, my children, and all my descendants.** Psalm115:12

ORIGINAL SCRIPTURE: "Don't worry about anything; instead, pray about everything. Tell God what you need, and thank him for all he has done. Then you will experience God's peace, which exceeds anything we can understand. His peace will guard your hearts and minds as you live in Christ Jesus." Philippians 4:6–7, NLT

PERSONALIZED SCRIPTURE: **Thank You, Lord, I don't have to worry about anything, instead I will just pray about it. I will tell You what I need and I will thank You for what You have done. When I experience Your peace, it exceeds my ability to understand it. Your peace guards my heart and mind as I think on Christ Jesus.** Philippians 4:6–7

PARAPHRASED SCRIPTURE: **Thank You, Lord, for Your promise that destroys the worry in my life. Instead of worrying I will pray and tell You my needs and then I will thank You even before Your answers come. Your peace is so amazing; it's greater than I can even fathom. As I meditate on and believe in Your promises, Your peace envelops my heart and mind.** Philippians 4:6–7

As you read the scriptures below be sure to personalize or paraphrase them as I did in the example above.

Additional Scriptures: Matthew 10:30–31, Isaiah 49:15, Hebrews 13:5b, Psalm 55:22, Psalm 23:1

6. LIE: God does the best He can. God loves me conditionally. (Your misconception due to your earthly father and mother.)

TRUTH: *Read renouncing statement at the beginning of this section.* I decree and declare God loves all of me, every bit. You love me when I wake up; You love me when I'm asleep. You love me through good times and what appears to be bad times. You love me unconditionally. You promise a way out to escape sin. You do say we reap what we sow but when You offer correction, it is not punitive. Your plan is always perfect for me because You want to bless me. There is no evil in You. I will be taught of the Lord and great will be my peace. You have a great plan for me and my family and I choose today to believe You will prosper me in all my ways.

ORIGINAL SCRIPTURE: "Thou wilt show me the path of life: in thy presence is fullness of joy; at thy right hand there are pleasures for evermore." Psalm 16:11, KJV

PERSONALIZED SCRIPTURE: **Thank You for showing me the path of life. In Your presence there is always joy. At Your right hand are pleasures forever more.** Psalm 16:11

PARAPHRASED SCRIPTURE: **Lord thank You for planting my feet firmly on the path of life. Everything about You and Your kingdom is amazing. Your presence brings more joy than I can contain. At Your right hand are pleasures for all eternity.** Psalm 16:11

ORIGINAL SCRIPTURE: "God is not human, that he should lie, not a human being, that he should change his mind. Does he speak and then not act? Does he promise and not fulfil?" Numbers 23:19

PERSONALIZED SCRIPTURE: **God is not human so He does not lie; He is not human so He does not change his mind. He does what He says. Thank You for fulfilling what You promise.** Numbers 23:19

PARAPHRASED SCRIPTURE: **Lord, many people have disappointed me. I'm so glad You are not like humans. Because You are divine, I know I can always trust You. You follow through on what You say. You always fulfill Your promises to me. You are a trustworthy God.** Numbers 23:19

As you read the scriptures below be sure to personalize or paraphrase them as I did in the example above.

Additional Scriptures: Isaiah 40:12, NLT, Psalm 8:4

7. LIE: I'm not worthy for someone like God to love me.

TRUTH: *Read renouncing statement at the beginning of this section.* I decree and declare God loved me from the very beginning, before I was even born. You chose to put me on this earth to bless and prosper me. You love me no matter what. You love me unconditionally as I am Your child because I accepted You as Lord of my life. I am Your inheritance designed to live a joyous life filled with good things. I am worthy of Your love. I am worthy of Your love because You say I am! Thank You Jesus.

ORIGINAL SCRIPTURE: "See what great love the Father has lavished on us, that we should be called children of God! And that is what we are!" I John 3:1

PERSONALIZED SCRIPTURE: **Thank You Father for Your great love that is lavished on me, the right to be called children of God. That is what I am, Your child!** I John 3:1

PARAPHRASED SCRIPTURE: **Father, You have lavishly poured out Your love on me. You have given me the right to be adopted as Your child! Thank You I can boldly declare, "I am Your favorite child!"** I John 3:1

ORIGINAL SCRIPTURE: "We are able to hold our heads high no matter what happens and know that all is well, for we know how dearly God loves us, and we feel this warm love everywhere within us because God has given us the Holy Spirit to fill our hearts with his love." Romans 5:5 TLB

PERSONALIZED SCRIPTURE: **Thank You, Lord, no matter what happens I know all is well because You dearly love me. I feel this warm love within me because You have given me the Holy Spirit who fills my heart with His love.** Romans 5:5

PARAPHRASED SCRIPTURE: **Lord thank You regardless of what the circumstances look like, I can relax in Your love for me and know everything will work out okay. Thank You for Your exuberant love for me. I feel it through the Holy Spirit, which You gave me, who showers His love in my heart.** Romans 5:5

As you read the scriptures below be sure to personalize or paraphrase them as I did in the example above.

Additional Scriptures: Isaiah 43:4a, NASB, Zephaniah 3:17, Romans 5:7–8, Psalm 103:13–14

8. LIE: God can't really take care of all of my needs or desires.

TRUTH: *Read renouncing statement at the beginning of this section.*

I decree and declare God cares about every need and desire I have. You will provide for all my needs and not just barely, because my Father in Heaven has plenty of provision. You are the God of "more than enough" because You made the world and everything in it. I will share my needs/desires and trust You will provide. Your scripture says to, "Trust You with all of my heart and lean not on my own understanding but in all my ways acknowledge You and You will direct my path." I choose to trust and obey Your commandments. I will meditate on Your word listening to Holy Spirit direction. Thank You for providing for me even when it looks otherwise. I stand in alignment with You, Lord.

ORIGINAL SCRIPTURE: "If you, then, though you are evil, know how to give good gifts to your children, how much more will your Father in heaven give good gifts to those who ask him?" Matthew 7:11

PERSONALIZED SCRIPTURE: **Thank You for giving good gifts to me, Your child, because You are my father in Heaven.**

PARAPHRASED SCRIPTURE: **Thank You, Father in Heaven, for giving me good gifts when I ask and even when I don't ask, because I am Your child.**

ORIGINAL SCRIPTURE: "But seek first his kingdom and his righteousness, and all these things will be given to you as well. Therefore, do not worry about tomorrow, for tomorrow will worry about itself. Each day has enough trouble of its own." Matthew 6: 33–34

PERSONALIZED SCRIPTURE: **I am seeking the kingdom of God first and Your righteousness and all other things will be given to me. I'm not going to worry about tomorrow because tomorrow has enough trouble.**

PARAPHRASED SCRIPTURE: **I will seek the kingdom of God**

first and Your righteousness and all other things will be given to me. I'm not going to worry about tomorrow because it has enough challenges.

As you read the scriptures below be sure to personalize or paraphrase them as I did in the example above.

Additional Scriptures: Matthew 6:28–31, Matthew 6:25–27, Psalm 84:11–12, Psalm 22:26, Psalm 146:7, Psalm 107:9, Luke 12:31, Philippians 4:19, Psalm 34:10, Psalm 38:9, CEV, Isaiah 54:10, NIV, 1 John 3:1, Psalm 52:8b

9. LIE: I won't amount to anything because my (parents, teacher, boss, friends) said I won't.

TRUTH: *Read renouncing statement at the beginning of this section.* I decree and declare I am a child of the Most High God making me royalty. I break off the power of those word curses spoken over me in the name of Jesus. I declare I will be successful stepping into my God-designed purpose. God has a perfect plan for my life which is for good and will prosper me. I have a God-ordained destiny which is very important and I intend to fulfill it. I WILL flourish and be victorious in my life. I am perfectly made in Your eyes so that settles it! I choose to believe You and what You say about me.

ORIGINAL SCRIPTURE: "For God knew his people in advance, and he chose them to become like his Son, so that his Son would be the firstborn among many brothers and sisters." Romans 8:29, NLT

PERSONALIZED SCRIPTURE: **Thank You God for choosing me to become like Your Son, who would be the firstborn among many brothers and sisters.**

PARAPHRASED SCRIPTURE: **God, before the world was even**

created You chose me to come into Your marvelous kingdom and to be transformed into the image of Your Son. Christ is the preeminent member of Your family and is bringing more spiritual children to You.

ORIGINAL SCRIPTURE: "Commit to the Lord whatever you do, and he will establish your plans." Proverbs 16:3

PERSONALIZED SCRIPTURE: **Lord I commit whatever I do to You. I will watch as You complete your plans.** Proverbs 16:3

PARAPHRASED SCRIPTURE: **Lord I can relax knowing when I commit my to-do lists and problems to You, that You are always there for me and You complete Your plans in my life.** Proverbs 16:3

As you read the scriptures below be sure to personalize or paraphrase them as I did in the example above.

Additional Scriptures: Deuteronomy 11:26–27, Deuteronomy 30:19, Jeremiah 29:11, Habakkuk 2:3, Psalm 138:8

10. LIE: God is mad at me. God doesn't want to talk to me.

Truth: Read renouncing statement above. I decree and declare You are never mad at me. You knew I would make mistakes before I made them and You forgive my sins. I decree You love me unconditionally because I am Your special child. You always want to talk with me because You are my good Heavenly Father. You love it when I talk with You about everything including my day, my life, my dreams, my family (husband, wife, children, grandkids, aunts, uncles, brothers, sisters, friends), my job, my plans, my sorrow, my pain, my worries-every single detail. You are here for me 24/7 because you promise to never forsake me. You are the same yesterday, today and tomorrow so Your love and commitment to me will not change. Thank You Holy Spirit for always being available to talk with me.

ORIGINAL SCRIPTURE: "The LORD himself goes before you and will be with you; he will never leave you nor forsake you. Do not be afraid; do not be discouraged." Deuteronomy 31:8

PERSONALIZED SCRIPTURE: **Thank You, Lord, for going before me and You are with me. Thank You for promising You will never leave me or forsake me. I will not be afraid and I will not be discouraged**. Deuteronomy 31:8

PARAPHRASED SCRIPTURE: **Lord it so encouraging to know You are not only with me but You are out ahead of me. Thank You for Your promise that You will always be with me and You will never forsake me. Because of that, I will not give in to fear or discouragement.** Deuteronomy 31:8

ORIGINAL SCRIPTURE: "And we are confident that he hears us whenever we ask for anything that pleases him. And since we know he hears us when we make our requests, we also know that he will give us what we ask for." I John 5:14–15 NLT

PERSONALIZED SCRIPTURE: **Lord I am confident You hear me when I ask for anything that pleases You. I know You hear me when I make my requests and I also know You will give me what I ask for when it is in alignment with your Word.** I John 5:14–15

PARAPHRASED SCRIPTURE: **Lord I am thankful You always listen when I ask for anything according to Your will. I know You hear my requests and I am certain You will answer me.** I John 5:14–15

As you read the scriptures below be sure to personalize or paraphrase them as I did in the example above.

"The LORD is gracious and compassionate, slow to anger and rich in love." Psalm 145:8

"And I pray that you, being rooted and established in love, may have power, together with all the Lord's holy people, to grasp how wide and long and high and deep is the love of Christ, and to know this love that surpasses knowledge that you may be filled to the measure of all the fullness of God." Ephesians 3:17–19.

Revelation 22:13 Isaiah 54:9–10 Revelation 21:6–7

Emotional Accidental Agreements

NOTE: Before beginning, let's ask Holy Spirit if you have any hidden unforgiveness. Remember, unforgiveness blocks prayers! Unforgiveness manifests as these attitudes and feelings: bitterness, anger, resentment, hatred, accusation, retaliation, fighting, rage, passive aggressive behavior, indignation, violence, criticism, judgment, cynicism, and negativity. See *Forgiveness* section prayer.

Take a moment of silence and ask the Lord to download the names of people you have unforgiveness towards. Ask for forgiveness and repent to remove any unforgiveness or bitterness.

Next, renounce your specific agreement (the lie) with the enemy listed below. First, speak the renouncing statement followed by the Truth Statement. Read the personalized scriptures out loud (dunamis power).

Read the renouncing statement before all Truth Statements.

Renouncing Statement: "Lord, on behalf of me, my ancestors and my descendants, I ask for forgiveness, and repent and renounce my agreements with the enemy in regard to lie number _______. I submit my body, soul and spirit to the Lord and ask You to align me with Your Will. Cleanse my sin and cover me with the blood of Jesus. Fill my soul wounds with Your resurrection power and the Shekinah glory light of Jesus in my innermost being.

I ask You to silence the enemy. Thank You the power and legal rights of the enemy are broken. (Luke 10:19) I ask to be restored in full covenant with You. As I am in covenant with You, I enjoy the benefits and blessings of being Your royal child. Lord, You are the Sovereign Judge in the Courts of Heaven and also the Judge on earth. Lord, I ask You to rule in my favor in the Courts of Heaven and ask You to release the angels to enforce this judgment.

I ask Your will be done on earth as it is in Heaven. You have given me the legal right to trample on the enemy (Psalm 91). I reclaim everything the enemy has stolen from me, my family and all that concerns me. Thank you for restoring the generational blessings and liberating our DNA in alignment with Your original plan for our lives which is our Godly inheritance. I ask that our God-ordained blessings come forth in the name of Jesus. I ask You to activate our DNA correction and blessings. These blessings include wisdom, knowledge, understanding, discernment, gifts, talents and all other Godly generational blessings. Lord, I ask specifically for You to bless me with the talents of ______________________. (Fill in the blank with your God aligned desires. Examples: music, languages, artistic ability, dance, writing, business)"

1. LIE: I don't feel good about ____________________(situation, person or circumstance).

TRUTH: *Read renouncing statement at the beginning of this section.* I decree and declare I will not solely trust my feelings as they are not always reliable. Father, You know the truth about this situation. You are a good Father who wants the best for me and will give me the strength to handle it. You love me more than I can imagine! I ask for Your perspective about this and choose to trust You to work everything for my good. I will speak positive, scriptural affirmations believing You mean what You say in the Bible. I choose to align my heart with Your Word. Thank you for loving me unconditionally.

ORIGINAL SCRIPTURE: "The Lord will give strength unto his people; the Lord will bless his people with peace." Psalm 29:11, KJV

PERSONALIZED SCRIPTURE: **Thank You Lord, for giving me strength. Thank You for blessing me with peace.** Psalm 29:11

PARAPHRASED SCRIPTURE: **Lord, when I feel weak I can**

look to You for strength. When I feel stressed, I can come to You and receive Your peace. You are amazing. Thank You Lord for Your good gifts to me. Psalm 29:11

ORIGINAL SCRIPTURE: "And we know that in all things God works for the good of those who love him, who have been called according to his purpose." Romans 8:28

PERSONALIZED SCRIPTURE: **I'm grateful You work everything for good for me because I love You and every detail of my life is called according to Your plans.** Romans 8:28

PARAPHRASED SCRIPTURE: **Lord, I am so relieved to know it's impossible for me to make a mistake big enough You can't correct.** Romans 8:28

ORIGINAL SCRIPTURE: "For my thoughts are not your thoughts, neither are your ways my ways, declares the Lord. 'As the heavens are higher than the earth, so are my ways higher than your ways and my thoughts than your thoughts." Isaiah 55:8–9

PERSONALIZED SCRIPTURE: **Lord I acknowledge Your thoughts are not like my thoughts and Your ways are not like my ways. As the heavens are higher than the earth, Your ways are higher than my ways and Your thoughts higher than my thoughts.** Isaiah 55:8–9

PARAPHRAZED SCRIPTURE: **Lord will You remind me everything about You is perfect? As high as the heavens are above the earth, that is how much higher Your thoughts and ways are than mine. When I am making decisions I know You will help me remember to ask You for Your heavenly wisdom.** Isaiah 55:8–9

As you read the scriptures below be sure to personalize or paraphrase them as I did in the example above.

Additional Scriptures: Proverbs 16:7, Proverbs 4:20–22, TLB, 3 John 2, Ephesians 3:16, NKJV, Psalm 138:3, NKJV, 2 Timothy 1:7, AMP, Isaiah 48:17, John 16:33

2. LIE: I will always feel guilty about ______________.

TRUTH: *Read renouncing statement at the beginning of this section.* I decree and declare I will not solely trust my feelings as they are not reliable. Guilt and condemnation are not from the Lord so I dismiss them as lies. Holy Spirit conviction causes me to lean towards You. You died on the cross to forgive my sins and remember them no more. I faithfully confess my sins to you and refuse to be hindered by guilt but will be led by love. I am forgiven. Holy Spirit reveal Your view on this situation which has a positive outcome. I choose to look forward toward the blessings You have for me.

ORIGINAL SCRIPTURE: "Therefore, there is now no condemnation for those who are in Christ Jesus, because through Christ Jesus the law of the Spirit who gives life has set you free from the law of sin and death." Romans 8:1–2

PERSONALIZED SCRIPTURE: **Thank You, Lord, there is no condemnation for me because I am in You. Through the law of the Spirit who gives life I have been set free from the law of sin and death**. Romans 8:1–2

PARAPHRASED SCRIPTURE: **Lord, even though I have sinned a lot and deserve punishment You promise You will never condemn me! Thank You for convicting my heart by Your life-giving Spirit which has set me free from the bondage and penalty of my sin. You have given me life for death!** Romans 8:1–2

ORIGINAL SCRIPTURE: "If we say that we have no sin, we are deceiving ourselves and the truth is not in us. If we confess our sins, He is faithful and righteous to forgive us our sins and to cleanse us from all unrighteousness." I John 1:8–9

PERSONALIZED SCRIPTURE: **I acknowledge I have sinned. I will not be deceived because You are Truth and You are in me. I confess my sins to You. Thank You for being faithful and righteous to forgive and cleanse me from all unrighteousness.** I John 1:8–9

PARAPHRASED SCRIPTURE: **Lord, I would be deceiving myself if I said I am not a sinner. I'm so grateful when I come to You and confess what I've done, You never turn me away! You are always faithful and righteous. You not only forgive my sins, You wash me clean from any residue.** I John 1:8–9

As you read the scriptures below be sure to personalize or paraphrase them as I did in the example above.

Additional Scriptures: Galatians 2:15, Psalm 32:5, Proverbs 28:13, Psalm 86:15

3. LIE: I feel bad about myself when ______________________________ ________________ happens. It makes me sad and I get depressed.

TRUTH: *Read renouncing statement at the beginning of this section.* I decree and declare I will not trust my feelings as they are not reliable. You will redeem every loss, restore every broken part and repair every breach. I choose not to look back on situations. You promised You have an amazing plan for my life and it is better than I can even imagine. Thank you for healing my heart and filling it with Godly desires. You always have good thoughts towards me. You love everything about me. You want to help me be more like

You—kind, strong and courageous. I am lovable and You gently correct me. I am listening for Your kind words. Thank You Jesus. I choose to be joyful today. I choose life for me and my descendants today.

ORIGINAL SCRIPTURE: "Forget the former things; do not dwell on the past." Isaiah 43:18

PERSONALIZED SCRIPTURE: **Lord, thank You for helping me forget the former things. I will not dwell on my past.** Isaiah 43:18

PARAPHRASED SCRIPTURE: **Lord, thank You because of Your forgiveness I won't obsess on my past failures. Kicking myself and dwelling on my past is not productive because You have a bright and promising future for me to look forward to.** Isaiah 43:18

ORIGINAL SCRIPTURE: "He heals the brokenhearted and binds up their wounds." Psalm 147:3

PERSONALIZED SCRIPTURE: **Thank You Lord for healing my broken heart and binding up my wounds.** Psalm 147:3

PARAPHRASED SCRIPTURE: **Lord, because of my sins and because of others who sinned against me, I have areas of my heart that feel broken. Thank You for mending broken hearts! Thank You for doctoring the open wounds that still cause me pain.** Psalm 147:3

ORIGINAL SCRIPTURE: "Because of the Lord's great love we are not consumed, for his compassions never fail. They are new every morning; great is your faithfulness." Lamentations 3:22–23

PERSONALIZED SCRIPTURE: **Lord, thank You that Your great love keeps me from being devoured by the enemy. Your**

compassions never fail. Each morning they are new. Your faithfulness is great. Lamentations 3:22–23

PARAPHRASED SCRIPTURE: **God, because of my sin, I deserve to be consumed by Your wrath. But Your justice has been overridden by Your great love, focused like a laser beam on me. Your unconditional love toward me always supersedes my sin. Every morning when the sun arises I wake up and find that You are pouring out new compassion on me. Your faithfulness to me is unfathomable.** Lamentations 3:22–23

ORIGINAL SCRIPTURE: "For I am sure of this very thing, that the one who began a good work in you will perfect it until the day of Christ Jesus." Philippians 1:6

PERSONALIZED SCRIPTURE: **Lord I am sure that since You began a good work in me, You will perfect it until the day You return.** Philippians 1:6

PARAPHRAZED SCRIPTURE: **Thank You, Lord, You will help me to unwaveringly believe Your promises. Since You are the initiator of my faith, You will watch over and nurture it until the day You return to the earth.** Philippians 1:6

ORIGINAL SCRIPTURE: "We demolish arguments and every pretension that sets itself up against the knowledge of God, and we take captive every thought to make it obedient to Christ." 2 Corinthians 10:5

PERSONALIZED SCRIPTURE: **Thank You, Lord, for helping me demolish arguments and every pretension that sets itself up against Your knowledge. I take every thought captive and make it obey You!** 2 Corinthians 10:5

PARAPHRAZED SCRIPTURE: **Thank You for helping me**

demolish all negative thoughts which don't line up with Your Word. I make a commitment to take every destructive thought captive and make it obey You by replacing the lie with a truth from Your Word. 2 Corinthians 10:5

As you read the scriptures below be sure to personalize or paraphrase them as I did in the example above.

Additional Scriptures: James 1:2–3, Philippians 3:14, Joel 2:24–26a, Psalm 25:7, Ephesians 2:10, ESV, Romans 8:1, ESV, Galatians 3:26, ESV, John 15:15, ESV, 2 Peter 1:4, ESV, Philippians 3:14, Psalm 143:8, Philippians 4:13, ESV, Jeremiah 29:11

4. LIE: I get mad when I think about ______________________________. (List a person or situation.)

TRUTH: *Read renouncing statement at the beginning of this section.* I decree and declare I will not trust my feelings as they are not reliable. I choose not to be angry, mad or bitter as I do not want my prayers blocked. I choose to forgive them as You have forgiven me. Thank you that my sins are forgiven so I am not separated from You. I close the door I accidentally opened to the enemy. I choose to abound with the fruit of the spirit, including love, joy, peace, patience, kindness, goodness, gentleness, faithfulness and self-control. I choose to align my thoughts to believe the Lord's perspective about this person or situation. I choose to move forward and not look back, as You have commanded. You promised to work everything for my good. You said it. I believe it because Your word is true. That's good enough for me!

ORIGINAL SCRIPTURE: "Get rid of all bitterness, rage and anger, brawling and slander, along with every form of malice." Ephesians 4:31

PERSONALIZED SCRIPTURE: **Lord, thank You for helping me get rid of all bitterness, rage, anger, brawling and slander, along with revenge.** Ephesians 4:31

PARAPHRASED SCRIPTURE: **Lord, I have things in my heart and mind I wish weren't there. Thank You for helping me overcome these things: bitterness, rage, anger, brawling, slander and revenge. I want to be filled up and overflowing with the Fruit of the Spirit.** Ephesians 4:31

ORIGINAL SCRIPTURE: "So, chosen by God for this new life of love, dress in the wardrobe God picked out for you: compassion, kindness, humility, quiet strength, discipline. Be even-tempered, content with second place, quick to forgive an offense. Forgive as quickly and completely as the Master forgave you." Colossians 3:12–13 MSG

PERSONALIZED SCRIPTURE: **Thank You for having chosen me for a new life of love. I will display an attitude in my heart of compassion, kindness, humility, quiet strength and discipline. I will be even-tempered and content with second place. I will quickly and completely forgive like You have forgiven me.** Colossians 3:12–13

PARAPHRASED SCRIPTURE: **God, I'm so blessed You chose me to live a life filled with love! You've taken away my undesirable traits and replaced them with Godly traits of compassion, kindness, humility, quiet strength and discipline. Thank You for helping me to be even-tempered and content with second place. Since You have completely forgiven me I will offer the same forgiveness to those who offend me.** Colossians 3:12–13

As you read the scriptures below be sure to personalize or paraphrase them as I did in the example above.

Additional Scriptures: Psalm 51:10, James 1:19–20, Ephesians 4:26, Mark 11:25, Deuteronomy 30:19, 2 Peter 3:9, TLB, Matthew 5:44, KJV, Luke 6:37, NLT

5. LIE: When I'm depressed or stressed, what brings me comfort/happiness is ______________________________.

TRUTH: *Read renouncing statement at the beginning of this section.* I decree and declare I will not rely on my feelings from my soul. I confess I have been using my coping mechanism of ____________ (what you filled in the blank above) as a replacement for Your comfort. Lord, I ask for a personal scripture for my circumstances. I choose to believe Your promises and speak the scripture out loud now. ________________________. (Insert scripture) If depression reappears, I will pray, seek Your perspective and speak my scripture which comforts and soothes me. Thank you for working within me to energize and create the power and desire to both will and work for what pleases You. Thank You for changing me allowing self-control, love and peace to rule in my heart. I choose to believe You. Thank You for loving me no matter what.

ORIGINAL SCRIPTURE: "Heart, body, and soul are filled with joy. You have let me experience the joys of life and the exquisite pleasures of your own eternal presence." Psalm 16:9, 11 TLB

PERSONALIZED SCRIPTURE: **My heart, body and soul are filled with joy. Thank You for letting me experience the joys of life and the exquisite pleasures of Your eternal presence.** Psalm 16:9, 11

PARAPHRASED SCRIPTURE: **Because of You my heart, body, and soul are overflowing with joy! You have showed me joy in life that I never knew before. "Eternal pleasurable" is how I would describe Your presence surrounding me.** Psalm 16:9, 11

ORIGINAL SCRIPTURE: "And the Lord will continually guide you, and satisfy your soul in scorched *and* dry places, and give strength to your bones; and you will be like a watered garden, and like a spring of water whose waters do not fail." Isaiah 58:11 AMP

PERSONALIZED SCRIPTURE: **Thank You, Lord, for Your continued guidance. You satisfy my soul when I am frail and weak and strengthen my bones. I am a watered garden, with a continually flowing spring of water.** Isaiah 58:11

PARAPHRASED SCRIPTURE: **Lord, You are my guide on this God-adventure I call my life. When I get stuck in those dry places and my mouth is parched and even my bones are tired and achy, You will revive me and make me like a well-watered garden. I will be like a refreshing, babbling brook that never dries up.** Isaiah 58:11

As you read the scriptures below be sure to personalize or paraphrase them as I did in the example above.

Additional Scriptures: Matthew 11:28–30, John 14:27, Psalm 29:11, Psalm 139:17–18, TLB, 2 Corinthians 9:8, TLB, Ephesians 1:3, TLB, Ephesians 1:5–8, TLB, Romans 14:4, GNT, Deuteronomy 28:2, John 16:33, John 20:19

6. LIE: I'm an emotional person so I can't help it when I get mad, upset, short tempered or say hurtful things to my family, spouse, friend or coworker or ________________. I have a right to give someone a piece of my mind. What I say doesn't really matter. They'll get over it.

TRUTH: *Read renouncing statement at the beginning of this section.* I decree and declare I will not solely trust my feelings. They aren't always reliable as they originate from my soul, which can be influenced by the enemy. I am leaning on You Lord, to help me control my tongue, temper and emotions. I choose to bless people with my words and not curse or condemn. I choose to speak life, hope and love to every single person. They will receive a blessing from me today. Thank You, Lord, for helping me.

ORIGINAL SCRIPTURE: "May these words of my mouth and this meditation of my heart be pleasing in your sight, Lord, my Rock and my Redeemer." Psalm 19:14

PERSONALIZED SCRIPTURE: **Lord I desire the words of my mouth and the meditation of my heart to be pleasing in Your sight. Thank You for being my Rock and my Redeemer.** Psalm 19:14

PARAPHRASED SCRIPTURE: **Lord, all day long thoughts go through my mind and then tumble out my lips. I want to please You by speaking blessings to those around me. Thank You for purifying my heart and mind to deliberately speak words pleasing to You.** Psalm 19:14

ORIGINAL SCRIPTURE: "A soft answer turns away wrath, but a harsh word stirs up anger. The tongue of the wise commends knowledge, but the mouths of fools pour out folly.... A gentle tongue is a tree of life, but perverseness in it breaks the spirit." Proverbs 15:1–4 ESV

PERSONALIZED SCRIPTURE: **My soft answer to someone will turn away wrath. I will not speak harsh words as it stirs up anger. Thank You for helping me speak with wisdom and knowledge, not like a fool who pours out folly. My gentle words are like a tree of life, but perverseness breaks people's spirits.** Proverbs 15:1–4

PARAPHRASED SCRIPTURE: **Lord, Thank You for helping me bless people with my lips. I avoid harsh words which inflame and anger. I choose instead to speak kindly and with wisdom,**

not like a fool whose comments make people angry. My gentle words are like a life-giving tree, providing fruit and shade. I avoid deceitful and harsh words which can crush someone's spirit. Help my words to always bless the hearer. Proverbs 15:1–4

As you read the scriptures below be sure to personalize or paraphrase them as I did in the example above.

Additional Scriptures: Psalm 141:3, Matthew 12:36, ESV, Hebrews 13:15

7. LIE: If I were married I would be happy. If I weren't married I would be happy. If I were married to someone else, I would be happy.

TRUTH: *Read renouncing statement at the beginning of this section.* I decree and declare I will not trust my feelings as they are not reliable. Father, you value marriage as do I. Change me to love others the way You love me. I will love You with all of my heart, soul, mind and strength. I can do all things through Christ who strengthens me. I will seek first the kingdom of God above all else, and live righteously, and He will give me everything I need. I won't worry about tomorrow, for tomorrow will bring its own worries. Living faithfully is a large enough task for today. I can't change my spouse but You can. I surrender my control over my spouse to You. Help restore loving feelings towards my spouse and release unforgiveness. Give me Your positive perspective on me and my spouse. Teach me how to pray more effectively for him or her. I will confess my sins and pray, so we may be healed. You say, the effective, fervent prayers produce pleasant results. You promise to work everything for out for good in our lives. I choose to believe You, Lord. Thank You loving me unconditionally.

Referenced Scriptures: James 5:16 NKJV; Matthew 6:33–34

ORIGINAL SCRIPTURE: "Seek the Kingdom of God above all else, and live righteously, and he will give you everything you need. So don't worry about tomorrow, for tomorrow will bring its own worries. Today's trouble is enough for today." Matthew 6:33–34 NLT

PERSONALIZED SCRIPTURE: **I am seeking the Kingdom of God first, and living righteously so You will give me everything I will need.** Matthew 6:33

PARAPHRAZED SCRIPTURE: **Thank You, Lord, for helping me to seek the Kingdom of God first in my daily priorities. I will live righteously. Thank You for Your promise to meet all my needs.** Matthew 6:33

ORIGINAL SCRIPTURE: Dear friends, let us continue to love one another, for love comes from God. Anyone who loves is a child of God and knows God. I John 4:7 NLT

PERSONALIZED SCRIPTURE: **I love You Lord because You loved me first. I love others because I am Your child and You are love.** I John 4:7

PARAPHRASED SCRIPTURE: **God, You are love—it's who You are. Thank You for helping me love everyone. I want to be a person who loves well, just like You. Those who love well are Your children.** I John 4:7

As you read the scriptures below be sure to personalize or paraphrase them as I did in the example above.

Additional Scriptures: Proverbs 3:5–6, I Timothy 6:6–8, ESV, Isaiah 40:29–31, ESV, I Corinthians 10:13, ESV

8. **LIE: Distrust keeps me safe.**

TRUTH: *Read renouncing statement at the beginning of this section.* I decree and declare I will not trust my feelings as they aren't reliable. Jesus, You keep me safe.

The Lord is my rock, my fortress, and my Savior in whom I find protection. You are my shield, the power that saves me, and my place of safety. In Psalm 91, Your faithful promises are my armor and protection. I surrender my control over myself, my family, agenda and imagination to You. I align with Your divine purpose and plan for my life and my family's lives. You promise to complete the good work You have begun in me. You promise to work everything out for my advantage. I surrender my control over myself, my family, my agenda and imagination to You. I align with Your purpose and plan for my life and my family's lives. Thank You for hearing my prayers and concerns. I will not worry about anything but pray about everything. I will tell You what I need and thank you for what you have done. I choose to trust You.

ORIGINAL SCRIPTURE: "This I declare about the Lord: He alone is my refuge, my place of safety; he is my God, and I trust him. For he will rescue you from every trap and protect you from deadly disease. He will cover you with his feathers. He will shelter you with his wings. His faithful promises are your armor and protection." Psalm 91:2–4 NLT

PERSONALIZED SCRIPTURE: **Lord, I declare You alone are my refuge and place of safety. You are my God and I trust You. You will rescue me from every trap and protect me from deadly diseases. You will cover me with Your feathers. You will shelter me with Your wings. Your faithful promises are my armor and protection.** Psalm 91:2–4

PARAPHRASED SCRIPTURE: **Lord, You alone are my refuge and place of safety. I trust You God. You promise to rescue me from difficulties and deadly diseases. You will cover me with Your love and shelter me from problems. Your faithful promises are my armor and protection.** Psalm 91:2–4

ORIGINAL SCRIPTURE: "I called to the Lord, who is worthy of praise and I have been saved from my enemies." Psalm 18:3

PERSONALIZED SCRIPTURE**: I call to You Lord because You are worthy of praise. I have been saved from my enemies.** Psalm 18:3

PARAPHRASED SCRIPTURE: **Lord, You are worthy of praise. You have saved me from my enemies.** Psalm 18:3

Physical Accidental Agreements

NOTE: Randy Clark,[23] the founder of Global Awakening Ministry, has a training manual about physical illnesses. Randy suggests an easy way to quickly discover the root of many diseases is to ask yourself "What was going on in my life at the time the illness began?" You will be able to identify a stressful time or horrible situation that literally caused "dis-ease" in your body. If you have multiple health issues, ask the Holy Spirit what was going on in your life at the time each physical ailment appeared. Write this down. I have interviewed hundreds of people using this question and every person could answer it no matter how many years ago the incident occurred. Some illnesses were brought in at birth, indicating a generational bloodline issue. After completing this section and the lie and Truth Statements. See the Appendix for information on Curses and Hindrances to Healing.

NOTE: Before beginning, let's ask Holy Spirit if you have any hidden unforgiveness. Take a moment of silence and ask the Lord to download the names of people you have unforgiveness towards. Ask for forgiveness and repent to remove any unforgiveness or bitterness.

Remember, unforgiveness blocks prayers! Unforgiveness manifests as these attitudes and feelings: bitterness, anger, resentment, hatred, accusation, retaliation, fighting, rage, passive aggressive behavior, indignation, violence, criticism, judgment, cynicism, and negativity. See *Forgiveness* section prayer.

Next, renounce your specific agreement (the lie) with the enemy listed below. First, speak the renouncing statement followed by the Truth Statement. Read the Personalized Scriptures out loud (dunamis power).

Read the renouncing statement before all Truth Statements.

Renouncing Statement: "Lord, on behalf of me, my ancestors and my descendants, I ask for forgiveness, and repent and renounce my agreements with the enemy in regard to lie number _______. I submit my body, soul and spirit to the Lord and ask You to align me with Your Will. Cleanse my sin and cover me with the blood of Jesus. Fill my soul wounds with Your resurrection power and the Shekinah glory light of Jesus in my innermost being.

I ask You to silence the enemy. Thank You the power and legal rights of the enemy are broken. (Luke 10:19) I ask to be restored in full covenant with You. As I am in covenant with You, I enjoy the benefits and blessings of being Your royal child. Lord, You are the Sovereign Judge in the Courts of Heaven and also the Judge on earth. Lord, I ask You to rule in my favor in the Courts of Heaven and ask You to release the angels to enforce this judgment.

I ask Your Will be done on earth as it is in Heaven. You have given me the legal right to trample on the enemy (Psalm 91). I reclaim everything the enemy has stolen from me, my family and all that concerns me. Thank you for restoring the generational blessings and liberating our DNA in alignment with Your original plan for our lives which is our Godly inheritance. I ask that our God-ordained blessings come forth in the name of Jesus. I ask You to activate our DNA correction and blessings. These blessings include wisdom, knowledge, understanding, discernment, gifts, talents and all other Godly generational blessings. Lord, I ask specifically for You to bless me with the talents of ________________________. (Fill in the blank with your God aligned desires. Examples: music, languages, artistic ability, dance, writing, business)"

HEALTH VOWS (LIES)

Any time a sentence begins with "I will, I can't, I won't" followed by a negative comment it will be a lie and therefore an agreement with the enemy.

1. LIE: I will never get well. My doctor says I will always have this disease or limitation. This disease runs in my family so I will just have to live with it; it's genetic. My doctor says there is no cure for this. I was born this way. I will always have...

TRUTH: *Read renouncing statement at the beginning of this section.* I decree and declare You want me to be whole in my body, soul and spirit. I declare I am whole and in alignment with Your original will and master plan for my body. You are a good Father who is for me and who will rescue and protect me. I declare I am healed in the name of Yeshua. I will not come in agreement with the enemy that I am ill, have physical limitations, disease or infirmity of any kind. I am free. John 8:32 says, "And you shall know the truth, and the truth shall make you free." He who Jesus sets free is free indeed. I put all my faith and trust in the Lord without any doubt about my complete healing. Thank You Father for healing me by sending Your Son to die on the cross. By Your stripes I am healed. I declare I am healed of every kind of infirmity. I declare out loud, "I don't have infirmities, Satan, you have infirmities. Jesus loves to heal me!" You promised to bring abundant life. Thank You, Lord, my body is healing as my soul prospers. You are healing my soul right now with Your Dunamis power. I will have peace that I am healed. I will exercise my faith in Jesus. Thank You, Jesus, I am healed of ________________________________. Jesus loves to heal me."

ADD/ADHD/learning problems

Allergies

Arm/elbow/shoulder problems

Arthritis

Autism/problems socializing

Auto immune system/lymph problems

Back problems/pain

Blind/eye problems

Blood/cholesterol issues

Cancer/abnormal cells

Circulation problems

Crohn's

Cutting/suicidal thoughts

Cysts/tumors

Depression

Diabetes/blood sugar problems

Female issues/endometriosis

Fibromyalgia

Foot problems

Hearing loss/Deafness

Heart disease

High blood pressure

Hormone imbalances/menopause issues

Insomnia/sleep apnea

Kidney issues

Liver/gallbladder issues

Lou Gehrig's disease (ALS)/Parkinson's

Lung/breathing problems/asthma/COPD

Memory problems/dementia/Alzheimer's

Migraines

Mobility issues/leg/knee/hip problems

Multiple chemical sensitivity (MCS)/ environmental illness (EI)

Multiple sclerosis/epilepsy

Osteoporosis/bone issues

Overweight/underweight

Panic attacks/anxiety/PTSD

Schizophrenia/bipolar/OCD/DID and other mental problems

Skin disorders

Some kind of infirmity

Speech/muteness issues

Spiritual oppression

Stomach issues/GERD/ulcers/acid reflux/digestive/intestinal issues

Thyroid issues, hypo and hyper thyroidism

TIA/strokes

______________________ (Fill in your health issue.)

HEALTH DECLARATION STATEMENTS

I declare all my circumstances, including my health, will prosper just as my soul is prospering. "I pray that you may enjoy good health and that all may go well with you, even as your soul is getting along well." 3 John 1:2

I declare the Lord's power is bringing health, healing, abundant peace, and security to me, my family, and my nation. "Nevertheless, I will bring health and healing to it; I will heal my people and will let them enjoy abundant peace and security." Jeremiah 33:6

I declare with God's help I will love Him with all my heart, soul, strength and mind. I will make it a priority to love my neighbor as much as I love myself. "He answered, 'Love the Lord your God with all your heart and with all your soul and with all your strength and with all your mind' and 'Love your neighbor as yourself.'" Luke 10:27

I declare I am free indeed because the Lord has made it so. "So if the Son sets you free, you will be free indeed." John 8:36

I declare Jesus has imparted His authority to me. As I go throughout my day, I will look for those who are sick or afflicted by evil spirits, and my prayers will set them free. "Jesus called his twelve disciples to him and gave them authority to drive out impure spirits and to heal every disease and sickness." Matthew 10:1

I declare my sins and iniquities are forgiven, and I have peace and healing in my life because You were pierced, crushed, punished, and wounded for me. "He was wounded because of our rebellious deeds, crushed because of our sins; he endured punishment that made us well; because of his wounds we have been healed." Isaiah 53:5NET

I declare I am no longer a slave to sin; I am a prisoner of righteousness. I am healed spiritually, emotionally, and physically because You went

to the cross in my place. "He himself bore our sins in his body on the cross, so that we might die to sins and live for righteousness; by his wounds you have been healed." 1 Peter 2:24

I declare each day I will remember and thank the Lord for the blessings He has freely given me. My sins are forgiven, and my body is healed. Thank You, Jesus. Help me always to be grateful and thankful. "Praise the Lord, my soul, and forget not all his benefits who forgives all your sins and heals all your diseases," Psalm 103:2–3

2. LIE: My physical appearance matters more to people and God than my inner appearance. I don't need to exercise, stay in shape, or eat healthy. God doesn't really care about my health.

TRUTH: Read the renouncing statement at the beginning of this section. I decree and declare it is important to look my best. What is truly valuable to the Lord is my inner beauty and godly character. When I emulate the love of Jesus and His character, people will be attracted to me because they are attracted to Jesus. That's what is important. Lord help me look like and act like You daily. I decree and declare my body is a temple belonging to you, Lord. You gave meticulous directions when building Your Old Testament temple, You are meticulously guiding my personal temple maintenance-my body. I choose You to direct my exercise daily, to be strong and give glory to You. I choose to eat healthy, wisely, and in moderation. I will ask You about the food and water I consume. I ask You to bless my food to nourish my body, DNA, and cells. Thank you for providing the nutrients needed for good health.

ORIGINAL SCRIPTURE: "Your beauty should not come from outward adornment, such as elaborate hairstyles and the wearing of gold jewelry or fine clothes. Rather, it should be that of your inner self, the unfading beauty of a gentle and quiet spirit, which is of great worth in God's sight." I Peter 3:3–4

PERSONALIZED SCRIPTURE: **Lord I acknowledge my beauty should not come from outward adornment such as hairstyles, jewelry, and clothes. Thank You for helping me develop my inner self, the unfading beauty of a gentle and quiet spirit which has great value in Your eyes.** I Peter 3:3–4

PARAPHRASED SCRIPTURE: **Lord it's so easy to get caught up in what society tells us is beautiful. Set me free from the trap of believing beauty only comes with designer clothes, fancy jewelry, makeup and the latest hairstyle. Thank You for helping me develop the inner beauty of a gentle and quiet spirit that You say is much more valuable.** I Peter 3:3–4

ORIGINAL SCRIPTURE: "But the LORD said to Samuel, 'Do not look on his appearance or on the height of his stature, because I have rejected him. For the LORD sees not as man sees: man looks on the outward appearance, but the LORD looks on the heart.'" I Samuel 16:7

PERSONALIZED SCRIPTURE: **I will not judge by physical appearances because the Lord doesn't. The Lord sees not as I do. I look on the outward appearances but the Lord looks at the heart.** I Samuel 16:7

PARAPHRASED SCRIPTURE: **Lord, I am easily swayed by people's appearances or status. I know You don't care anything about those things. While I'm busy looking at someone's hairstyle, jewelry, clothes, car, or home, You are gazing at what really matters, their heart. Thank You for helping me to think and evaluate like You do.** I Samuel 16:7

ORIGINAL SCRIPTURE: "I appeal to you therefore, brothers, by the mercies of God, to present your bodies as a living sacrifice, holy and acceptable to God, which is your spiritual worship." Romans 12:1

PERSONALIZED SCRIPTURE: **By God's mercy I will present my body as a living sacrifice, holy and acceptable to You. This is an act of spiritual worship.** Romans 12:1

PARAPHRASED SCRIPTURE: **Lord, thank You for sending Your mercies to help me present my body as a living sacrifice to You. You view this as a holy sacrifice. I view this as an act of spiritual worship and obedience to You.** Romans 12:1

ORIGINAL SCRIPTURE: "But I discipline my body and keep it under control...." I Corinthians 9:27a

PERSONALIZED SCRIPTURE: **Thank You, Lord, for helping me discipline my body and keep it under control**. I Corinthians 9:27a

PARAPHRASED SCRIPTURE: **Lord, many times I find it challenging to eat healthy and exercise. I'm so glad You help me when I ask, to use self-discipline and self-control over my body when I am tempted.** I Corinthians 9:27a

As you read the scriptures below, be sure to personalize or paraphrase them as I did in the example above.

Additional Scriptures: I Timothy 4:8, Romans 6:13, I Corinthians 10:31, Proverbs 31:30, John 7:24, Ephesians 2:10, Psalm 139:14, Ecclesiastes 3:11a, Genesis 1:31a

3. LIE: If I had a different ______________________ I would be happier or more effective for the kingdom. People would like me better. My life would be better. I wish I had a different: ________________, head, ears, nose, mouth, eyes, cheeks, neck, body, legs, arms, torso, feet, knees, fingers, etc., If illness is associated with the body part, pray the Truth Statement from lie #1, the health declarations and the stronghold-breaking prayer.

TRUTH: Read the renouncing statement at the beginning of this section. I decree and declare I am fearfully and wonderfully made in Your image. I speak life into my body and soul and specifically speak life into___________. I release the dunamis power within my spirit and the glory light of Jesus to penetrate all my body parts and soul wounds. I receive the blessings of the Lord for prospering my health and my body. Give my heart Your perspective to align with Your word. As my soul prospers, my health will prosper, as well as all areas of my life. You are the giver of all good gifts. Thank You, Lord, for all You are doing for me.

ORIGINAL SCRIPTURE: "For You formed my inward parts; You wove me in my mother's womb. I will give thanks to You, for I am fearfully and wonderfully made; Wonderful are Your works, And my soul knows it very well. My frame was not hidden from You, When I was made in secret," Psalm 139:13–15a

PERSONALIZED SCRIPTURE: **Lord, You formed my inward body parts and wove me in my mother's womb. Thank You because I am fearfully and wonderfully made. Your works are wonderful, and my soul know this. My frame wasn't hidden from when I was made in secret.** Psalm 139:13–15a

PARAPHRASED SCRIPTURE: **Lord, You are the only life-giver. When my mother was carrying me, Your eyes were upon me. You were actually forming my body and giving me my personality and temperament. Even in the darkness of the womb, I wasn't hidden from You. I acknowledge everything You do is wonderful, and I thank You for the gift of my life.** Psalm 139:13–15a

ORIGINAL SCRIPTURE: "Then God said, 'Let us make man in our image, after our likeness. And let them have dominion over the fish of the sea and over the birds of the heavens and over the livestock and over all the earth and over every creeping thing that creeps on the earth.' So God created man in his own image, in the image of God he created him; male and female he created them." Genesis 1:26–27

PERSONALIZED SCRIPTURE: **God You said, "Let us make man in our image, after our likeness." You have given me dominion over the fish, birds, livestock, over all the earth and over every creeping thing on the earth. Thank You for creating me in Your own image, male and female.** Genesis 1:26–27

PARAPHRASED SCRIPTURE: **Lord, You had an amazing idea, "Let us make man in our image." Your desire is for me to reign over the earth and the animals: the fish, the birds, the livestock, and all the animals that roam the planet. You wanted to share Your vast love, so You created men and women. You created me after Your very own image.** Genesis 1:26–27

As you read the scriptures below, be sure to personalize or paraphrase them as I did in the example above.

Additional Scriptures: Jeremiah 1:5, I Peter 3:3–4, I Samuel 16:7, Psalm 139:14

Financial Accidental Agreements

Take a moment of silence and ask the Lord to download the names of people you have unforgiveness towards. Ask for forgiveness and repent to remove any unforgiveness or bitterness. See *Forgiveness* section prayer.

Next, renounce your specific agreement (the lie) with the enemy listed below. First, speak the renouncing statement followed by the Truth Statement." Read the personalized scriptures out loud (dunamis power).

Read the renouncing statement before all Truth Statements."

Renouncing Statement: "Lord, on behalf of me, my ancestors and my descendants, I ask for forgiveness and repent and renounce my agreements with the enemy in regard to lie number _______. I submit my body, soul, and spirit to the Lord and ask You to align me with Your will. Cleanse my sin and cover me with the blood of Jesus. Fill my soul wounds with Your resurrection power and the shekinah glory light of Jesus in my innermost being.

I ask You to silence the enemy. Thank You the power and legal rights of the enemy are broken. (Luke 10:19) I ask to be restored in full covenant with You. As I am in covenant with You, I enjoy the benefits and blessings of being Your royal child. Lord, You are the sovereign judge in the courts of heaven and also the judge on earth. Lord, I ask You to rule in my favor in the courts of heaven and ask You to release the angels to enforce this judgment.

I ask Your will be done on earth as it is in heaven. You have given me the legal right to trample on the enemy (Psalm 91). I reclaim everything the enemy has stolen from me, my family, and all that concerns me. Thank you for restoring the generational blessings and liberating our DNA in alignment with Your original plan for our lives, which is our godly inheritance. I ask that our God-ordained blessings come forth in the name of Jesus. I ask You to activate our DNA correction and blessings. These blessings include wisdom, knowledge, understanding, discernment, gifts, talents, and all other godly generational blessings. Lord, I ask specifically for You to bless me with the talents of ______________________. (Fill in the blank with your God aligned desires. Examples: music, languages, artistic ability, dance, writing, or business.)

1. LIE: I won't ever have enough _______________(Fill in the blank).

TRUTH: Read the renouncing statement at the beginning of this section. Break off the vow made in the above statement. I decree and declare You want to prosper me even as my soul prospers. You are for me, God, not against me. All things are possible with You by my side. You are my God who has "more than enough!" You give me the ability to produce wealth confirming Your covenant to my ancestors. This covenant is still in effect today. I choose to believe You will provide me with more than enough provision in this area. If I have an accidental agreement in this area, highlight the root cause to me. I ask for forgiveness and repent. I renounce any agreements with the enemy tying up my financial freedom. I align myself with Your promises about money and provision. I will listen and adjust my thinking and actions as You direct. I believe all things are possible with You. Thank You for blessing me.

ORIGINAL SCRIPTURE: "With man this is impossible, but with God all things are possible." Matthew 19:26

PERSONALIZED SCRIPTURE: **Thank You God that ALL things are possible.** Matthew 19:26

PARAPHRASED SCRIPTURE: **With man's ability, this situation is impossible, but with my powerful God, ALL things are possible.** Matthew 19:26

ORIGINAL SCRIPTURE: But remember the Lord your God, for it is He who gives you the ability to produce wealth, and so confirms his covenant, which he swore to your ancestors, as it is today. Deuteronomy 8:18

PERSONALIZED SCRIPTURE: **You have given me power to get wealth, and this fulfills Your promise to my ancestors.** Deuteronomy 8:18

PARAPHRASED SCRIPTURE: **Thank You, Lord, for giving me the power to get wealth by listening to Your wisdom. This fulfills Your promise to my ancestors.** Deuteronomy 8:18

As you read the scriptures below be sure to personalize or paraphrase them as I did in the example above.

Additional Scriptures: Luke 12:24, Psalm 37:25, Psalm 9:18, Psalm 22:26, Psalm 146:7, Amos 9:13–15

2. LIE: I don't have enough time to ___________. (Example: balance my checkbook, make a budget, find coupons, cook at home, research finance options to buy a house or rent to own, learn about or improve my credit score, pay off debt, earn extra money, learn new computer skills, or complete continuing education.) God can't help me organize my time and schedule.

TRUTH: Read the renouncing statement at the beginning of this section. I decree and declare God does want to bless me financially now. The Lord wants to prosper me in all areas, including finances, and this means even my smallest needs. I ask You Lord to reveal where I have an accidental agreement and Holy Spirit help me remove it now. I decree I will have enough time and resources to fulfill the next step toward my God-ordained destiny. My time is in Your hands. I am trusting You, Lord, to give me wisdom, guidance, and discernment as to what I am to do, what doors I am to knock on, and which doors I am to walk through. Thank You, Lord, for prospering me in everything I do according to Your will. Thank You for organizing my time and giving me the strength I need. With God's help: I do have time to balance my checkbook. I do have time to make and stick to a weekly and monthly budget. I do have time to find coupons. I do have time to research finance or lease options with God's help. I can earn extra money. God will give me ideas. I can improve my credit score. God will direct me. I can pay off debt. God will give me ideas. I can learn computer skills. I can complete continuing education. I can organize my schedule to be more efficient. Help me make the most of every opportunity and be wise in the way I act. Let all I do give You glory.

ORIGINAL SCRIPTURE: "But I trust in you, Lord. I say, "You are my God. My times are in your hands." Psalm 31:14–15

PERSONALIZED SCRIPTURE: **I trust you, Lord, and I say You are my God. My time is in Your hands.** Psalm 31:14–15

PARAPHRASED SCRIPTURE: **I trust you, Lord, and I declare You are my God who holds all of my time in Your hands.** Psalm 31:14–15

ORIGINAL SCRIPTURE: "Be wise in the way you act toward outsiders; make the most of every opportunity." Colossians 4:5

PERSONALIZED SCRIPTURE: **I will be wise in the way I act toward outsiders and make the most of every opportunity.** Colossians 4:5

PARAPHRASED SCRIPTURE: **I will be wise in my interaction with others and will make the most of every opportunity You give me Lord.** Colossians 4:5

As you read the scriptures below, be sure to personalize or paraphrase them, as I did in the example above.

Additional Scriptures: Psalm 90:12, Proverbs 10:44, Proverbs 21:5, Proverbs 28:19

3. LIE: God can't or won't bless me financially. He won't help me make money or provide for my needs or the needs of my children.

TRUTH: Read the renouncing statement at the beginning of this section. I decree and declare God DOES want to bless me financially and in other ways. He loves to bless His children. He made the world and is in charge of it, including finances and provision. He knows my needs before I even ask. I declare God loves me and will prosper me even as my soul prospers. I will trust Him with the small things and look forward to having Him bless me. I will not worry because I choose to trust You, my Heavenly Father. I will first seek You, Your kingdom, and Your righteousness. You will add everything else I need. I will honor the Lord by faithfully tithing. I am listening, and I choose to obey Your guidance. I ask Holy Spirit to reveal any area in which I have an accidental agreement. Holy Spirit, thank You for pulling down every stronghold which has set itself up against You. I ask You to illuminate the light of Your word and take every thought captive to the obedience of Christ. Thank You for closing the original door of disobedience, and I ask You, Jesus, to be set up as the permanent doorkeeper. I ask my God-ordained destiny, and my descendants' destiny, to come forth in the name of Jesus.

ORIGINAL SCRIPTURE: "Honor the Lord with your wealth, with the first fruits of all your crops," Proverbs 3:9

PERSONALIZED SCRIPTURE: **I will honor the Lord with my wealth and with the first fruits of all my crops.** Proverbs 3:9

PARAPHRASED SCRIPTURE: **I will honor the Lord with all my wealth and with the first and best of everything You give me.** Proverbs 3:9

ORIGINAL SCRIPTURE: "Therefore do not be anxious, saying, 'What shall we eat?' or 'What shall we drink?' or 'What shall we wear?' For the Gentiles seek after all these things, and your Heavenly Father knows that you need them all. But seek first the kingdom of God and his righteousness, and all these things will be added to you." Matthew 6:31–32

PERSONALIZED SCRIPTURE: **I will not be anxious about**

anything, including what I eat, drink, or wear. You, my Heavenly Father, know all I will need, so I am seeking the kingdom of God and Your righteousness first, and You will provide the rest. Matthew 6:31–32

PARAPHRASED SCRIPTURE: **Thank You, Heavenly Father, for providing everything I need even before I ask. I am seeking You and Your will first, before anything else, and you will provide my food, drink, clothing, and all other provisions. I will not worry about anything.** Matthew 6:31–32

As you read the scriptures below be sure to personalize or paraphrase them as I did in the example above.

Additional Scriptures: 1 Samuel 2:7, Proverbs 28:25, Psalm 115:14, Psalm 34:10, Malachi 3:10, 3 John 1:2, Deuteronomy 8:18, Amos 9:13–15, Psalm 67:1, Psalm 80:3, Psalm 119:135, Proverbs 19:8, Isaiah 33:2, Daniel 9:17

4. LIE: I have lost money and provision through fraud and theft. This lost or stolen money and provision can't be restored.

TRUTH: Read the renouncing statement at the beginning of this section. I decree and declare God can and will restore all money and provision lost, stolen, or hijacked by the enemy. Thank You for promising to restore everything the locust has eaten. You promise to bless seven times greater when the enemy is caught. Thank You, Lord, that You have plenty of money and provision and You intend to bless me and my family. Reveal the lie I am believing concerning a lack of finances. I repent and renounce this accidental agreement with the enemy and ask You cover me, my ancestors, and descendants' sins with Your blood. I ask You to release your dunamis power to heal my soul wounds. I trust You to direct the use of my finances and provision and will not lean on my own understanding. I will listen for instruction as to how You want them spent and invested because You make my path straight. Thank You for revealing the truth about every situation and helping me make the correct decisions. Thank You for breaking the financial patterns inherited from my ancestors. Thank You, Holy Spirit, for leading me into all truth and freedom.

ORIGINAL SCRIPTURE: "Trust in the Lord with all your heart and lean not on your own understanding; in all your ways submit to him, and he will make your paths straight." Proverbs 3:5–6

PERSONALIZED SCRIPTURE: **I will trust in the Lord with all of my heart and will not lean on my own understanding. In all my ways, I will submit to God, and He will make my paths straight.** Proverbs 3:5–6

PARAPHRASED SCRIPTURE: **I am trusting in the Lord with all of my heart, and I will not depend upon my own understanding in life. I will submit to Him in everything I do, and the Lord will make my path straight in life.** Proverbs 3:5–6

ORIGINAL SCRIPTURE: "The threshing floors will be full of grain, And the vats will overflow with the new wine and oil. Then I will make up to you for the years that the swarming locust has eaten, the creeping locust, the stripping locust, and the gnawing locust, My great army which I sent among you. "You will have plenty to eat and be satisfied and praise the name of the Lord your God, who has dealt wondrously with you." Joel 2:24–26a

PERSONALIZED SCRIPTURE: **Thank You that my threshing floors will be full of grain and my vats will overflow with new wine and oil. Thank You for making up the years the swarming locust has eaten, the creeping locust, the stripping locust, and the gnawing locust by sending Your great army to us. Thank**

You I will have plenty to eat and be satisfied and praise the name of the Lord your God who has dealt wondrously with me. Joel 2:24–26a

PARAPHRASED SCRIPTURE: **Thank You, Lord, for filling my home with plenty of food and provision, which will be more than enough. Thank You for redeeming everything the enemy has stolen from me and my family, and restoring it better than before.** Thank You for dealing miraculously with me. Joel 2:24–26a

As you read the scriptures below, be sure to personalize or paraphrase them as I did in the example above.

Additional Scriptures: Proverbs 10:22, AMP, 3 John 1:2, NKJV, Jeremiah 30:18–22, Deuteronomy 30:3, MSG

5. LIE: I don't know how to manage money or provision and I can't learn.

TRUTH: Read the renouncing statement at the beginning of this section. I decree and declare the Lord will give me wisdom, and from Your mouth comes knowledge and understanding. I will call out for Your insight as to where Your money is to be spent. I choose to listen and obey Your instructions because the fear of the Lord leads to divine knowledge. I trust You to teach me how to spend righteously in accordance with Your will for my life. Thank You for changing my heart's desires to line up with Your desires. Thank You for pulling down every stronghold in my life masquerading as truth that is really a lie from the enemy. Illuminate the light of Your word in my innermost being. Take every thought captive to the obedience of Christ. Jesus, I ask You to be the permanent gatekeeper for my life. I am excited to fulfill my God-ordained destiny. Thank You I am being set free from these hidden lies to receive the hidden treasures and blessings You have reserved for me!

ORIGINAL SCRIPTURE: "Wisdom is a shelter as money is a shelter, but the advantage of knowledge is this: wisdom preserves those who have it." Ecclesiastes 7:12

PERSONALIZED SCRIPTURE: **Thank You, Lord, for giving me wisdom, which is a strong shelter, stronger than money. Thank You for giving me knowledge and wisdom, which will preserve me.** Ecclesiastes 7:12

PARAPHRASED SCRIPTURE: **Thank You, Lord, for giving me wisdom and knowledge to help me with money. Your wisdom will cause me to preserve it.** Ecclesiastes 7:12

ORIGINAL SCRIPTURE: "Indeed, if you call out for insight and cry aloud for understanding, and if you look for it as for silver and search for it as for hidden treasure, then you will understand the fear of the Lord and find the knowledge of God. For the Lord gives wisdom; from his mouth come knowledge and understanding." Proverbs 2:3–6

PERSONALIZED SCRIPTURE: **Thank You Lord, since I have cried out for insight and understanding and searched for You more than for silver and gold, I will understand the fear of the Lord and find the knowledge I need. Thank You for giving me godly wisdom, knowledge, and understanding**. Proverbs 2:3–6

PARAPHRASED SCRIPTURE: **Thank You, Lord, for giving me insight, understanding, respect for your greatness, and all of the knowledge I need to make decisions. Thank You for giving me godly wisdom, knowledge, and understanding from your very mouth.** Proverbs 2:3–6

As you read the scriptures below, be sure to personalize or paraphrase them as I did in the example above.

Additional Scriptures: Proverbs 10:21, Proverbs 3:13–14, Proverbs 8:10–11, Proverbs 9:10, Isaiah 48:17

6. LIE: I can't possibly get out of debt. I must go into debt to succeed in life. I must borrow money my whole life. I must have debt on credit cards to live. It doesn't matter if I go into debt when I really want something.

TRUTH: Read the renouncing statement at the beginning of this section. I decree and declare You do not want me to be in debt. I ask for forgiveness and repent for believing I had to live in debt to survive. I come out of agreement with the enemy You do not have enough to provide us with money, resources, food, clothes, or any other need I or my family have. I choose to trust and align myself with You. You promise to give me the ability to produce wealth, confirming Your covenant which You swore to my ancestors. This covenant is still in effect today. You can and will provide for my needs without incurring debt. You promise a way out, so I ask You, Lord, to provide a way for my debt to be paid off, forgiven, or removed. I have renounced my accidental agreement with the enemy with regards to debt. Thank You for cleansing me and my sin with the blood of Jesus. I will listen for Your voice, guidance, and wisdom as to where to spend Your money and when to NOT spend Your money. Thank You for removing the wrong desires in my heart to spend money as a substitute for You and Your love. Take me deeper into Your truth in the Bible so I can understand how deep Your love is for me. Teach me Your ways and plans to help me prosper me in all areas of my life. Thank You for loving and caring for me. You are a good Father.

ORIGINAL SCRIPTURE: "The rich rules over the poor, And the borrower is slave to the lender." Proverbs 22:7

PERSONALIZED SCRIPTURE: **Thank You that I will not**

borrow to become a slave. Proverbs 22:7

PARAPHRASED SCRIPTURE: **The rich rules over the poor and the borrower is a slave to the lender. Thank You Lord, that I am not a slave, and You will provide a way out of debt.** Proverbs 22:7

ORIGINAL SCRIPTURE: "Let no debt remain outstanding, except the continuing debt to love one another, for whoever loves others has fulfilled the law." Romans 13:8

PERSONALIZED SCRIPTURE: **I will let no debt remain outstanding, except the continuing debt to love one another because whoever loves others has fulfilled the law.** Romans 13:8

PARAPHRASED SCRIPTURE: **I will not be in debt, and I will love others as the Lord has commanded.** Romans 13:8

ORIGINAL SCRIPTURE: "But remember the Lord your God, for it is He who gives you the ability to produce wealth, and so confirms his covenant, which he swore to your ancestors, as it is today." Deuteronomy 8:18

PERSONALIZED SCRIPTURE: **I will remember the Lord my God, for it is He who gives me the ability to produce wealth and so confirms His covenant, which He swore to my ancestors, as it is today.** Deuteronomy 8:18

PARAPHRASED SCRIPTURE: **I will remember the Lord my God, for He gives me the ability to produce wealth and prosper. This confirms His covenant, which He promised my ancestors, and it continues today to me.** Deuteronomy 8:18

As you read the scriptures below, be sure to personalize or paraphrase them as I did in the example above.

Additional Scriptures: Ezekiel 36:26, Matthew 6:24, Proverbs

28:25, Ephesians 3:20, Proverbs 21:5

7. LIE: I may have to compromise my integrity and biblical principles to get ahead.

TRUTH: Read the renouncing statement at the beginning of this section. I decree and declare the Lord is a God of truth and justice. I trust He will honor me because I will honor Him. I choose to seek God and biblical principles first in everything I do to live a righteous life. You promise the righteous will be rewarded with prosperity. Thank You that I will prosper, even as my soul prospers. I will seek the kingdom of God first, and You will take care of the rest of my needs. I will be careful to live a blameless life, and I will lead a life of integrity in my home, family, friends, and work. Thank You for promising to protect me as I live a life of integrity and honesty. I seek Your counsel before making decisions and thank You for answering. I choose to put my hope in you, Lord. Thank You for loving me unconditionally. Your word says, "Joyful are people of integrity, who follow the instructions of the Lord. He grants a treasure of common sense to the honest. He is a shield to those who walk with integrity." I trust the Lord to advance me and prosper me with favor as I am His favorite child, filled with integrity!

ORIGINAL SCRIPTURE: "Better the little that the righteous have than the wealth of many wicked; for the power of the wicked will be broken, but the LORD upholds the righteous." Psalm 37:16–17

PERSONALIZED SCRIPTURE: **It's better to have little wealth that I, being righteous through Christ have, than the wealth of many wicked; the power of the wicked will be broken, but the Lord upholds me because I am righteous. Psalm 37:16-17**

PARAPHRASED SCRIPTURE: **It's better for me to have little wealth and remain righteous than have the wealth of the wicked; The Lord will break the power of the wicked, but the Lord will advocate and defend me because I am righteous as I belong to Him. Psalm 37:16–17**

ORIGINAL SCRIPTURE: "Adversity pursues sinners, But the righteous will be rewarded with prosperity." Proverbs 13:21

PERSONALIZED SCRIPTURE: **I am righteous through Christ, so I will be rewarded with prosperity and adversity will not follow me.** Proverbs 13:21

PARAPHRASED SCRIPTURE: **I am righteous and justified as a child of Christ, so I will be rewarded with prosperity and adversity will not follow me.** Proverbs 13:21

ORIGINAL SCRIPTURE: "Better a little with righteousness than much gain with injustice." Proverbs 16:8

PERSONALIZED SCRIPTURE: **I will be righteousness through Christ and will not gain with injustice.** Proverbs 16:8

PARAPHRASED SCRIPTURE: **I'm better off with a little righteousness than much wealth obtained through injustice.** Proverbs 16:8

As you read the scriptures below, be sure to personalize or paraphrase them as I did in the example above.

Additional Scriptures: Matthew 6:24, Exodus 20:15, Proverbs 13:11, Luke 3:14, Ephesians 4:28, Proverbs 21:17, Proverbs 28:6, Proverbs 13:11

8. LIE: God doesn't notice or care if I tithe. God won't withhold blessings if

I don't tithe.

TRUTH: Read the renouncing statement at the beginning of this section. Thank You Lord for being very clear that tithing brings blessings. I decree I will tithe on everything I earn, receive, or have because it is all a gift from You. I repent for not tithing in the past and ask for forgiveness. I ask the curse be removed from me, my ancestors, and my descendants from stealing the tithes from You. I decree I will tithe and thank You for this opportunity to honor You. Thank You, Father, for teaching me how to trust You. Help me understand Your love and provision has no limit when I am in alignment with Your will. Holy Spirit, prompt me to give Your money where You desire. Adjust my heart's desires to be in sync with Your thoughts. You say, "blessed is the man who fears the Lord, who finds great delight in His commands. Wealth and riches are in His house." I love You, and I commit to tithe fully.

ORIGINAL SCRIPTURE: "Will a mere mortal rob God? Yet you rob me. 'But you ask, "How are we robbing you?" 'In tithes and offerings. You are under a curse, your whole nation, because you are robbing me.'" Malachi 3:8–9

PERSONALIZED SCRIPTURE: **Thank You, Lord, that I will properly tithe and not rob. Thank You that I will not be under a curse nor will my family or nation.** Malachi 3:8–9

PARAPHRASED SCRIPTURE: **I will not rob God by withholding tithes and offerings. It brings a curse on me, my family and nation. In my tithe and offerings I will honor You, because everything I have belongs to You.** Malachi 3:8–9

ORIGINAL SCRIPTURE: "'Bring the whole tithe into the storehouse, that there may be food in my house. Test me in this,' says the LORD Almighty, 'and see if I will not throw open the floodgates of heaven and pour out so much blessing that there will not be room enough to store it.'" Malachi 3:10–11a, 12

PERSONALIZED SCRIPTURE: **Because I bring my whole tithe into the church, You have opened up the windows of Heaven and have poured more blessings on me than I can even contain. You have rebuked the devourer of my money and blessings. People see me and call me blessed; both me and my land are a delight.** Malachi 3:10–11a, 12

PARAPHRASED SCRIPTURE: **Thank You for opening the windows of heaven and pouring out so many blessings on me I cannot count them because I brought my whole tithe into the church. Thank You for rebuking the enemy from stealing my money and blessings. People see me and call me and my land blessed by the Lord.** Malachi 3:10–11a, 12

ORIGINAL SCRIPTURE: "Blessed is the man who fears the Lord, who finds great delight in his commands. Wealth and riches are in his house." Psalm 112:1–3 NIV

PERSONALIZED SCRIPTURE: **I fear you, Lord, and delight in Your commands, so wealth and riches are in my home.** Psalm 112:1–3

PARAPHRASED SCRIPTURE: **I greatly respect and revere you Lord, and I delight in following Your commands in the Bible. Thank You that wealth and riches are in my household.** Psalm 112:1–3

As you read the scriptures below, be sure to personalize or paraphrase them as I did in the example above.

Additional Scriptures: Ecclesiastes 5:10, 1 Samuel 3:10, NKJV, Luke 11:42, Proverbs 3:9–10, 2 Corinthians 9:7

9. LIE: God doesn't notice or care if I don't give to others. God doesn't expect me to help other people I don't even know.

TRUTH: Read the renouncing statement at the beginning of this section. Your word says to love others as You love yourself. I decree and declare I choose to give generously, knowing You, Father, have more than enough for me and my family. I will not make an agreement with the enemy that You do not have enough provision. I choose to agree with Your word You will provide for all of my needs according to Your riches in glory by Christ Jesus. I will show godly compassion and be generous. Thank You, Holy Spirit, for prompting my heart to be kind and charitable. Thank You I am blessed by You to be a blessing to others. I choose to live a lifestyle displaying compassion and love for others as Christ demonstrated.

ORIGINAL SCRIPTURE: "Evil men borrow, but do not repay their debt, but the godly show compassion and are generous." Psalm 37:21, NET

PERSONALIZED SCRIPTURE: **I am godly, so I will show compassion, be generous and not borrow money, putting me in debt.** Psalm 37:21

PARAPHRASED SCRIPTURE: **I am a godly person who follows the Lord's commands, so I will not go into debt. I will show compassion on people in need and be generous because everything really belongs to You.** Psalm 37:21

ORIGINAL SCRIPTURE: "If anyone is poor among your fellow Israelites in any of the towns of the land the LORD your God is giving you, do not be hardhearted or tightfisted toward them." Deuteronomy 15:7

PERSONALIZED SCRIPTURE: **I will be kindhearted and**

generous in any towns where it is needed. Deuteronomy 15:7

PARAPHRASED SCRIPTURE: **Thank You for sharing Your land with me, Lord, and I will be generous and kindhearted to my fellow man.** Deuteronomy 15:7

ORIGINAL SCRIPTURE: "Jesus answered, 'If you want to be perfect, go, sell your possessions and give to the poor, and you will have treasure in heaven. Then come, follow me.'" Matthew 19:21

PERSONALIZED SCRIPTURE: **Since I am a follower of Jesus, I will sell my possessions as the Lord directs to give to the poor. I look forward to my treasure in Heaven.** Matthew 19:21

PARAPHRASED SCRIPTURE: **As a disciple of Jesus, I will sell my possessions as the Lord directs to help the poor, because I know my real treasure is in Heaven.** Matthew 19:21

As you read the scriptures below, be sure to personalize or paraphrase them as I did in the example above.

Additional Scriptures: Acts 4:34, Psalm 112:5, Matthew 6:21, Exodus 22:25

10. LIE: God isn't interested in my career or work. God can't help me advance my career. I don't have time to finish my work. God doesn't care if I'm sloppy in my work. God isn't interested in my work details.

TRUTH: Read the renouncing statement at the beginning of this section. I decree and declare You care about every detail in my life, including my career. I declare God is in charge of my life, job, and everything affecting me. First, I will ask You about every concern about my life, job, career moves, relationships, education, and training. I will trust You to organize my calendar and prioritize my day. I will listen and obey Your prompts without running ahead. I know You will speak clearly to direct my path. You say the steps of a good man are ordered by the Lord. I will trust You with all my heart and lean not on my own understanding, but in all my ways acknowledge You. I will seek Your advice about every detail of Your God-ordained plan. Thank You for blessing the work of my hands. Thank You for sending Your angels before me and as my rear guard to protect and guide me in all matters, great and small.

ORIGINAL SCRIPTURE: "Trust in the Lord with all your heart and lean not on your own understanding; in all your ways submit to him, and he will make your paths straight." Proverbs 3:5–6

PERSONALIZED SCRIPTURE: **I trust in You Lord with all my heart and I don't lean on my own understanding. I submit all my ways to You, and You make my paths straight.** Proverbs 3:5–6

PARAPHRASED SCRIPTURE: **Thank You, Lord, for helping me to trust You with all of my heart. Even when it doesn't look like you're paying attention to my situation, help me to let go of trying to figure things out. I will submit my ways to You as we walk together, hand-in-hand, on pleasant paths.** Proverbs 3:5–6

ORIGINAL SCRIPTURE: "The Lord will open the heavens, the storehouse of his bounty, to send rain on your land in season and to bless all the work of your hands. You will lend to many nations but will borrow from none." Deuteronomy 28:12

PERSONALIZED SCRIPTURE: **Thank You, Lord, for opening the heavens, Your storehouse, for sending rain on the land and blessing the works of my hands. I will lend to many nations, but I will not borrow from any.** Deuteronomy 28:12

PARAPHRASED SCRIPTURE: **Thank You for sending a deluge of heavenly blessings my way. Thank You for sending rain at**

the perfect time to make my crops flourish and provide for my needs. Thank You for blessing the works of my hands so abundantly that I will have the finances to help others instead of being the one who needs financial help. Deuteronomy 28:12

As you read the scriptures below, be sure to personalize or paraphrase them as I did in the example above.

Additional Scriptures: Matthew 7:7, Mark 11:24, 2 Corinthians 5:7, Psalm 115:11–12

Relational Accidental Agreements

Take a moment of silence and ask the Lord to download the names of people you have unforgiveness towards. Ask for forgiveness and repent to remove any unforgiveness or bitterness. See *Forgiveness* section prayer.

Next, renounce your specific agreement (the lie) with the enemy listed below. First, speak the renouncing statement followed by the Truth Statement." Read the personalized scriptures out loud (dunamis power).

Read the renouncing statement before all Truth Statements.

Renouncing Statement: "Lord, on behalf of me, my ancestors, and my descendants, I ask for forgiveness and repent and renounce my agreements with the enemy with regards to lie number _______. I submit my body, soul, and spirit to the Lord and ask You to align me with Your will. Cleanse my sin and cover me with the blood of Jesus. Fill my soul wounds with Your resurrection power and the shekinah glory light of Jesus in my innermost being.

I ask You to silence the enemy. Thank You the power and legal rights of the enemy are broken. (Luke 10:19) I ask to be restored in full covenant with You. As I am in covenant with You, I enjoy the benefits and blessings of being Your royal child. Lord, You are the sovereign judge in the courts of heaven and also the judge on earth. Lord, I ask You to rule in my favor in the courts of heaven and ask You to release the angels to enforce this judgment.

I ask Your will be done on earth as it is in heaven. You have given me the legal right to trample on the enemy (Psalm 91). I reclaim everything the enemy has stolen from me, my family, and all that concerns me. Thank you for restoring the generational blessings and liberating our DNA in alignment with Your original plan for our lives, which is our godly inheritance. I ask that our God-ordained blessings come forth in the name of Jesus. I ask You to activate our DNA correction and blessings. These blessings include wisdom, knowledge, understanding, discernment, gifts, talents, and all other godly generational blessings. Lord, I ask specifically for You to bless me with the talents of ______________________. (Fill in the blank with your God aligned desires. Examples: music, languages, artistic ability, dance, writing, or business.)

1. LIE: I don't have enough time to ____________________ (relationships).

> TRUTH: Read the renouncing statement at the beginning of this section. I decree and declare this is the day You have made, so I will be glad and rejoice in it. Father God, I ask You to be in charge of my day, and I surrender my calendar to You. Thank You for organizing my time, allowing me to follow Your agenda. The steps of a good man are ordered by the Lord. Thank You for revealing hidden problems in relationships and correcting my perspective. Reveal the healthy relationships and end relationships not part of my God-ordained destiny. I will guard my heart with all diligence because out of it flows the issues of life. Align my heart with Your word. I choose to listen and obey Your instructions. The fear of the Lord leads to divine knowledge. Thank You for arranging my time to pursue healthy relationships.

ORIGINAL SCRIPTURE: "This is the day the LORD has made. We will rejoice and be glad in it." Psalm 118:24 NLT

PERSONALIZED SCRIPTURE: **Thank You Lord for today, the day You have made. I will rejoice and be glad today.** Psalm 118:24

PARAPHRASED SCRIPTURE: **Lord, You are the giver of life, and every day is a gift from Your hand. I acknowledge You gave me today as a gift, and regardless of what happens, I will have a grateful attitude today.** Psalm 118:24

ORIGINAL SCRIPTURE: "Walk with the wise and become wise, for a companion of fools suffers harm." Proverbs 13:20

PERSONALIZED SCRIPTURE: **Lord, I choose to walk with wise people and become wise. Having fools as companions brings me harm, so I will walk with wise people.** Proverbs 13:20

PARAPHRASED SCRIPTURE: **Lord, because I value wisdom, I choose to develop friendships with people who are wise in Your eyes. I know being influenced by people who do not value Your ways produces bad fruit. Thank You for bringing me wise friendships.** Proverbs 13:20

As you read the scriptures below, be sure to personalize or paraphrase them as I did in the example above.

Additional Scriptures: Proverbs 18:24, 1 Corinthians 15:33, ASV, Ecclesiastes 3:1–8

2. Why do I keep dating or marrying the same type of guy, who doesn't care and love me the way I deserve to be loved? Am I stupid? What's wrong with me?

TRUTH: Read the renouncing statement above. I declare and decree the Lord is my source of hope. The Lord will fill me completely with His joy and shalom peace because I trust in him. I will overflow with confident hope through the power of the Holy Spirit. I will not be afraid or discouraged, for the Lord will personally go ahead of me to help me with relationships. He will be with me. He will neither fail me or abandon me. Many plans are in my mind and imagination about how my life will turn out, but the Lord's divine plan for my life will be the best plan which will delight my heart! It will succeed! I will not fear the future. I will let my character and personality be free from the love of money including: greed, avarice, lust, and cravings for earthly possessions. I will be satisfied with my present circumstances and with what I have. God, Himself, has said, He will not in any way fail me, give me up, or leave me without support. He will not, he will not, he will not, in any way, leave me helpless, forsake me, or let me down. He will not let go of me! He promises! Thank You, Lord, for guiding and training me in the path I should follow. Thank You for providing job training, child rearing help, godly mentors, and a church family. You know my needs before I ask. Thank You for Your divine intervention. Jesus, Your name is all powerful!

ORIGINAL SCRIPTURE: "Do not be afraid or discouraged, for the Lord will personally go ahead of you. He will be with you; he will neither fail you nor abandon you." Deuteronomy 31:8 NLT

PERSONALIZED SCRIPTURE: **I will not be afraid or discouraged, for the Lord will personally go ahead of me. He will be with me; he will neither fail me nor abandon me. Deuteronomy 31:8** NLT

PARAPHRASED SCRIPTURE: **I will not be afraid or discouraged because the Lord will personally go ahead of me in life. He will be with me throughout life. He will neither fail nor abandon me in any circumstances.** Deuteronomy 31:8 NL)

ORIGINAL SCRIPTURE: "Let your character *or* moral disposition be free from love of money [including greed, avarice, lust, and craving for earthly possessions] and be satisfied with your present [circumstances and with what you have]; for He [God] Himself has said, I will not in any way fail you *nor* give you up *nor* leave you without support. [I will] not, I will] not, [I will] not in any degree leave you helpless *nor* forsake *nor* let [you] down nor relax My hold on you! Assuredly not!" Hebrews 13:5–6 AMPC

PERSONALIZED SCRIPTURE: **I will let my character or moral disposition be free from the love of money, including greed, avarice, lust, and cravings for earthly possessions. I will be satisfied with my present circumstances and with what I have. God Himself, has said, He will not in any way fail me nor give me up nor leave me without support. He will not, he will not, he will not, in any degree, leave me helpless nor forsake nor let me down nor relax His hold on me! Assuredly not!** Hebrews 13:5–6 AMPC

PARAPHRASED SCRIPTURE: **I will let my character and personality be free from the love of money, including greed, avarice, lust, and cravings for earthly possessions. I will be satisfied with my present circumstances and with what I have. God Himself, has said, He will not in any way fail me, give me up, or leave me without support. He will not, he will not, he will not, in any way leave me helpless, forsake me, or let me down. He will not let go of me! He promises!** Hebrews 13:5–6 AMPC

ORIGINAL SCRIPTURE: "Many plans are in a man's mind, but it is the Lord's purpose for him that will stand." Proverbs 19:21 AMPC

PERSONALIZED SCRIPTURE: **Many plans are in my mind, but the Lord's purpose for me will stand.** Proverbs 19:21 AMPC

PARAPHRASED SCRIPTURE: **Many plans are in my mind about how my life will turn out, but the Lord's divine plan for my life will prevail.** Proverbs 19:21 AMPC

ORIGINAL SCRIPTURE: "I pray that God, the source of hope, will fill you completely with joy and peace because you trust in him. Then you will overflow with confident hope through the power of the Holy Spirit." Romans 15:13 NLT

PERSONALIZED SCRIPTURE: **I pray that God, the source of my hope, will fill me completely with joy and peace because I trust Him. I will overflow with confident hope through the power of the Holy Spirit.** Romans 15:13 NLT

PARAPHRASED SCRIPTURE: **I pray that God, the source of all my hope, will fill me completely with His joy and peace. I trust Him. I am thankful I will overflow with confident hope of my future through the power of the Holy Spirit.** Romans 15:13 NLT

3. LIE: I enjoy the excitement of romance novels, reality shows, pornography, and R-rated movies with sex and violence. There's nothing wrong with masturbation. It helps me relax and gives me pleasure.

TRUTH: Read the renouncing statement above. I decree and declare I will not try to escape from reality by living in a fantasy world. I choose to have You cleanse my mind. I choose to believe You have a wonderful life planned for me. "For I know the plans I have for you," declares the Lord, "plans to prosper you and not to harm you, plans to give you hope and a future." I will delight myself in the Lord, and You will give me the desires of my heart. I surrender my eyes, ears, thoughts, will, emotions, heart, and control to You Lord. I command my body, soul, and spirit to submit to the Holy Spirit. I exchange my escape mechanisms, hijacking my future, for greater understanding of You and Your perspective on sex. You made man and woman to be together, so intimacy is part of Your plan for marriage. I declare I will seek You with all my heart, soul, mind, and strength. Thank You for providing freedom for healthy relationships to live and love, completing my God-ordained destiny.

ORIGINAL SCRIPTURE: "'I have the right to do anything,' you say but not everything is beneficial. 'I have the right to do anything' but not everything is constructive." I Corinthians 10:23

PERSONALIZED SCRIPTURE: **Thank You, Lord, for helping me realize even though I have the right to do anything, not everything is beneficial. Though I have the freedom to do anything, not everything is constructive for me.** I Corinthians 10:23

PARAPHRASED SCRIPTURE: **Lord, thank You for giving me the freedom to choose, but help me to choose wisely, because many things are not beneficial for me. Give me godly wisdom in everything I do and everywhere I go.** I Corinthians 10:23

ORIGINAL SCRIPTURE: "For out of the heart come evil thoughts, murder, adultery, sexual immorality, theft, false testimony, and slander." Matthew 15:19

PERSONALIZED SCRIPTURE: Thank You, Lord, that I will trust You and nothing else. **Thank You, Lord, for helping me not to trust my heart apart from You; the heart can be filled with evil thoughts—murder, adultery, sexual immorality, theft, false testimony, and slander.** Matthew 15:19

PARAPHRASED SCRIPTURE: Lord, I trust You and will not rely

on my own thinking or feelings. **Thank You, Lord, for helping me not to be led by what's in my heart—murder, adultery, sexual immorality, theft, false testimony, and slander. Thank You for promising to give me a new heart. Help me always to be led by You into doing what is right in Your eyes.** Matthew 15:19

As you read the scriptures below, be sure to personalize or paraphrase them as I did in the example above.,

I Peter 2:16, Proverbs 4:23, I Peter 1:14–16, Psalm 51:10, Job 31:1, AMPC, Matthew 5:8, Titus 1:15

4. LIE: The media says I have to be prettier, thinner, and sexier than I am in order to be more attractive and lovable to men.

TRUTH: Read the renouncing statement at the beginning of this section. I decree and declare this is a big, fat lie from the enemy, which I renounce. I choose to believe what Your word says about me and not believe the media. I will not allow underwear and swimsuit models to determine whether I am lovable. I am a daughter of the King of Kings. I am royalty with special privileges reserved for His children. I choose to believe my Heavenly Father when He declares over me, as I am made in His image. This means I am perfect in His eyes. I am beautiful inside and out. Thank You for valuing inward beauty and a gentle, quiet spirit. Gentleness does not mean weakness. It means humility and thankfulness towards God and conveying a polite, restrained behavior towards others. Thank You for molding me into a gentle, godly woman. You adore me and want to bless me. Thank You for wanting to prosper me even as my soul prospers. You want the best for me which is to help me, not condemn me. I am listening to Your instructions to adjust my heart and values. Thank You I am lovable the way I am.

ORIGINAL SCRIPTURE: "Your beauty should not come from

outward adornment, such as elaborate hairstyles and the wearing of gold, jewelry, or fine clothes. Rather, it should be that of your inner self, the unfading beauty of a gentle and quiet spirit, which is of great worth in God's sight." I Peter 3:3–4

PERSONALIZED SCRIPTURE: **Lord, I acknowledge my beauty should not come from outward adornment such as hairstyles, jewelry, and clothes. Thank You, Lord, for helping me to develop my inner self, the unfading beauty of a gentle and quiet spirit which has great value in Your eyes.** I Peter 3:3–4

PARAPHRASED SCRIPTURE: **Lord, it's so easy to get caught up in what society tells me is beautiful. Thank You for helping set me free from the trap of believing beauty only comes with designer clothes, fancy jewelry, makeup, and the latest hairstyle. Thank You for adjusting my attitude and beliefs to believe and understand the truth—a godly inner self and a gentle and quiet spirit are what are valuable. Thank You Lord for helping me develop my inner beauty just as You have ordained.** I Peter 3:3–4

ORIGINAL SCRIPTURE: "But the LORD said to Samuel, 'Do not consider his appearance or his height, for I have rejected him. The LORD does not look at the things people look at. People look at the outward appearance, but the LORD looks at the heart.'" I Samuel 16:7

PERSONALIZED SCRIPTURE: **Thank You, Lord, for helping me not judge people based on their appearance, but accept them as You do. Help me to set aside outward appearance and look at a person's heart.** I Samuel 16:7

PARAPHRASED SCRIPTURE: **Thank You, Lord, for showing me how to evaluate people by Your standard—a standard of love. Thank You I do not judge by outward appearances, nor do**

I judge, because this is Your job. I choose to look at their heart and love them as You love. I Samuel 16:7

As you read the scriptures below, be sure to personalize or paraphrase them as I did in the example above.

Additional Scriptures: Proverbs 31:30, John 7:24, Genesis 1:31a, Psalm 139:14, Ecclesiastes 3:11a, Ephesians 2:10

5. LIE: Waiting to have sex until I get married is totally unnecessary and outdated. There's no harm in not waiting. Everyone does it, and the guys expect it. We love each other and will probably get married. We are already engaged. It doesn't matter if I want to have sex for one night and "give him or her my love."

TRUTH: Read the renouncing statement at the beginning of this section. I decree and declare I will not follow what others do, having sex with partners before marriage. I will value myself and my body as special gift from the Lord. I will serve You Lord with all my heart, soul, mind, and strength. I will seek Your will for my life before making major decisions such as living together. This is against Your counsel in the Bible. Your commandments are for my good, not to harm me. I will not follow my feelings or emotions, but will trust in the Lord with all my heart and not depend on my own understanding. Thank You for protecting me, as You want the best for me. Thank You for speaking to my heart and making my path straight. I declare I will not misplace my love, lust, or look for love in the wrong places, which is a manifestation of a hole in my heart. If I have had sex or sexual touching outside of marriage, I ask for forgiveness for defiling my body. I ask You to cleanse me with the blood of Jesus Christ. You promise to heal my broken heart and satisfy my deepest longings. Thank You for protecting me by giving me these biblical decrees.

Note: The truth is when you have sex with someone, you receive everything they have inside of them—spiritually, physically, mentally, or emotionally—PLUS all their other sexual partners. Yikes! That's a lot of germs, spirits, and baggage!

ORIGINAL SCRIPTURE: "Who among you is wise and understanding? Let him show by his noble conduct that his actions are done humbly and wisely." James 3:13 ISV

PERSONALIZED SCRIPTURE: **Lord, thank You that I am becoming wise and have understanding of You and Your ways because You are causing me to conduct myself nobly. Thank You for making my actions humble and wise.** James 3:13

PARAPHRASED SCRIPTURE: **Lord, it's my earnest desire to be wise and have great understanding of You and Your Word. Thank You for helping me conduct myself in a manner which is noble, humble, and wise.** James 3:13

ORIGINAL SCRIPTURE: "But since sexual immorality is occurring, each man should have sexual relations with his own wife, and each woman with her own husband." I Corinthians 7:2

PERSONALIZED SCRIPTURE: **Thank You Lord for helping me flee sexual immorality. I acknowledge men and women should only have sexual relations with their own spouse.** I Corinthians 7:2

PARAPHRASED SCRIPTURE: **Lord, sexual immorality is rampant in our culture and sometimes it's a temptation to me. Thank You for helping me only desire my spouse. I surrender my thoughts, will, emotions, body, and spirit to You.** I Corinthians 7:2

ORIGINAL SCRIPTURE: "But whoever looks intently into the perfect law that gives freedom, and continues in it, not forgetting what they have heard, but doing it, they will be blessed in what they do." James 1:25

PERSONALIZED SCRIPTURE: **Thank You Lord for blessing me because I am looking intently at and following Your perfect law, which brings me freedom and blessings. Help me continue to walk in freedom and not forget what I have heard. I want to receive all of Your blessings.** James 1:25

PARAPHRASED SCRIPTURE: **Thank You, Lord, for helping me study Your perfect teachings which set me free. Help me not forget what I have learned but to put it into practice. Thank You for helping me because I want the blessing You give to those who follow You and Your teachings.** James 1:25

ORIGINAL SCRIPTURE: "'I have the right to do anything,' you say but not everything is beneficial. 'I have the right to do anything' but not everything is constructive." I Corinthians 10:23

PERSONALIZED SCRIPTURE: **Thank You, Lord, for helping me realize even though I have the right to do anything, not everything is beneficial. Even though I have the right to do anything, not everything is constructive and profitable for me.** I Corinthians 10:23

PARAPHRASED SCRIPTURE: **Lord, thank You for giving me the freedom to choose and for helping me to choose wisely due to Your supernatural discernment. Many things I could do are not beneficial or productive for me. Thank You for helping me to always choose wisely and knowledgeably.** I Corinthians 10:23

As you read the scriptures below, be sure to personalize or paraphrase them as I did in the example above.

Additional Scriptures: 1 Corinthians 6:18, 1 Peter 2:16, Luke

10:27, Romans 6:6, Isaiah 61:1, 1 Peter 2:16, Ephesians 5:3, 1 Corinthians 7:2, Ephesians 6:11–12, Hebrews 13:4

6. LIE: As a divorced or widowed person, the Bible says Jesus is my husband and He cares for widows and orphans. But I don't get it—I'm not seeing blessings, and I feel abandoned by Jesus, my church, and even my church friends. This is too hard so there must be something wrong.

TRUTH: Read the renouncing statement at the beginning of this section. I decree and declare the Lord is my husband. You love me, and I choose to trust You. Thank You for protecting me from harmful situations or people. You know my future and what relationships are healthy for me. As my husband, I will count on You to understand my deepest desires, to give me love, wisdom, revelation, discernment, guidance, and fill my mouth and life with good things. This renews my youth like the eagle's. I choose not to look at the negative events but to align with Your word which speaks life. You promise to work all things out for good, so I choose to view past events positively. In Isaiah 55:8–9, You say, **"Your thoughts are not my thoughts, nor are your ways my ways. Just as the heavens are higher than the earth, My ways are higher than your ways, and My thoughts than your thoughts."** Teach me Your ways.

Thank You for directing me to a church that welcomes divorced women, children, and widows. Thank You for giving me God-ordained mentors, prayer partners, and friends. Thank You for putting my name on their hearts to intercede. I will faithfully serve in the church You have for me. I will look to You for my blessings: spiritually, relationally, physically, emotionally, mentally, financially, and willfully. Thank You for promising to prosper me even as my soul is prospering and healing. I choose to believe Your promises because You never lie. You love me no matter what.

You're for me and not against me. You promise never to forsake me or betray me. Thank You for giving us good promises, Heavenly Father, who can and will keep His Word.

ORIGINAL SCRIPTURE: "You, Lord, know every one of my deepest desires, and my noisy groans are no secret to you." Psalm 38:9 CEV

PERSONALIZED SCRIPTURE: **Thank You, Lord, for knowing all my deepest desires as well as my painful groans. I have no secrets from You.** Psalm 38:9

PARAPHRASED SCRIPTURE: **Lord, You know all my deepest desires, the good ones and the bad ones. You know everything about me and You still love me unconditionally. When I am in distress and I sigh or groan, You are always listening. You are attentive to all my emotional needs.** Psalm 38:9

ORIGINAL SCRIPTURE: "For I am convinced that neither death, nor life, nor angels, nor principalities, nor things present, nor things to come, nor powers, nor height, nor depth, nor any other created thing, will be able to separate us from the love of God, which is in Christ Jesus our Lord." Romans 8:38–39

PERSONALIZED SCRIPTURE: **Thank You that neither death, nor life, nor angels, nor principalities, nor things present, nor things to come, nor powers, nor height, nor depth, nor any other created thing, will be able to separate me from Your love which is in Christ Jesus.** Romans 8:38–39,

PARAPHRASED SCRIPTURE: **Lord, You promise nothing in the world can separate me from Your love. Whether I encounter: death, life, angels, principalities, things present, things to come, unclean powers, height, depth, or any other created thing—none of these can separate Your love from me! Yay God!** Romans 8:38–39

ORIGINAL SCRIPTURE: "Since we live by the Spirit, let us keep in step with the Spirit." Galatians 5:25

PERSONALIZED SCRIPTURE: **Thank You for helping me stay in step with the Holy Spirit since I am filled with Your Spirit.** Galatians 5:25

PARAPHRASED SCRIPTURE: **Lord, thank You for sending the Holy Spirit to live inside of me; guiding me with Your divine judgment.** Galatians 5:25

ORIGINAL SCRIPTURE: "He fills my life with good things. My youth is renewed like the eagle's!" Psalm 103:5 NLT

PERSONALIZED SCRIPTURE: **Thank You for filling my life with good things and renewing my youth like the eagle's.** Psalm 103:5

PARAPHRASED SCRIPTURE: **Thank You, Lord, for filling my life with good things from Your kingdom. Even as I age, You will preserve my youth. You will give me the same characteristics as an eagle—strong, overcoming, and soaring above all my problems.** Psalm 103:5

As you read the scriptures below, be sure to personalize or paraphrase them as I did in the example above.

Additional Scriptures: Psalm 16:11, KJV, Numbers 23:19, Isaiah 54:10, Matthew 10:30, 1 Corinthians 6:13, Ephesians 5:3–7.

7.LIE: My marriage is beyond repair. My spouse won't change. He or she will never be as religious as I am. My marriage will be disappointing at best. If my spouse would change, everything would be okay.

TRUTH: Read the renouncing statement at the beginning of this section. I decree and declare I ask the Lord to take charge of my marriage. I surrender my agenda, opinions, and feelings about my spouse and marriage to You. Thank You for refining me, changing my heart, and healing my soul to align with Your will for my life. The word says, "For if you forgive other people when they sin against you, your Heavenly Father will also forgive you. But if you do not forgive others their sins, your Father will not forgive your sins." I ask for forgiveness and repent for harboring anger, bitterness, and resentment. Teach me to love the way You love. Give me godly, spiritual eyes to see my spouse the way You view them. **Thank You, Lord, for helping me to be kind, tenderhearted and forgiving, just as God forgave me**. Thank You for working everything out for my good. Lord, I choose to trust my marriage and future to You. I ask You to fulfill our God-ordained destinies.

ORIGINAL SCRIPTURE: "For if you forgive other people when they sin against you, your Heavenly Father will also forgive you. But if you do not forgive others their sins, your Father will not forgive your sins." Matthew 6:14–15

PERSONALIZED SCRIPTURE: **Lord, Your word says if I forgive other people when they sin against me, my Heavenly Father will also forgive me. I choose to forgive others of their sins.** Matthew 6:14–15

PARAPHRAZED SCRIPTURE: **Lord, I choose to forgive everyone I have held unforgiveness, bitterness, anger, resentment, rage, retaliation, accusation, hatred, blaming, a critical spirit, or judgment toward. Your word says if I don't forgive people who sin against me, my sins won't be forgiven, and I don't want anything to separate me from You, Your love and protection. Sometimes, I really don't want to forgive. Sometimes, I want to forgive, and I pray to release the person who hurt me, but I'm still mad. Thank**

You for teaching me what true forgiveness is and Your perspective on the person. Regardless of how I feel, I choose to forgive because You already forgave me. Matthew 6:14–15

ORIGINAL SCRIPTURE: "Be kind to one another, tenderhearted, forgiving one another, as God in Christ forgave you." Ephesians 4:32 ESV

PERSONALIZED SCRIPTURE: **Thank You, Lord, for helping me to be kind, tenderhearted, and forgiving, just like God forgave me.** Ephesians 4:32

PARAPHRAZED SCRIPTURE: **Lord, I make a choice right now to be kind and tenderhearted to everyone—even those who hurt or offended me. I choose to forgive because Christ forgave me so who am I to withhold forgiveness?** Ephesians 4:32

As you read the scriptures below, be sure to personalize or paraphrase as I did in the example above.

Additional Scriptures: Colossians 3:13, Luke 6:37b, Mark 11:25, ESV, Ephesians 5:21–28, Proverbs 12:4, Proverbs 20:6–7, Proverbs 31:10, Matthew 19:6

8. LIE: My family is so messed up, God can't straighten them out. He can't help my children learn or grow, so I have to take charge. I have to fix my family, or they won't get to heaven. My children and family run from God. I don't know how He will get their attention to save them. I'm too far away physically and emotionally to be able to fix, help, or save my family.

TRUTH: Read the renouncing statement at the beginning of this section. I decree and declare Lord, You are in charge of my family, and I don't have to be responsible for fixing them. I surrender my perceived control over them and their lives. I entrust their care to

You. You promise to complete the good work You have begun and will work everything out for our good. I surrender myself, my family, my agenda, and imagination to You and align with Your purpose and plan for my family's lives. Thank You, Father, for hearing my prayers for my family to be saved, to serve You, to fulfill their God-ordained destinies, and for us to share heaven together. You created them, You love them, and You want the best for them. I will not worry, but I choose to trust You. Isaiah 49:25b says, "I will contend with those that contend with you and your children I will save." I will continue to fervently pray but trust You for the outcome. Thank You that my children will be taught by the Lord and great will be their peace.

ORIGINAL SCRIPTURE: "All your children will be taught by the LORD, and great will be their peace." Isaiah 54:13 This includes spiritual children.

PERSONALIZED SCRIPTURE: **Thank You Lord that all my children will be taught by You and their peace will be great.** Isaiah 54:13

PARAPHRAZED SCRIPTURE: **Lord, being a parent is a challenging job, and I thank You for Your help. I am grateful for Your promises that you will teach my children and spiritual children, and they will experience great peace. The next time I'm worried, I will remember Your promise to me.** Isaiah 54:13

ORIGINAL SCRIPTURE: "Therefore I tell you, whatever you ask for in prayer, believe that you have received it, and it will be yours." Mark 11:24

PERSONALIZED SCRIPTURE: **Thank You, Lord, for promising whatever I ask for in prayer, in alignment with Your will, if I believe, I have received it and it will be mine.** Mark 11:24

PARAPHRAZED SCRIPTURE: **Thank You, Lord, for increasing**

my faith. I want to take You up on Your amazing promise that if I have faith, whatever I have asked for in prayer will be mine. Thank You for aligning my requests with Your will on earth as it is in heaven. Mark 11:24

ORIGINAL SCRIPTURE: "'As for me, this is my covenant with them,' says the LORD. 'My Spirit, who is on you, will not depart from you, and my words that I have put in your mouth will always be on your lips, on the lips of your children, and on the lips of their descendants from this time on and forever,' says the LORD." Isaiah 59:21

PERSONALIZED SCRIPTURE: **Thank You, Lord, for making a covenant with me that Your Spirit will not depart from me and the words You have given me will always be on my lips, my children's lips, and the lips of my descendants.** Isaiah 59:21

PARAPHRAZED SCRIPTURE: **Thank You for being a Covenant God, and for the covenant You made with me. You have given me Your Holy Spirit who will always be with me. You have put Your words in my mouth and promised they will never depart from me, my children and my descendants. Thank You for Your amazing goodness to me.** Isaiah 59:21

As you read the scriptures below, be sure to personalize or paraphrase them as I did in the example above.

Additional Scriptures: Colossians 2:15, Colossians 1:13, NLT, Isaiah 49:25

9. LIE: My family or extended family is too messed up to fix. They suffer from stress, anxiety, disorders, depression, and other mental health issues. They are addicted to alcohol, pills, drugs, or pornography, etc. I don't know how this unhealthy cycle will get broken. I don't know if they will ever get free from bondage and find God.

TRUTH: Read the renouncing statement at the beginning of this section. I decree and declare You are a God of Truth. You say, "You shall know the truth, and the truth shall set you free." Thank You, Lord, for illuminating the light of Your word and taking every thought captive to the obedience of Christ. Thank You for closing the original door of disobedience opened by us, our children, and/or our ancestors. I ask You Jesus, to set Yourself up as the permanent doorkeeper. Thank You for arranging for our God-ordained destinies to come forth in the name of Jesus of Nazareth. Thank You for removing every obstacle or assignment of the enemy to interfere with opening the door for our freedom. Where Your Spirit is, there is freedom. I declare Jesus is the way, the truth, and the life. I declare we will not die, but will live and declare the works of the Lord in the land of the living. Thank You for sending Your angels on assignment to help us overcome Accidental Agreements with the enemy in every area of our lives. I choose to believe God is in charge of our children and family. We are being set free from all bondage, all addictions, and anything unclean or unrighteous. Thank You for our freedom because we have sought Your precepts. Whom the Lord sets free is free indeed.

ORIGINAL SCRIPTURE: "Then you will know the truth, and the truth will set you free." John 8:32

PERSONALIZED SCRIPTURE: **Thank You, Lord, that I know You, the truth, and You are setting me free.** John 8:32

PARAPHRASED SCRIPTURE: **Lord, thank You for being truth. Thank You for revealing the truth to me so I will be set free from anything I'm in bondage to. There is no chain that You cannot break. Thank You for complete freedom with Christ inside of me.** John 8:32

ORIGINAL SCRIPTURE: "I will walk about in freedom, for I

have sought out your precepts." Psalm 119:45

PERSONALIZED SCRIPTURE: **I walk in freedom because I have sought after Your commandments.** Psalm 119:45

PARAPHRASED SCRIPTURE: **Thank You, Lord, for letting me walk in freedom because I have sought after our commandments and precepts. Thank You for teaching me how to pursue You, study, and memorize Your commandments. I am confident in Your promise if I do this, You will enable me to walk in freedom in every area of my life I surrender to You.** Psalm 119:45

ORIGINAL SCRIPTURE: "Now the Lord is the Spirit, and where the Spirit of the Lord is, there is freedom." 2 Corinthians 3:17

PERSONALIZED SCRIPTURE: **Thank You, Lord, for filling me with the Holy Spirit, because where Your Spirit is, there is freedom.** 2 Corinthians 3:17

PARAPHRAZED SCRIPTURE: **Lord, You are spirit and You are truth, and where Your Spirit is there is liberty, emancipation from bondage and true freedom. Thank You for filling me with Your Holy Spirit.** 2 Corinthians 3:17

ORIGINAL SCRIPTURE: "We are destroying sophisticated arguments and every exalted and proud thing that sets itself up against the [true] knowledge of God, and we are taking every thought and purpose captive to the obedience of Christ." 2 Corinthians 10:5 AMP

PERSONALIZED SCRIPTURE: **Lord, together we are destroying arguments and every exalted and proud thing that has set itself up against the true knowledge of God. We are taking every thought captive and making it obedient to You and Your will for my life.** 2 Corinthians 10:5

PARAPHRAZED SCRIPTURE: **Lord, I am partnering with You to destroy reasoning, logic, theories, arguments, imagination, and any other proud thing that would come against my thoughts, hijacking the true knowledge of God. With Your help, I take captive all the thoughts I have and make them obey You and Your awesome plans for my life.** 2 Corinthians 10:5

As you read the scriptures below, be sure to personalize or paraphrase them as I did in the example above.

Additional Scriptures: Psalm 119:45, Luke 4:18, 2 Corinthians 3:17, James 1:25, 2 Corinthians 10:25, 2 Corinthians 10:5, Luke 4:1

10. LIE: God can't help me heal my broken relationships. He can't help me find godly friends. I may have to hang out with people who are a bad influence on me or I will be alone and lonely. God can't help my children quit hanging around bad influencers and form godly, healthy relationships.

TRUTH: Read the renouncing statement at the beginning of this section. I decree and declare You are Jehovah Rapha, the God who heals. Thank You for prospering our souls, our health, relationships, and all that concerns us with abundant blessings! Thank You for being a relational God who desires a real, earthly relationship with me, my family and friends. Lord, either change our friends to be authentic followers of Jesus or remove them. Thank You for eliminating every obstacle for me and my family. Thank You for pursuing us and never leaving or forsaking us. I declare You are Emmanuel, God with us. You say, "Ask and it will be given to you; seek and you will find; knock and the door will be opened to you." I am asking You for godly mentors and influencers. You have a perfect plan for me and my family with a wonderful future and hope. I trust Your Will be done on earth as it is in heaven. Thank You for Your abundant blessings.

ORIGINAL SCRIPTURE: "Dear friend, I pray that you may enjoy good health and that all may go well with you, even as your soul is getting along well." 3 John 2

PERSONALIZED SCRIPTURE: **Thank You I am enjoying good health and all will go well with me, as my soul is prospering now.** 3 John 2

PARAPHRAZED SCRIPTURE: **Lord, thank You for helping my soul prosper. I know as this happens my body will be healthy, and all things will go well for me.** 3 John 2

ORIGINAL SCRIPTURE: "Ask and it will be given to you; seek and you will find; knock and the door will be opened to you." Matthew 7:7

PERSONALIZED SCRIPTURE: **Thank You for promising when I ask You, it will be given, when I seek, I will find, and when I knock the door will be opened. Thank You for alignment with Your will on earth as it is in heaven.** Matthew 7:7

PARAPHRASED SCRIPTURE: **Thank You, Lord, for helping me believe this amazing promise: when I pray in accordance with Your will, it is heard loudly and clearly in Heaven. Thank You when I ask, You will give to me. Thank You when I seek, You will let me find. Thank You when I knock, You will swing the door wide open for me!** Matthew 7:7

ORIGINAL SCRIPTURE: "For I know the plans I have for you, declares the Lord, plans to prosper you and not to harm you, plans to give you hope and a future. Then you will call on me and come and pray to me, and I will listen to you. You will seek me and find me when you seek me with all your heart. I will be found by you," declares the Lord, "and will bring you back from captivity." Jeremiah 29:11–14A

PERSONALIZED SCRIPTURE: God, You know the thoughts and plans You have for me and my family. They are for our good and not for evil. We will have great hope for the final outcome because we will seek you in prayer with all of our heart, and You will set us free from bondage. Jeremiah 29:11–14A

PARAPHRASED SCRIPTURE: God, thank You that Your thoughts, plans, and purposes for our lives are good—no, great! We will continue to call on Your great name, Jesus, and seek You with all of our heart in prayer. You promise to hear us, and we will find Your will for our lives, which will set us free to prosper in everything we do. Jeremiah 29:11–14A

As you read the scriptures below, be sure to personalize or paraphrase them as I did in the example above.

Additional Scriptures: Mark 11:24, Proverbs 27:17, NLT, 1 John 1:3, John 15:15, ESV, James 5:16, NASB

11. LIE: My children lack maturity, guidance, and wisdom. I'm never going to get them out of my house. They are never going to be able to stand on their own. My children are never going to hold a job, connect with others in a healthy manner, or make a living for themselves.

TRUTH: Read the renouncing statement above. First, ask for forgiveness and repent for word-cursing them by saying the words, "They will never…" Ask the Lord to heal their soul wounds created by these words and fill them with His resurrection glory light of Jesus. Ask the Lord to bring forth the blessings which were sidetracked due to these word curses.

I decree and declare the Lord is in charge of my family. I trust You to direct us in every phase of our lives, including our jobs, education, wisdom, knowledge and understanding of Christ, relationships, stability, and maturity. All my children will be taught by the LORD, and great will be their peace. The Bible says, "He will cleanse your hearts and the hearts of your children and of your children's children so that you will love the Lord your God with all your hearts and souls." I will trust in the Lord with all my heart and not depend on my own understanding. I will seek Your will in all I do. You will show me which path to take. Thank You, Lord, there is no limit to Your resources and opportunities. I declare You are in charge of developing our lives to align with the purpose and plan You predestined before time. Thank You every knee will bow and every tongue will confess Jesus is savior above earth, on earth, and below earth. Thank You for increasing us in wisdom and stature and in favor with God.

ORIGINAL SCRIPTURE: "All your children will be taught by the LORD, and great will be their peace." Isaiah 54:13 (This includes spiritual children.)

PERSONALIZED SCRIPTURE: **Thank You, Lord, that all my children will be taught by You and their shalom peace will be great.** Isaiah 54:13

PARAPHRASED SCRIPTURE: **Lord, being a parent is a challenging job, and I thank You for Your help. I am grateful for Your promises to teach my children and spiritual children. They will experience Your shalom peace full of contentment, wholeness, soundness, tranquility, and prosperity. The next time I'm worried, I will remember Your promise to me.** Isaiah 54:13

ORIGINAL SCRIPTURE: "Trust in the Lord with all your heart; do not depend on your own understanding. Seek his will in all you do, and he will show you which path to take." Proverbs 3:5–6 NLT

PERSONALIZED SCRIPTURE: **I trust You Lord, with all my**

heart, and do not try to figure out everything with my own understanding. I give You credit in all I do, so You are now directing my paths. Proverbs 3:5–6, NLT

PARAPHRASED SCRIPTURE: **I choose to trust You Lord in everything and I do not rely on my knowledge or intelligence but instead seek Your advice in each situation. You will direct me in the way I should go.** Proverbs 3:5–6 NLT

ORIGINAL SCRIPTURE: "He will cleanse your hearts and the hearts of your children and of your children's children so that you will love the Lord your God with all your hearts and souls, and Israel shall come alive again!" Deuteronomy 30:6 TLB

PERSONALIZED SCRIPTURE: **Thank You for cleansing our hearts and the hearts of our children to love You, Lord, with all of our heart and soul, to be alive with Your Spirit inside of us.** Deuteronomy 30:6

PARAPHRASED SCRIPTURE: **You have cleansed our hearts, our children's hearts, and future generations so we will love you with all of our heart and soul. By abiding in You, we will be alive with the Holy Spirit leading us.** Deuteronomy 30:6

ORIGINAL SCRIPTURE: "And Jesus increased in wisdom and stature and in favor with God and man." Luke 2:52, KJV

PERSONALIZED SCRIPTURE: **Thank You, Lord, that our children have grown in wisdom, stature, and favor with You and man.** Luke 2:52

PARAPHRASED SCRIPTURE: **Thank You, Lord, that our children will continue to grow more like Jesus daily. They will grow in wisdom, stature, and favor with You and others.** Luke 2:52

ORIGINAL SCRIPTURE: "Then you will know the truth, and the truth will set you free." John 8:32

PERSONALIZED SCRIPTURE: **Thank You, Lord, that we will know You, the truth, and You are setting us free.** John 8:32

PARAPHRASED SCRIPTURE: **Lord, thank You for being truth. Thank You for revealing the truth to us so we will be set free from anything we are in bondage to. There is no chain You cannot break. Thank You for complete freedom with Christ.** John 8:32

As you read the scriptures below, be sure to personalize or paraphrase them as I did in the example above.

Philippians 2:9–11, James 1:5, KJV, Matthew 7:7, Mark 11:24, Psalm 102:28, Psalm 112:1–2, Matthew 6:33, ESV, Ephesians 1:17

12. LIE: I'm too old, and it's too late to see my family restored. My children and siblings are adults who aren't serving God.

TRUTH: Read the renouncing statement at the beginning of this section. I decree and declare the Lord is good and You will work everything out for my good and the good of my family. Thank You that Your timing is always perfect. You promise to finish the good work You have begun in me and my family. Thank You for hearing and answering every prayer because the prayers of a righteous person are effective and accomplish much. Thank You Lord for teaching me how to pray consistently in alignment with Your will for our lives. Thank You for being a God who restores things better than they were before. You promise everything the locust or enemy has eaten or stolen will be restored. Holy Spirit, teach me to hear Your voice with clarity. Thank You for removing every stronghold in me and my family. You say, "You shall know the Truth and the Truth shall set you free. Thank You for setting us free. I ask You to close the original door of disobedience opened by me or my ancestors. I ask Jesus to be the permanent doorkeeper. (Pray the stronghold prayer in the Appendix here.) Thank You that my children (insert name) are taught of the Lord and great is their peace. Your ways are perfect. I choose to live a righteous life so my children will be blessed. I choose to trust You."

ORIGINAL SCRIPTURE: "For I am sure of this very thing, that the one who began a good work in you will perfect it until the day of Christ Jesus." Philippians 1:6

PERSONALIZED SCRIPTURE: **Lord, I am sure since You began a good work in me, You will perfect it until the day You return.** Philippians 1:6

PARAPHRASED SCRIPTURE: **Thank You, Lord, for helping me to unwaveringly believe Your promise that since You were the initiator of my faith, You will watch over and nurture me and my faith until the day You return to the earth.** Philippians 1:6

ORIGINAL SCRIPTURE: "And we know that in all things God works for the good of those who love him, who have been called according to his purpose." Romans 8:28

PERSONALIZED SCRIPTURE: **Thank You for working everything for good for me because I love You and am called according to Your purpose.** Romans 8:28

PARAPHRASED SCRIPTURE: **Lord, I am so relieved to know it's impossible for me to make a mistake big enough that You can't correct it because You love me that much.** Romans 8:28

ORIGINAL SCRIPTURE: "We demolish arguments and every pretension that sets itself up against the knowledge of God, and we take captive every thought to make it obedient to Christ." 2 Corinthians 10:5

PERSONALIZED SCRIPTURE: **Thank You, Lord, for helping me demolish arguments and every pretension that has set itself up against Your knowledge. I take every thought captive and make it obey You!** 2 Corinthians 10:5

PARAPHRASED SCRIPTURE: **Thank You, Lord, for helping me demolish all thoughts that don't line up with Your word. I make a commitment to take every negative thought captive and make it obey You by replacing the lie with a positive truth from Your word.** 2 Corinthians 10:5

ORIGINAL SCRIPTURE: "The righteous lead blameless lives; blessed are their children after them." Proverbs 20:7

PERSONALIZED SCRIPTURE: **I choose to live a righteous life so my children will be blessed.** Proverbs 20:7

PARAPHRASED SCRIPTURE: **Lord, thank You for the gift of righteousness You have given me. I choose to always follow Your teachings. Thank You for Your promise my children will be blessed by You.** Proverbs 20:7

As you read the scriptures below, be sure to personalize or paraphrase them as I did in the example above.

Additional Scriptures: Psalm 92:12–14, James 5:16, NASB, Isaiah 54:13, Ruth 4:15, Proverbs 16:31, Psalm 71:18–19, 1 Corinthians 1:8, Deuteronomy 4:40, Proverbs 14:26, Jeremiah 32:39, Isaiah 49:25b

Willful Accidental Agreements

Take a moment of silence and ask the Lord to download the names of people you have unforgiveness towards. Ask for forgiveness and repent to remove any unforgiveness or bitterness. See *Forgiveness* section for prayer.

Next, renounce your specific agreement (the lie) with the enemy listed below. First, speak the renouncing statement followed by the Truth Statement." Read the personalized scriptures out loud (dunamis power).

Read the renouncing statement before all Truth Statements.

Renouncing Statement: "Lord, on behalf of me, my ancestors, and my descendants, I ask for forgiveness and repent and renounce my agreements with the enemy with regards to lie number _______. I submit my body, soul, and spirit to the Lord and ask You to align me with Your will. Cleanse my sin and cover me with the blood of Jesus. Fill my soul wounds with Your resurrection power and the shekinah glory light of Jesus in my innermost being.

I ask You to silence the enemy. Thank You the power and legal rights of the enemy are broken. (Luke 10:19) I ask to be restored in full covenant with You. As I am in covenant with You, I enjoy the benefits and blessings of being Your royal child. Lord, You are the sovereign judge in the courts of heaven and also the judge on earth. Lord, I ask You to rule in my favor in the courts of heaven and ask You to release the angels to enforce this judgment.

I ask Your will be done on earth as it is in heaven. You have given me the legal right to trample on the enemy (Psalm 91). I reclaim everything the enemy has stolen from me, my family, and all that concerns me. Thank you for restoring the generational blessings and liberating our DNA in alignment with Your original plan for our lives, which is our godly inheritance. I ask that our God-ordained blessings come forth in the name of Jesus. I ask You to activate our DNA correction and blessings. These blessings include wisdom, knowledge, understanding, discernment, gifts, talents, and all other godly generational blessings. Lord, I ask specifically for You to bless me with the talents of ________________________. (Fill in the blank with your God-aligned desires. Examples: music, languages, artistic ability, dance, writing, or business.)

1. LIE: I can't break the habit of ________________________. Every time I try to stop this habit, it seems to creep back into my life. I've asked God to help but He's not helping enough.

TRUTH: Read the renouncing statement at the beginning of this section. I decree and declare all things are possible with God. You are for me, not against me, so I trust You to help me control my will. Show me where I need to adjust my habits and give me Your perspective on this situation. Thank You for giving me the tools to permanently break this habit. **Thank You no temptations will come against me except the ones that are common to everyone. You are faithful and will not allow me to be tempted more than I can bear. Thank You when I am tempted, You will also provide a way out so I can endure it.** (I Corinthians 10:13) Teach me to meditate on Your words, day and night, and to seek You with all of my heart, soul, mind, and strength. Thank You for removing every stronghold in my life and setting me free. You say I shall know the Truth and the Truth shall set me free. I trust You to show me how to break free from these stronghold habits. Illuminate the light of Your word and take captive all of my thoughts to the obedience of Christ. Jesus, close the original gate of disobedience opened by me or my ancestors to the enemy. I ask You to be the permanent gatekeeper of my mind, will, and emotions. Thank You for bringing forth my God-ordained destiny. Thank You for being a good Father who loves me and blesses me.

ORIGINAL SCRIPTURE: "So if the Son sets you free, you will be free indeed." John 8:36

PERSONALIZED SCRIPTURE: **Thank You, Lord, for setting me free. I am free indeed.** John 8:36

PARAPHRASED SCRIPTURE: **Lord, You are my freedom. No sin or demon can keep me bound because You freed me from the enemy's kingdom. I am free indeed!** John 8:36

ORIGINAL SCRIPTURE: No temptation has overtaken you except what is common to mankind. And God is faithful; he will not let you be tempted beyond what you can bear. But when you are tempted, he will also provide a way out so that you can endure it. I Corinthians 10:13

PERSONALIZED SCRIPTURE: **Lord, thank You no temptations come against me except the ones that are common to everyone. You are faithful and will not allow me to be tempted more than I can bear. Thank You when I am tempted, You will also provide a way out so I can endure it.** I Corinthians 10:13

PARAPHRASED SCRIPTURE: **Lord, sometimes it seems like every time I turn around the enemy is flinging another temptation at me. You are faithful because You will not allow me to be tempted beyond what I can stand. I'm glad You always provide a way for me to overcome. Therefore, I will ask for Your wisdom.** I Corinthians 10:13

As you read the scriptures below, be sure to personalize or paraphrase them as I did in the example above.

Additional Scriptures: Philippians 4:13, KJV, Romans 13:14, 1 Corinthians 6:12, 2 Corinthians 5:17

2. LIE: I can't stand up to ____________________. My voice isn't heard when I'm speaking to ______________________.

TRUTH: Read the statement at the beginning of this section. I decree and declare when You created the world, You were a God of boundaries. With the help of Holy Spirit, I will be a person with firm boundaries. If my God-ordained boundaries have been moved, I ask You to realign them with Your plan. Your word says, "since we live by the Spirit, let us keep in step with the Spirit." Galatians 5:22 (NLT) says, "But the Holy Spirit produces this kind of fruit in our lives: love, joy, peace, patience, kindness, goodness, faithfulness, gentleness, and self-control." I will have self-control in all areas of my life and will require the same from everyone around me. Thank You for creating me for love. I will love with good boundaries, protecting myself, my dignity, and my children in all situations. I will not allow myself to stay in unhealthy relationships or situations which can harm my mind, will, or emotions. You keep me in perfect peace because I trust in you. All my thoughts are fixed on you! Thank You for heightening my awareness when I need to remove myself, speak up, or stay silent and pray. Speak to me and convict me when I am going astray. I will be anxious for nothing, but in everything, by prayer and supplication, with thanksgiving, let my requests be made known to God; and the peace of God, which surpasses all understanding, will guard my heart and mind through Christ Jesus. (Philippians 4:6–7) Thank You for hearing and answering my prayers.

ORIGINAL SCRIPTURE: "But the Holy Spirit produces this kind of fruit in our lives: love, joy, peace, patience, kindness, goodness, faithfulness, gentleness, and self-control." Galatians 5:22 NLT

PERSONALIZED SCRIPTURE: **Thank You, Lord, the Holy Spirit produces these characteristics in my life: love, joy, peace, patience, kindness, goodness, faithfulness, gentleness, and self-control.** Galatians 5:22

PARAPHRASED SCRIPTURE: **Holy Spirit, thank You for partnering with me to produce the following godly characteristics in my life: love, joy, peace, patience, kindness, goodness, faithfulness, gentleness, and self-control.** Galatians 5:22

ORIGINAL SCRIPTURE: "Since we live by the Spirit, let us keep in step with the Spirit." Galatians 5:25

PERSONALIZED SCRIPTURE**: I will live by the leading of the Holy Spirit and keep in step with Him.** Galatians 5:25

PARAPHRASED SCRIPTURE: **Lord, thank You for sending the Holy Spirit to live in me. Teach me to always be guided by Him, not my own judgment.** Galatians 5:25

As you read the scriptures below be sure to personalize or paraphrase them as I did in the example above.

Additional Scriptures: Ephesians 4:15, NLT, 1 Thessalonians 5:13b

---

[23] Clark, Randy, (2011). *Ministry Team Training Manual,* Mechanicsburg, PA: Apostolic Network of Global Awakening.

MEET THE AUTHOR

NATALIE S. WOLFE

Natalie S. Wolfe has dedicated years learning how the Lord loves to bless and heal His people. She is the author of The ABC Blessing Book: Anointing, Blessing and Covering Your Home in Prayer.

She completed the intensive Christian Healing Certification Program by Randy Clark through Global Awakening. This curriculum was focused on inner healing, deliverance and physical healing. In 2016, Natalie graduated from the Complete Healing School and was ordained through Joan Hunter Ministries. She is a member of the Women In Ministry Network, through Patricia King Ministries. Natalie has facilitated numerous bible studies and does speaking and counseling for groups.

She is the founder and president of Wolfe Real Estate Company. Natalie worked in commercial real estate for 27 years as a top producer with the largest real estate company in the world. While there, she leased, sold and developed office buildings in Kansas City and throughout the Midwest.

Natalie was one of the first women in commercial real estate where she broke records for production. She developed the Office Building

Industry Standard for Office Absorption in Kansas City, later adopted by national real estate companies. She annually addressed national real estate investors as the authority on Office Investments.

Known for her financial acumen, she approached real estate problems from a creative perspective, repositioning assets. She created opportunities for investors to gain "territory."

Her business training of expanding territory for owners was the genesis of preparing her to segway into the biblical realm. Her training in Randy Clark's Healing School taught her the spiritual reality of reclaiming God's territory. She became trained in reclaiming God's territory which applies to His land, His people and their future inheritance.

Natalie is the founder of Your Family Blessings, LLC. She is passionate about teaching believers how to reclaim their spiritual health, physical well-being, family unity, property, home and past generational blessings; recovering their God-ordained domain and promised blessings. She is enthusiastic in unlocking each person's hijacked blessings and restoring their spiritual family bloodline.

If you would like to learn more or to invite Natalie to speak for your group or organization, please visit:

AccidentalAgreements.com

ACCIDENTAL AGREEMENT CITATIONS

Bennett, Rita (1982). *You Can Be Emotionally Free.* Alachua, Florida: Bridge-Logos.

Botari, Pablo (2000). *Free In Christ.* Lake Mary, FL: Charisma House Media.

Crandall, Chauncey W. IV, MD (2010). *Raising The Dead.* New York, NY: FaithWords, Hachette Book Group.

Crandall, Dr. Chauncey W. IV, MD (2015). *Touching Heaven.* New York, NY: FaithWords, Hachette Book Group.

Frangipane, F. (2011). *The Three Battlegrounds.* Cedar Rapids, IA: Arrow Publications, Inc.

Horrobin, P.J. & Prince, D. (2008). *Healing through Deliverance: The Foundation and Practice of Deliverance Ministry.* Ada, MI: Chosen Books.

Hunter, Joan (2006). *Healing The Whole Man.* New Kensington, PA: Whitaker House.

Johnson, Bill (2016). *God Is Good.* Shippensburg, PA: Destiny Image Publishing, Inc.

Johnson, Bill and Kris Vallotton (2006). *The Supernatural Ways of Royalty.* Shippensburg, PA: Destiny Image Publishing, Inc.

Kirkwood, Kerry (2016) *The Power Of Right Thinking.* Shippensburg, PA: Destiny Image Publishing, Inc.

Leaf, Caroline Dr. (2013). *Switch On Your Brain*. Grand Rapids, MI: Baker Books, Baker Publishing Company.

Wilson, Ralph F. (2010) *Names and Titles of God*. Loomis, JesusWalk Publications.

Wright, Henry W., MD (2009). *A More Excellent Way To Be In Health*. New Kensington, PA: Whitaker House.

ARE YOU READY FOR GOD TO RESTORE, REBUILD, AND REPAIR YOUR LIFE—YOUR FAMILY?

Do you need a miracle in your family? Do you need protection? Do you need God's blessing as you make decisions, face the future, or plan your finances? I have wonderful news for you!

- God has a plan for you (Jeremiah 29:11–13).
- God wants to bless you and your family (Jeremiah 33:3).
- God wants to answer your prayers (John 15:7–8).

The ABC Blessing Book is your practical guide to inviting God's blessing into your home. Your home will be more loving, experience more joy and laughter, be safe from the onslaught of the enemy, and become a place of peace where there are harmonious relationships. You can have the good, healthy, wholesome life you desire!

To order your copy, go to www.ABCBLESSING.com.

Also available on Kindle.

BIBLE COPYRIGHT STATEMENTS

Made in the USA
Columbia, SC
20 June 2021